DIGNITY AND HUMAN RIGHTS

THE IMPLEMENTATION OF ECONOMIC, SOCIAL AND CULTURAL RIGHTS

BERMA KLEIN GOLDEWIJK
ADALID CONTRERAS BASPINEIRO
PAULO CÉSAR CARBONARI
(eds.)

Intersentia
Transnational Publishers
In cooperation with the
T·M·C·ASSER PRESS

Distribution for the UK:
Hart Publishing
Salter's Boat Yard
Folly Bridge
Abingdon Road
Oxford OX1 4LB
UK
Tel: + 44 1865 24 55 33
Fax: + 44 1865 79 48 82

Distribution for North America:
Transnational Publishers
410 Saw Mill River Road
Ardsley
New York 10502-2615
USA
Tel: + 1 914 693 5100
Fax: + 1 914 693 4430

Distribution for Switzerland and Germany:
Schulthess Verlag
Zwingliplatz 2
CH-8022 Zürich
Switzerland
Tel: + 41 1 251 93 36
Fax: + 41 1 261 63 94

Distribution for other countries:
Intersentia Publishers
Churchilllaan 108
2900 Schoten
Belgium
Tel: + 32 3 680 15 50
Fax: + 32 3 658 71 21

Dignity and Human Rights
The Implementation of Economic, Social and Cultural Rights
Berma Klein Goldewijk, Adalid Contreras Baspineiro and Paulo César Carbonari (eds.)

Book Series: The Implementation of Economic, Social and Cultural Rights
English Translator: Carolyn Brissett – Global Multilingüe (Brazil) Translation of Latin American contributions

ISBN 1-57105-253-4
ISBN 90-5095-219-4
D/2002/7849/14
NUGI 698

TABLE OF CONTENTS

FOREWORD

Virginia DANDAN (Philippines)
Chair of the United Nations Committee on Economic, Social and Cultural Rights
&
Miloon KOTHARI (India)
United Nations Special Rapporteur on Adequate Housing as a Component of the Right to an Adequate Standard of Living

The global climate today is characterised by two contradictory phenomena. Firstly, there is the increased insecurity generated by the September 11, 2001 attack in the United States including the unequal and disproportionate military response. Secondly, there is the remarkable confluence and solidarity that has characterised global civil society's response to the serious impact of economic globalisation on the world's poor. This is best characterised by the first World Social Forum held in Porto Alegre and even more the vast participation globally that has marked the preparations for the next World Social Forum – and the millions who have joined the clarion call 'Another World is Possible'.

The first scenario creates an uncertain world climate and the second a world full of hope. It is critical to ensure that this transition period that the world is going through is used to reaffirm universally accepted principles of human rights and to breathe fresh air into inalienable principles that must guide our short and long term action if we are serious about both getting to the 'root causes' of global terrorism and to give direction and a legal basis to the alternatives being proposed by civil society alliances.

This is all the more pertinent and timely as the Nobel Peace Prize this year has been awarded to the United Nations and to its Secretary-General Kofi Annan. Such recognition serves to highlight for us the mission of the United Nations led by 'We the People's...' – the promotion of peace, security and human rights.

The foundation of human rights that has emerged from the UN over the past 50 years, in the form of instruments and mechanisms, has evolved out of an overarching thrust provided by inviolable principles that elaborate upon and substantiate human dignity and well-being. Such principles are non-discrimination; self-determination; non-retrogression; international cooperation; gender equality; the right to a remedy. These principles bear strong implications on the notions of universality and indivisibility, interdependence and interrelatedness of human rights.

These principles and the instruments that give practical direction for their implementation comprise unambiguous directions for State responsibility at local, national and international levels.

Take for example, in today's interdependent world, the essential but underutilised principle of international cooperation. This principle, firmly entrenched in the UN Charter (articles 55 and 56) and the Universal Declaration of Human Rights (article 28), and elaborated upon in the International Covenant on Economic, Social and Cultural Rights, has significant implications if put into practice. It calls upon States to take 'joint' and 'separate' action through international assistance and cooperation to promote the realisation of human rights. The implications of this are that resources have to be made available and actions taken in 'solidarity' and 'fraternity'. Such a direction, if taken seriously by the world's States would call for:

- International action on the right to food, housing, work, education;
- Finally tackling the critical issue of land and wealth distribution;
- Implications for globalisation policies to ensure that the primacy of human rights takes precedence in international policy formulation including the full integration of economic, social and cultural rights into global and regional trade, investment, finance, debt and structural adjustment policies;
- Implications for poverty reduction strategies such that collective action is taken by States.

The principle and codification of international cooperation in the international instruments also has obligations that developing countries can utilise to ensure that no action is taken or no global policies are adopted that could inhibit the ability of States to implement the commitments they have to their people stemming from the international human rights instruments. Moreover, these States can use these obligations on the world's governments to counter the ongoing negative implications of iniquitous debt, adjustment, trade, investment and finance agreements.

Also, take as an example of the momentous implications of the implementation of the fundamental human rights principle of *non-discrimination.* This is the core value of human rights which has implications for the world's disadvantaged and demands affirmative action by States consistent with the cardinal human rights approach of meeting the needs of the vulnerable people, those whose dignity is most under assault, first.

In the current global climate of growing income disparity and the growing gulf between the rich and the poor it is important to remember that discrimination and segregation in economic, social and cultural rights are not only based on grounds of race, class or gender, but can also result from poverty and economic marginalization. As the Committee on Economic, Social and Cultural Rights has pointed out in its statement on Poverty and the Covenant on Economic, Social and Cultural Rights:

"*Non-discrimination and equality are integral elements of the international human rights normative framework, including the International Covenant on Economic, Social and Cultural Rights. Sometimes poverty arises when people have no access to existing resources because of who they are, what they believe or where they live. Discrimination may cause poverty, just as poverty may cause discrimination. Inequality may be entrenched in institutions and deeply rooted in social values that shape relationships within households and communities. Accordingly, the international norms of non-discrimination and equality, which demand that particular attention be given to vulnerable groups and individuals from such groups, have profound implications for anti-poverty strategies*".

In the current state of institutionalised discrimination that is found in the patterns of violation of economic, social and cultural rights it is critical that at all levels of civil society and States a concerted effort is made. This is a concerted effort to implement the human rights principles of non-discrimination and equality including through the implementation of the Declaration and Programme of Action that has emerged from the 2001 Durban World Conference on Racial Discrimination.

Strategies have to be evolved that operationalise these human rights principles through the implementation of human rights instruments including through civil society struggle and advocacy work including human rights education and learning and through the sustenance of tension between international institutions (especially the UN system and the International Financial Institutions) until there is a full integration of human rights principles and instruments into global trade policies.

The ideological moorings required to rescue the world from the consolidation of a 'militaristic mindset' needs to draw upon and adhere scrupulously to international human rights principles and instruments. The need to meet this challenge head-on is an inescapable task. The challenge is to forge a structure of multilateralism that is underpinned by a moral, ethical and legal basis that is steeped in the enduring value of the dignity and well-being of all human beings – the very foundation of human rights – the very foundation of the formation and the continued relevance of the United Nations – the only way in which this year's Nobel Peace Prize will lead to a lasting legacy. In addition to the required and inevitable role of States it is critical that civil society itself embrace, through the integration into the alternative blueprint being outlined, as their own the principles and provisions of the international human rights instruments and the mechanisms that are the pillars of the UN human rights system. We owe the world's poor nothing less than the full human rights that the pursuit of their dignity deserves and our actions will be judged by nothing less than whether we are able to achieve this inevitable task.

SECTION I
INTRODUCTION AND CONTEXT

FROM SEATTLE TO PORTO ALEGRE: EMERGENCE OF A NEW FOCUS ON DIGNITY AND THE IMPLEMENTATION OF ECONOMIC, SOCIAL AND CULTURAL RIGHTS

Berma KLEIN GOLDEWIJK (The Netherlands)

Introduction

On the occasion of the first World Social Forum in Porto Alegre (Brazil, January 2001), the implementation of economic, social and cultural rights has come to the fore as one of the most relevant issues.[1] This group of human rights encompasses basic rights, such as the right to adequate housing, the right to health, the right to food, which comprises the right to safe drinking water, and the right to education. In the context of globalisation and shifting power dynamics, no task other than the implementation of economic, social and cultural rights could be more urgent.

Global economic integration may contribute to the improvement of living standards and the reduction of inequity and inequality. Yet, the way the current global economic system is being developed puts at risk the very objectives for which it has been created. There is a growing gap between a global trade system that relates economic integration to political liberalization, and an international human rights system that calls for justice, fundamental freedoms, non-discrimination and regulation of markets. This gap has some serious implications for the further operationalization of all human rights in their universal dimension, above all the *right to an adequate standard of living*. In recent years, the human rights community has expressed its concerns about such current developments, and has been sending urgent appeals to the World Bank, the International Monetary Fund and the World Trade Organization.

---

1 In Porto Alegre, at World Social Forum I, three endorsing networks introduced the focus on the implementation of economic, social and cultural rights. These were: the National Brazilian Movement for Human Rights (MNDH), the Inter-American Platform for Human Rights, Democracy and Development (PIDHDD), and the International Forum on the Implementation of Economic, Social and Cultural Rights (CEDAR International, Centre for Dignity and Rights). The events on economic, social and cultural rights at WSF I were mainly supported by the Co-Financing Agency Icco. These networks converged in bringing together different types of human rights organizations on a national, continental and international scale. The events were realised in the Aula Maior of the Catholic University of Porto Alegre.

The further development of economic, social and cultural rights responds to a new momentum and to shifting approaches in the field of international human rights, particularly through the commitment and the consistent work of civil society. From the side of the human rights community, the primacy of human rights obligations over economic policies has been restated on several occasions. This has also been expressed by civil society at the World Social Forum in Porto Alegre. In this respect it is highly significant that the World *Social* Forum was conceived as a counterweight to the annual World *Economic* Forum, until recently held in Davos. The World Social Forum focuses explicitly on the *social domain*, where the impacts of economic, political and cultural globalisation are being identified and challenged by a diversity of actors that work in the fields of gender, environment, debt crisis, human rights and so forth. After its first realization, the city of Porto Alegre became a symbol of the creation of *viable proposals and alternatives* on an international scale.[2] Already during the 1990s, when a series of UN World Conferences was realized, different cities have in fact received a symbolic significance, such as Vienna (1993), Cairo (1994), Beijing (1995) and Kopenhagen (1995). Other cities have now been added: Seattle (1999), where the World Trade Organisation met, is being seen now as the birthplace of a new type of global civil coalition.[3] Other remarkable cities are Melbourne, where the World Economic Forum met (2000); Prague, where the main annual meetings of the World Bank and the IMF took place, and, of course, Genua (2001). Against these backgrounds, Porto Alegre (2001) made it very clear that if global economic forces intend to prevent the violations of human rights, promote sustainable development and the reduction of poverty and inequality, they will have to respond to and be made compatible with the international human rights system. It was clearly demonstrated that human rights require the global advancement of a legal protection system that embodies the needed change in economic, political, social, and cultural living conditions.

Main Objective: Transformation of Inadequate Living Conditions

The title of this book, *Dignity and Human Rights*, refers above all to the urgent *transformation* of humiliating and dehumanizing realities. The current developments in the trade agenda and the implementation of trade agreements -international, regional and bilateral- have raised major

---

2 François Houtart, *La tirania del mercado y sus alternativas*, Madrid (Editorial Popular), 2001.

3 Emir Sader, 'Antes e depois de Seattle', in: *Resistencias y alternativas a la mundialización neoliberal*, Buenos Aires (OSAL – CLACSO, Consejo Latinoamericano de Ciencias Sociales), Año I, No.3, 2001, p. 5-9.

concerns within the human rights community.[4] The number of homeless persons is still increasing, the enjoyment of the right to health -in particular poor people's access to basic health care- along with food security, is not realized for the majority of people. Basic living conditions, including the right to education and to work, are reflected in the *right to an adequate standard of living,* which is part of the Universal Declaration of Human Rights (1948).

This book aims in particular at a more effective implementation and operationalization of economic, social and cultural rights while focusing at the many existing gaps: between policy and implementation, between legal recognition and everyday practice. The collective of authors that created this book highlights at least four dimensions of the problematique of implementation. Firstly, the emergence of rights-based approaches to development and their impact on international cooperation. Secondly, the creation and enhancement of new instruments for the implementation of economic, social and cultural rights. Such an instrument can be found in the civil society reports on State compliance with the International Covenant on Economic, Social and Cultural Rights. Much attention is being paid to those reports in this book. The third dimension of implementation relates to the subjects and processes that shape and develop rights-based approaches and use the new instruments for transformation of society. And fourthly, there is the need to further develop concerted strategies. Both instruments and strategies are being taken up here as part of a *multi-actor approach,* which involves civil society and the state, and -in a different way- the corporate sector and international financial institutions.

This book has been produced by a collective of authors who belong to different (inter)national networks, work in the field of economic, social and cultural rights, and are committed to a substantive debate. All were present at World Social Forum I in Porto Alegre. All participated in and actively contributed to the major debates on human rights. This book tries to capture the dynamism and richness of the dialogues, placing emphasis both on fundamental and operational issues, global alternatives and practical recommendations. The coming together of these networks for substantive debate is, in itself, a unique experience. The contributions to this book can therefore be seen as components of a framework for further co-operation. This framework is being processed through the Dignity and Human Rights Caucus, which emerged in the course of events that prepare

---

4 See for instance *Globalisation and its impact on the full enjoyment of all human rights,* U.N. Doc. E/CN.4/SUB. 2/RES/2001/5; *Intellectual Property and Human Rights,* U.N. Doc. E/CN.4/SUB; *Liberalization of trade in services and human rights,* U.N. Doc. E/CN.4/SUB.2/RES/2001/4.

the next World Social Forum II. This Caucus is being endorsed by several (inter)national networks that co-operate in the field of implementation of economic, social and cultural rights, and will get a more permanent structure after World Social Forum II.

Human Dignity and its Downside: Humiliation

Human dignity needs to be brought to the centre of the international human rights debate. That is the heart of the argument of this book. Dignity as the source of human rights law is also protected by law. Indeed, whereas human dignity is the core and the foundation of human rights, it is through the operationalization of rights that dignity is protected. This is clearly stated in the Universal Declaration of Human Rights (1948), in particular in its Preamble. In processes of the implementation of human rights this interaction between dignity and rights is being realised.

Dignity is inherent to each and every person simply because of his or her being human. As such, dignity is a category of *being*, not just of *having*. Indeed, human dignity cannot be limited to something that people 'have'; it must first of all be seen as belonging to their 'being'. Human dignity does not come from status, nationality, ethnicity or any human accomplishment. Whereas your dignity can be severely damaged, no one can take your dignity away from you – not if you are poor, or belong to an ethnic minority, or are physically or mentally disabled. Along the same line, dignity means respect for all other persons, no matter what their capacities or living conditions are. There are, as Gustavo Gutiérrez has put it, no 'no-personas', no 'nobodies'.[5] Therefore, the starting point from where to get access to human rights is dignity. Everyone knows when they are humiliated and their human dignity is violated. Human dignity is part of the human condition of everyone, is a fundamental standard for humanity, for human rights law and for humanitarian law.[6] Addressing the violations of human dignity can therefore be seen as the *hard core of strategies* to protect human rights. This issue has received a high profile during recent United Nations discussions of *minimum humanitarian standards*, both in the Commission on Human Rights and the Sub-Commission on the Prevention of Discrimination and the Protection of Minorities.

---

5 Gustavo Gutiérrez, *La Fuerza Histórica de los Pobres*, Salamanca (Sígueme), 1982, p. 248.

6 See Berma Klein Goldewijk & Bas de Gaay Fortman, *Where Needs Meet Rights, Economic, Social and Cultural Rights in a New Perspective*, (Risk Book Series, No.88), Geneva (WCC Publications), 1999, see in particular Chapter 5 'Human dignity and humiliation'.

The notion of human dignity is used extensively in some cultures, and is hardly at all in others. Violations of human dignity are therefore also understood differently. Indeed, what one person may experience as humiliating, may be seen by someone else as just an embarrassment or a dishonour but not as humiliation. How then to identify humiliation? Which practices and institutions are humiliating and what implications would this have for strategy-building?

The downside of human dignity is, indeed, maltreatment, humiliation and dehumanization. At least four main types of maltreatment have been distinguished so far: maltreatment that is causing suffering, that is restricting freedom, that is violating rights and that is perpetrating injustice.[7] Such forms of maltreatment are interrelated. Maltreatment easily brings about humiliation, the injury of self-respect.[8] Whereas humiliation has always existed, it has almost never been seen as a central notion in discussions of human rights policies and strategies, where concepts like injustice, inequality, discrimination, non-recognition, marginalization and exclusion have often prevailed.

Humiliation, in Avishai Margalit's view, is a form of cruelty that destroys people's capacity to believe in themselves, to take initiatives and to change their own situation. Humiliation and dehumanization matter so much not only because of their effects on people's fundamental freedoms, but also because of the effect they have on the capacity of individual persons to be agents of change in their own situation. The notion of *human agency* is very crucial, indeed: people respect each other on the basis of their autonomy and their ability to act as human agents, to change, to reshape their lives.[9]

In addressing the elimination of *systematic institutional humiliation*, a distinction can be made between a *civilized* society and a *decent* society. A civilized society is one in which individuals do not humiliate each other; a decent society is one whose institutions do not humiliate its members, a society which fights conditions that constitute a justification for its dependents to consider themselves humiliated.[10] This distinction between a decent and a civilized society needs to be further debated, since the

---

7 Steven Lukes, 'Humiliation and the Politics of Identity', in: *Social Research*, Vol.64, No.1, 1997, p. 36-52; Frederic Schick, 'On Humiliation', in: *ibid.*, p. 131-47.

8 Avishai Margalit is an Israeli political philospher. His most famous book, in which he elaborated the notion of humiliation, is *The Decent Society*, Cambridge MA (Harvard UP), 1996, p. 9.

9 Avishai Margalit, *The Decent Society*, *o.c.*, p. 70.

10 *Ibid.*, p. 10.

distinction between individual behaviour and institutional behaviour is not always easy to make.[11]

Human rights offer legal protection of basic human dignity. For many people, however, their human rights remain abstract and far away. Finding a starting point in human dignity is therefore so important. Poor people are first of all people with rights: their dignity needs to be protected.[12] Economic, social and cultural rights offer precisely this protection by law of human dignity, of people's basic human needs and of their fundamental freedoms. This implies that economic, social and cultural rights have a transformative character. They present a legal framework for processes of social, political and cultural change. As such, human rights need to be seen as legal resources *and* as political instruments for transformation.

Instruments and Strategies for the Implementation of Rights

There might be a broad consensus on the level of shared values and principles, when it is affirmed that everyone has a right to food, health, housing and education. It may also be evident that development projects, which unjustifiably displace people, are a violation of the right to housing. The question is: how to come from a more general belief in human rights principles to effective human rights practices and mechanisms at a local, national and international level.[13] In this regard, I want to address two major challenges. In the first place, the substantive components of economic, social and cultural rights, such as the right to housing, food, health, education. And in the second place, the legal and institutional

---

[11] See also Bas de Gaay Fortman & Berma Klein Goldewijk, *Dios y las cosas. La economia global desde una perspectiva de civilización* (Coll. Presencia Social, 26), Santander (Ed. Sal Terrae), 1999 (or. engl. *God and the goods. Global economy in a civilizational perspective*, Geneva, WCC Publications, 1998).

[12] Berma Klein Goldewijk, 'The Quest for human dignity. Human rights and religion, State and civil society in a context of globalisation and conflict', in: J. Nacpil-Manipon & C. Perez (eds.), *Challenging globalisation: Solidarity and search for alternatives*, Asia-Europe Joint Consultation on Challeging Globalisation & Hong Kong Baptist University, Hong Kong, 1999, p. 102-113.

[13] In 1976, both the Covenant on Economic, Social and Cultural Rights (CESCR) and the Covenant on Civil and Political Rights (CCPR) entered into force. These treaties, as well as the treaty bodies, composed of independent experts, have developed standards, have elaborated on the substance, and have been instrumental in making the supervisory procedures more meaningful. Both in the context of the state reporting procedure and the individual complaints procedure (which thus far only exists under the CCPR) the Committees adopt conclusions. Under the reporting procedure they adopt Concluding Comments/Observations which follow the examination of a State report, and substantial General Comments, which address different rights.

mechanisms through which such rights can be fully enjoyed by those affected.

These challenges bring us to the core of the problematique of the implementation of economic, social and cultural rights, which can be outlined, in my view, in the following points.

The Contents of Rights and the Institutional Protection Mechanisms

– Firstly, there is the need to create the institutional protection mechanisms, at the same time as the (minimum) contents of economic, social and cultural rights are advanced and interpreted. There is a persistent lack of clarity regarding the meaning and interpretation, the enjoyment and implications of these rights. Furthermore, economic, social and cultural rights are not only systematically threatened and violated, they are also widely unknown and largely ignored. The implementation of economic, social and cultural rights has to be seen as a long-term struggle for both developing the contents and the institutionally recognised protection mechanisms. As part of concrete history, institutional protection mechanisms will have to arise together with -and not in advance of- a clear understanding of the contents and meanings of the different economic, social and cultural rights. In this struggle, the rights-violated people need to be recognised as the primary movers of the process of implementation. As in the field of civil and political rights, the institutional framework and the legal and social protection mechanisms emerge out of the struggles for human rights by those affected.

Poverty and the Supply-Side of Rights

– Secondly, economic, social and cultural rights advance rights to something most poor people have never had, such as adequate housing and food, good health conditions, access to education. This implies that the implementation of these rights needs to be accompanied by complex social transformation processes with significant redistributive implications. The point I want to raise here regards the much debated supply-side of rights.[14] There is often the assumption that a right to food or housing could be realised by merely establishing an obligation on the national and local government to *provide* more housing. In fact, the

---

[14] Bruce Porter (Canada) contributed decisively to my approaches in human rights. See for instance Bruce Porter, 'Socio-Economic Rights Advocacy – Using International Law: Notes from Canada', in: *ESR Review* (Economic and Social Rights in South Africa), Vol 2, No 1, July 1999.

right to food or the right to adequate housing place decisive obligations on governments. Under the International Covenant on Economic, Social and Cultural Rights, as well as under the articles 25 and 26 of the Universal Declaration of Human Rights, States are responsible for ensuring the provision of accessible basic social services, as they are referred to in both instruments. Yet, seen from a critical perspective, the underlying assumption seems to be that if there were an adequate supply of food or houses, the rights would be enjoyed. Another -related- assumption appears to be that getting access to a right can simply be realised by increasing the supply.[15] This is a misconception, namely that the rights to food, housing or education are primarily realised by the provision of goods and services, or by offering financial assistance. By just focusing on the supply-side of rights, people's basic inequality just remains. In the end, people have not increased their access to human rights, but more dependency on their government.

So, how to come to grips with the supply-side of rights? Indeed, under the International Covenant on Economic, Social and Cultural Rights, States are legally bound to take appropriate steps to ensure the respect for economic, social and cultural rights. This means that the delivery of basic social services by the State needs to be connected to regulatory activities of States in the fields of global economy and governance. This connection is fundamental for the realization of basic rights. The current liberalisation and privatization of all kinds of social services seriously affects the equitable and non-discriminatory access to basic services. Basic social services are increasingly out of reach of the poor. Therefore, the implementation of economic, social and cultural rights can not be simplified to people claiming their rights and can not merely be equated with the delivery of basic social services by the State. Implementing these rights relates -above all- to people's everyday struggle for equity and equality in getting access to universal human rights, and to the State taking appropriate measures to regulate and remedy situations that lead to human rights violations or clash with its legally binding human rights obligations.

Rights, Social Goals and Policies

– Thirdly, economic, social and cultural rights are often *invoked as a social goal*, or are seen as a social aspiration, rather than understood as

---

15 Berma Klein Goldewijk & Bas de Gaay Fortman, *Where needs meet rights. Economic, social and cultural rights in a new perspective* (Risk Book Series, No.88), Geneva (WCC Publications), 1999.

institutionalising a practice. Indeed, the traditional conception of economic, social and cultural rights, which was explicitly rejected by the drafters of the South African Constitution, characterised economic, social and cultural rights as being of the nature of *social goals or aspirations*, agreed upon by states but not enforceable by citizens. What are the implications of this view in terms of a global market economy? Under economic globalisation, people often have to rely on privatized markets to find adequate health conditions or adequate housing. Realising the right to food, health or adequate housing in such a setting has in the first place to do with the government's obligation to *protect* and *fulfil* these rights by regulating the market or intervening in the market, to protect poor and vulnerable groups.[16]

Development and Democracy

– In current implementation debates, it is not always sufficiently taken into account that economic, social and cultural rights are part of the fundamental values of *democracy*. This relates to a set of social and political practices rooted in the participation and free self-determination of citizens and peoples.[17] Now more than ever before, human security has entered the agenda of democracy and good governance, extending the classical concept of state security. Human security is not restricted to the sovereignty of states anymore, but now includes people's security and environmental security as well. Effective enjoyment of the right to an environment that is not harmful to health and well-being, of the right to food and clean water, and thus to human security, is a concrete manifestation of democracy and the sustainability of development.[18] Indeed, a lack of economic and social development cannot, under any circumstance, be presented as a justification of violations of civil and political rights, or of economic, social and cultural rights. In her 'Plan of Action to Strengthen the Implementation of the International Covenant on Economic, Social and Cultural Rights', the United Nations

---

16 See also Celso Lafer & Paulo Sergio Pinheiro, 'Globalização econômica, políticas neoliberais e os direitos econômicos, sociais e culturais', in: *1o Encontro Brasileiro de Direitos Humanos*, São Paulo (Centro de Estúdos), 2001, p. 47-55.

17 This has been explicitly recognised by the *Quito Declaration,* On the enforcement and realization of economic, social, and cultural rights in Latin America and the Caribbean, July 24, 1998.

18 See for this element also the *IUCN Draft Covenant on Environment and Development* (deposited at the UN, 1995). *Our Creative Diversity,* Report World Commission on Culture and Development, 1995. *Our Global Neighbourhood,* Report Commission on Global Governance, 1995. *Caring for the Future,* Report Independent Commission on Population and Quality of Life, 1996.

High Commissioner for Human Rights expressed her explicit concern in this regard. She highlighted that the present global context, in which economic, social and cultural rights are being denied to most of the world's population, puts at risk the fundamentals and the assumptions on which the international human rights system is based.

Framework of this Book: Summary of the Contributions

The contributions by the collective of authors are organized here into four sections. In *Section I*, Cândido Grzybowski (Brazil) offers an introduction to the emergence and backgrounds of the World Social Forum. He discusses globalisation and explains how active global citizenship networks have developed during the 1990s, in the course of the World Conferences run by the United Nations. While illustrating the different dimensions of the World Social Forum, Grzybowski highlights the emergence of global proposals that might contribute to a reshaping of current international economies and policies.

Section II presents the meaning and relevance of *rights-based approaches*. Has the development paradigm reached its limits now, while gradually being substituted by rights-based approaches? Or have development approaches and rights-based approaches to be seen as complementary? Co-editor Paulo César Carbonari (Brazil) introduces this section, by elaborating on the core notion of human dignity, which is intrinsic to development and human rights. He reaffirms dignity as a basic concept of ethics and a cornerstone of rights. From a philosophical point of view, Carbonari clarifies the meaning of dignity, seen as a fundamental standard for humanity and a basic notion of a universally valid system of ethics. Carbonari expressly relates universal values and principles to the far more complex issue of diversity. He concludes with citizenship, understood as an historical aspect of dignity. Jayme Benvenuto Lima (Brazil) explains the roots and reasons for the affirmation of the indivisibility and enforceability of human rights. He clearly demonstrates the inadequacy of the so-called generation-based classification of human rights. Benvenuto Lima expresses the view that there is no way of denying the legitimacy of human rights, in particular of economic, social and cultural rights. Indeed, rights are social constructions that have gradually been shaped in history by human needs and requirements and thus reflect the basic conditions of life. Seen in this light, the enforceability of rights is fully justified.

Miloon Kothari (India), UN Special Rapporteur on the right to adequate housing, presents this particular right as a cornerstone human right, and as a legal and advocacy tool. He offers a clear understanding of the links between processes of economic globalization and the implementation of the right to adequate housing, while outlining some components of the housing rights framework. Kothari analyses the priority issues and the impediments to realizing the right to adequate housing in the context of the current privatization of housing services and markets, land speculation, the commodification of housing, and the application of user fees for resources such as water, sanitation and electricity. Venitia Govender (South Africa) writes on economic, social and cultural rights as entitlements, and how they are different from policy options. She highlights the great sensitivity in South Africa regarding aspects of cultural rights and explains how the relationship between dominant and subjugated cultures has profoundly influenced South Africa's history. The connection between the issues of cultural identity, self-determination and traditional leadership on the one hand, and the implementation of economic and social rights on the other hand, remains critical. Furthermore, she explicitly takes up the basic issues of democracy and poverty, and discusses the right to education, food -including clean water. Wieteke Beernink & Harry Derksen (The Netherlands) elaborate on the implications of the search for the right(s) approach for development NGOs, in particular for Icco, being one of the Dutch Co-Financing Agencies. Such an approach, they affirm, requires a rethinking of current policies, a change of attitudes and learning abilities, a change in core-practices, a resetting of agenda's and strategies. Following a rights-based approach, they conclude, means adopting a process- and action-orientation that challenges existing power structures at all levels.

Section III highlights the question of the *instruments for the implementation* of economic, social and cultural rights. Co-editor Adalid Contreras Baspineiro (Bolivia) introduces this section with the statement that the enforceability of all human rights has been strengthened nowadays, as a result of the impacts that current adjustment policies have and the related upsurge in citizen demands. He presents the Inter-American instruments that underpin the enforceability of economic, social and cultural rights, and relates them to international tools and regulations, and remarkable civil society documents, such as Declaration of Quito and the Social Charter of the Americas. In her article, Flávia Piovesan (Brazil) furthers on this, particularly addressing the scope of the instruments for the implementation of economic, social and cultural rights within the particular Latin American context. She makes up the balance of practices and experiences of implementing these rights in Brazil, and discusses the implications thereof for strategies towards the further operationalization of these rights. Her analysis of litigation involving economic, social and cultural rights, comprises four different arenas: local (judiciary authority) and international courts, legislative authority, executive authority, and the private sector.

Areli Sandoval Terán (Mexico) analyses the experience of elaborating and lobbying the Alternative Report on economic, social and cultural rights in Mexico. One of the main strengths of this Mexican civil society document is that it is grounded on official sources and that it produces concrete proposals. Examinations and analyses were undertaken by well-known academics. Case studies of violations of economic, social and cultural rights were documented, with more elaborate sections on Chiapas, the North American Free Trade Treaty (NAFTA) and the Federal Budget. The preparation of this Alternative Report indeed produced a vital tool for lobbying and political pressure. Marcio Alexandre Gualberto (Brazil) follows up with the Brazilian experience of the Civil Society Report on State Compliance with the International Covenant on Economic, Social and Cultural Rights. This report has provided a great deal of the input the Committee needs in order to analyse the status of these rights in Brazil. Most remarkable in the case of Brazil was the methodology used to prepare the report, with 2.000 organisations in the different states of Brazil. The output that was generated from the public hearings was systematized in various rounds into the final report, which was presented and very well received by members of the Committee on Economic, Social and Cultural Rights.

Section IV introduces *subjects and processes*. The introduction to this section is made by Pedro Cláudio Cunca Bocayuva (Brazil), with a contribution on social subjects, human rights and their political meaning. He analyses the significance of the dispute on the concept of rights as tools for emancipation and equality. He compares this with notions of rights that have historically become part of the ideology of domination and the logic of the global expansion of capital. The core challenge he is presenting, regards the relation between democracy and human rights. Marcio Alexandre Gualberto (Brazil) focuses on the Afro-Brazilian populace as a social subject with rights. He examines three areas: the right to education, the right to culture and the use of legal mechanisms for implementing these rights. He brings out how racial issues intrinsically relate with human rights, and studies the inequalities based on race and gender.

The notion of the 'human' attached to subjects and their human rights implies that people enjoy dignity as inherent to all human beings and by virtue of their shared humanity. What, then, does the human element means in regard to the dignity of *all* living creatures? In his contribution to this book, Aziz Ab'Saber (Brazil) launches the discussion on the respect and care for humankind and the earth. In explaining -what he calls- the 'essence' of the Earth Charter, he moves at the crossroads between the ecological sciences, the geographical and the space sciences. Patricia Morales (Argentina), in her article on the moral and global challenges to implement the Earth Charter, compares the Charter to other global documents, such as the Universal Declaration of Human Rights. As part of this comparison, she elaborates on the objective that the Earth Charter be adopted by the United Nations as soft law. Moreover, she expressly brings out the specific intra- and inter-generational dimensions as they are present in the Charter, as a specific challenge to its implementation. Ricardo Vega Posada (Peru) concludes this section, sketching out the peasant land struggles and the entitlements to land rights in Puno. His focus is on the legal aspects of land titles and ownership, as components of the implementation of agrarian development policies in the region.

Section V discusses the issue of *strategies for implementing rights.* With her contribution on economic globalization, civil society and rights, Ger Roebeling (The Netherlands) introduces this section. She discusses the reform of the National State, the limits of the Social Welfare State, and how the State reduces the social costs of the country, while continuing to borrow money from international financial institutions. She elaborates on the impacts the free market mechanisms have on the poor, including the extremely contradictory way in which market actors deal with their social responsibility. This broader context paves the way for M.C. Raj (India) to present different strategies of the Dalit People, the Outcast(e)s, in the particular context of Brahminism, Hindu Nation building and casteism. He explains the origins of casteism as a system of graded inequality, legitimized by the division of laborers. The Dalit community is a casteless community, seen as untouchable and impure. Raj further elaborates on the roots of untouchability under the caste system and the way untouchability is used as a tool for violations of people's dignity and rights, to such an extent that it assumes barbaric dimensions. Against these backgrounds he presents the outline for the further development of a programme for strategy building.

Francisco Whitaker Ferreira (Brazil) analyses corruption as part of the capital flows brought in by organised crime and drug traffic. He interprets corruption as one of the ingredients of the inequitable living conditions of the poor. Corruption is indeed a serious type of theft that absorbs government resources away from social welfare purposes into private pockets. This endangers the common good and the social cohesion of society, and seriously affects the morale and the future of people. He further elaborates on anti-corruption strategies. Dale McKinley (South Africa) analyses the struggle for a People's Budget in South Africa. He presents the budget as a tool for setting policy priorities and deciding how the wealth and resources of the country are being utilised. Under Apartheid, the budget was used to institutionalise economic inequality and social injustice. In his contribution, McKinley discusses electoral politics and the extent to which South African people themselves are involved in the decisions that affect their everyday lives. He explicitly deals with the redistributive implications of the people's struggle for their budget. Miloon Kothari (India) presents the extensive work undertaken in the last decade on the right to housing. He encourages in particular the further strengthening of linkages between his mandate as Special Rapporteur and the human rights treaty bodies. He suggests the promotion of interagency cooperation among United Nations bodies and other international organizations, and highlights the need to further integrate the right to adequate housing in the operational activities of the United Nations. Joe Louis Washington (USA) concludes this section with a symbolic presentation of the gap between policy and implementation. In the light of the richness of all these contributions, this book indeed marks a moment and intends to contribute to an on-going dialogue.

WORLD SOCIAL FORUM: YES, ANOTHER WORLD IS POSSIBLE

Cândido GRZYBOWSKI (Brazil)

Introduction

Held in Porto Alegre from January 25 – 30, 2001, the World Social Forum had everything needed to become one of those landmark events that punctuate the history of our generation. These are the occasions that seem to divide time into before and after their occurrence, through a break that redirects the flow of history, at least in terms of understanding what is happening and the conditions of the human adventure. The changes they trigger may be practical and come into effect immediately or – which is more probable – they reshape the ways in which the possibilities and constraints on human actions are perceived and assessed in a wide variety of situations, relationships, structures, cultures and historical processes. Nevertheless, we women and men are making history through what we really are and what we believe we are. Imagining that another world is possible is an act of creating for making it possible. An event such as the World Social Forum spotlights contradictions and works on them, releasing tremendous amounts of creative energy. This is without doubt a hopeful start to the millennium for the lovers of freedom and human dignity.

The driving force behind the World Social Forum lies in its innovative aspects. This is an initiative undertaken by an emerging planet-wide civil society. It is designed to enhance and appreciate citizen participation and struggles in many different societies, while striving to endow the proposals that they prompt with global dimensions. It is eager to develop into a broad-ranging movement of ideas nourished by the wide diversity of human possibilities, in contrast to a single dominant line of thought. Interpretations for or against are the best indicators of its impact, even if it is difficult to reach agreement on its novelty, consistence and social and cultural importance.

This analysis is based on my privileged position as a Director of Ibase and a member of the Organising Committee of the first edition of the World

Social Forum.[1] But more than avoiding the possible and even inevitable bias of my viewpoint, the main concern here is to express a point of view that is militantly engaged in the construction of this initiative. This means contributing to ensure that – as a collective project – it is as broad-ranging and open as possible to a wide variety of issues and the participation of diversity, certainly ensuring that we think about the world globally, but also in a radically democratic and citizen-focused way.

What Brings Us to the World Social Forum

The World Social Forum is in fact an initiative undertaken by certain players at specific places and times. It is nurtured by a political and cultural broth that must be redeemed in order to understand its catalytic capacities, set against the backdrop of globalisation and the struggle against it.

But why does globalisation prompt so much passion and hate? Why does it make people so uncomfortable? Much of this is due to its own craftsmen and heralds: figures in themselves prompting strongly-polarised reactions. It is enough to recall here Reagan the Cowboy, or Margaret Thatcher the Iron Lady, to make our hair stand on end. And what can be said about their followers and imitators all over the world? It would consequently be a strategic error not to acknowledge the entire neo-liberal economic school at the service of these figures, which has been penetrating respectable academic institutions and spreading its wings as a hegemonic form of thought.

This school of thought and these policies have put down long roots in old but renewed multilateral institutions, like the IMF and the World Bank, or their newer – and already global – counterparts such as the WTO. Since the late 1970s, legitimising policies and ideas have been forged, designed to reconstitute a capitalistic hegemony that is no longer a Nation-State

---

1 The following entities sat on the Organising Committee of the World Social Forum in Brazil:
Brazilian NGOs Association (ABONG – *Associação Brasileira de ONGs*);
Action to Tax Financial Transactions for Supporting Citizens (Attac – *Ação pela Tributação das Transações Financeiras em apoio aos Cidadãos*);
Brazilian Committee for Justice and Peace, National Council of Brazilian Bishops (CBJP/CNBB – *Comissão Brasileira Justiça e Paz*);
Brazilian Association of Entrepreneurs for Citizenship (Cives – *Associação Brasileira de Empresários pela Cidadania*);
Central Workers Union (CUT – *Central Única dos Trabalhadores*);
Brazilian Institute for Social and Economic Analyses (Ibase – *Instituto Brasileiro de Análises Sociais e Econômicas*);
Global Centre for Justice (*Centro de Justiça Global*);
Landless Peasants Movement (MST – *Movimento dos Trabalhadores Rurais Sem Terra*).

imperialism, but rather a worldwide system serving huge privately-owned economic and financial corporations. The driving force behind all this is the idea of the free market, the law of the quest for total productivity, and competition at a global scale. The driving force behind all this is liberalisation and privatisation, deregulation and the reduction of the role of State in economic administration. Even the principal leaders and intellectuals of these ideas and policies define them as being globalisation, an irreversible process that – according to them – marks the end of history. The real end of the bipolar order and the Cold War that developed after World War II was the collapse of true socialism in Eastern Europe, which seemed to establish the definitive conditions for consolidating and expanding the new world (dis)order of economic and financial capital.

In practical terms, however, this globalisation has resulted in a systematic transfer of the power to formulate policies from the Nation-States to the international sphere, concentrating power in global institutions that are not at all democratic or transparent. Outstanding among its results is the speed-up in the concentration of wealth in just a few hands, with rising inequality and social exclusion at the global scale, which jeopardises the sustainability of the Planet to an even greater extent, where daily life is subject to the whims and wagers of stock exchange speculators and the "economic health" of corporations and governments, endangering the life to undertake an in-depth analysis of what is commonly called globalisation. However, it is well worthwhile highlighting two elements in order to understand the widespread discomfort that this causes, and the rising – and increasingly irate – waves of protest sweeping around the world. Initially, globalisation fostered by huge economic and financial conglomerate is synonymous with denying historical conquests and dismantling rights. In order to allow this globalisation to expand, there is a social and historical standpoint of expanding the public and grassroots space in question. Everything that has been built up through hard struggle and social participation, with discussions and agreements among opponents and many different sides, expressed in the relationships, processes, structures and policies of a democratic State of Law is now being dismantled, although this was designed to foster and extend the collective well-being. Despite the vast variety of situations of one type or another, this dismantling process is spreading through all societies, producing a new phenomenon that consists of the interiorisation of the poverty of the South by the developed North, and to an even greater extent in Eastern Europe, while at the same time the wealth of the North is trickling down to benefit a privileged few in the impoverished South. To an increasing extent, more and more people are protesting against this dismantling of citizenship rights.

A second aspect that is directly associated with its predecessor is related to globalisation as the dominant ideology and world view. Here, globalisation is dealt with as a single type of thinking, and as a value that claims to be universal. Much has been written about the intrinsic speciousness of the driving idea of the free market, which lies at the heart of the elaboration of neo-liberalism, its much touted triumphs and arrogance that neither see nor admit alternatives other than variants on itself. It is sufficient to recall that no market exists without a political and institutional framework, and consequently without an authority. The free market and the global market are in fact a worldwide power system that is forging structure of suprastate authorities and institutions such as the WTO, the IMF, the WB, G-7, the European Union, NATO and many others, placing the United Nations and powerful States such as the USA at its service, together with their armies and central banks. The free market – where almost nothing is free other than the law of the jungle that always benefits the strongest – is in fact a concept of the world, of the way of organising the economy, the State authorities and civil society itself. This concept views the world from the accumulation-based standpoint of mega-corporations, with the well-being of society seen as a natural outcome of enhance economic health.

Globalisation takes an economicistic and reductionist view of the human situation. However, saying that it has no values would be a mistake in our combat strategy. Neo-liberalism springs from the restoration and re-enthronement of the old ideas of individualism as the core value in human relationships. This does not mean denying the individuality of each individual and unique man and woman. The problem lies in rating this as the exclusive value, as undertaken by individualism. The idea of citizenship contradicts this specifically because it views common rights and values through different individuals. Freedom, equality and diversity are core factors in the concept of citizenship. As values are not individual properties, they are rights that only exist when common to different individuals. This gives rise to the clash between the standpoints of citizenship and individualism. This also lies at the root of all cultural and political opposition of emerging global citizenship to the individualism preached and practiced by globalisation. In brief, it may be said that neo-liberalism expropriates citizenship in the name of individualism, which in practical terms means depriving men and women citizens of the power of decision over their own lives within society.

It is vital to view the World Social Forum as deeply imbued with this cultural broth of opposition to the dominant globalisation that is at the service of major economic groups, seeking one of the ways to encourage collective awareness and the theoretical preparation of alternatives. This is why the underpinnings of the Forum and its vitality are intrinsically linked to the trenches holding back the avalanche of globalisation, dug by groups of men and women there where they live and build up the conditions of their economic, social and cultural lives.

Similarly, it is impossible to understand this initiative without associating it with the rising wave of public protests and demonstrations against globalisation noted over recent years, particularly in Seattle, Washington, Prague and Nice. What makes this Forum both possible and feasible are all those men and women who have taken up this struggle through movements, associations and organisations, in actions both small and large, local or nationwide, regional or global, this does not matter. It is the confluence of the diversity of networks and movements at the widest possible global scale that directs the World Social Forum.

The appearance of global civil society and planetary-wide citizenship seems to be a key factor, or even a rallying-cry, but it is not, and warrants analysis in order to offset the lack of reflection, together with technical and political systematisation that is vital for anyone whose benchmarks are freedom and human dignity, engaged in the radicalisation of democracy. It would be a mistake to limit them to globalisation itself, as though they were its effects. Worldwide social movements exist through the power of the players themselves who establish them. Leaving no doubts on this matter, I recall the feminist and environmental movements as examples here. On a broader-ranging basis, we can associate the human rights movement with them, although it has not yet forged a collective global subject as its flag-bearer. These movements created and still create global facts, not due to economic and financial globalisation, but rather as the natural outcome of the grassroots issues that fuel them, which are global by nature. But we are facing another globalisation movement. It is not by chance that they are fighting on the front lines.

Contradictorily, there is no doubt that the struggle against globalisation is expanding the process of establishing global civil movements and networks. The agenda and the event "of the others" at the international level have been and still are fields where new players are appearing together with networks focused on globalisation as the core issue. Building up links among civil organisations throughout the lengthy Uruguay Round of the GATT Talks from 1986 through 1994, that resulted in the WTO as its final act in Marrakech, was a workshop in building up a global prospective on citizenship. The next step led us to Seattle in late 1999, when militant global citizenship managed to abort the establishment of a new round of talks for deregulating world trade, under the aegis of the WTO. This was clearly already a strategic alliance of civil networks and players, as well as NGOs and trade unions in particular. A similar process took place over the issue of the World Jubilee Campaign in 2000.

These particularly active global citizenship networks emerged during the cycle of conferences run by the United Nations during the 1990s. Specific examples are networks such as Social Watch and Development Alternative with Women for a New Era (DAWNE). But many other networks have also been set up, such as the Structural Adjustment Participatory Review International Network (SAPRIN), Alliance pour un Monde Responsable et Solidaire, Red Interamericana Agricultura y Desarrollo (RIAD), Agricultures Paysannes et Modernisation (APM), Via Campesina, One World and many others. In general, theme-focused networks that build up basic expertise, know-how and experience progress to consider alternatives to globalisation.

Once viewed without free market blinkers, the world seems to be fertilised by the values, thoughts and acts that are ushering in another future for humankind. Anyone who thinks that economic and financial globalisation is barely running up against old interests and opposing forces is quite wrong. They certainly exist, there is no doubt about that, but are characterised by also being against the emerging worldwide civil society and planetary-wide citizenship. Those "on the other side" who supported the World Social Forum have a fresh flavour of powers that are being renewed through struggles, taking to the streets in order to defend their causes, getting organised into worldwide networks to exchange experiences and draw up collective proposals, participating in remodelling States, economies and even their own societies, while exploring the possibilities of the place where they live.

The World Social Forum seeks to be yet another meeting-place, a cross-roads, an open university for global citizenship, in order to reflect and exchange knowledge, expertise, know-how and experience. This is a public affirmation of diversity and the construction of alternatives, when faced with the wearisome, homogenising and single-minded rationale of neo-liberal globalisation. The World Social Forum attempts to extract the common constructive essence of our diversity through global grassroots initiatives, in parallel to the dominant globalisation.

This is where the World Social Forum found an echo. The rest consisted of the daring and courage of the players who became involved in making it a reality: the Organising Committee in Brazil, the International Support Committee, the vital support of the Rio Grande do Sul State Government and the Porto Alegre Town Council. There is no doubt that the social fabric of organisations and movements in Brazil, together with the political density of its experience in participative administration of local governments were crucial conditions for its implementation, while sending an unchallenged signal to the world of its intentions. Finally, the political sense cannot be ignored of our colleagues who so ably identified an immediate target in counterpoint to everything that we wish through the World Social Forum. Consequently, this selection of the World Economic Forum in Davos could not have been better, while also setting the dates for our event.

World Social Forum I: A Cauldron of Ideas, Happiness and Hope

Something new was born in Porto Alegre. For many years, a meeting like this has not been seen, a true "Now!" call to action for world democracy, complete with all the bustle and muddle appropriate to an event as huge as this. It was heart-warming to be a part of such a historic event, as a witness. Floating in the air was an invitation to daring dreams, because another world is possible, timely and necessary. But this task is very demanding, and this was merely a good start.

Quite some time will still be needed to confirm and highlight the steps taken at this I Forum. Reclaiming everything will be quite impossible. The available data are merely educated guesses – as delegates, representing entities and movements in civil society, academic institutions, churches, parliamentarians and mayors – there were over 4,700 people there, with over 1,500 international participants registered from 117 countries. Guest celebrities totalled 165 (77 Brazilian and 88 international) of whom 96 were panellists (27 Brazilian and 69 international). The number of youngsters in the Youth Camp was estimated at 2,000, with 700 representatives from the indigenous nations. Over 1,300 people were accredited to help with the organisation, communications, logistics support, translation and security. Additionally, a further 1,870 journalists were accredited, 386 of whom were international.

The interest prompted in the media by this Forum is also very clear through the communications media to which these journalists belong: 764 outlets (television, radios, leading newspapers through to the alternative media published by movements and entities) of whom 322 were international from 52 countries. This picture is completed by a further 10,000 – 12,000 participants who were drawn to the World Social Forum and followed its many different scheduled activities in some way. The Events Centre at the Pontifical Catholic University, the nerve centre of the Forum, was a microcosm of emerging world citizenship, for a few days. With the support of the *Perseu Abramo* Institute in São Paulo, a sampling survey is being completed (400 people) undertaken in the heat of the event in an attempt to capture the expectations and assessments of this participant universe.

The Organising Committee opted for a structure working with three types of basic activities, divided into three phases: the panel sessions in the morning; initiative workshops run by the delegates in the afternoon; and testimonial sessions in the evening session from leading names in the struggle for citizenship all over the world. A basic theme was proposed for the panel sessions divided into four sections, each assigned four core issues:

- The production of wealth and social reproduction
- Access to wealth and sustainability
- The affirmation of civil society and public areas
- Political power and ethics in the new society

Consequently, four panel sessions were held simultaneously every morning at the Forum. Despite large audiences at these morning panel sessions and the importance of their discussions, the true value of the Forum and its innovative power sprang from the workshops proposed by the participants. Here diversity was not only well to the fore, but was also creative in analysing these issues in depth, putting forward proposals, exchanging experiences and building up links among the participants themselves.

Over 420 workshops were scheduled, with more than 300 of them actually taking place. Over 80 workshops were proposed by the participants focused on Core Theme I, stressing issues related to work and supportive economics, with almost 40 workshops. Core Theme II prompted 110 workshops, 70 of which discussed human rights and the distribution of wealth. Core Theme III drew almost 120 proposed workshops, highlighting the issue of strengthening the capacity of civil societies and building up public areas, with 90 workshops. Over 110 workshops focused on Core Theme IV were split largely between the issue of democracy and the new power (55) and mediating conflicts and the construction of peace (40). In fact, all these workshops were important, precisely because they showcased the practice, theoretical reflections and proposals of the participants. Unfortunately, it was not possible to set up an operation that could systematically garner information from all these workshops. Over 115 data-sheets produced and the documents forwarded to the organisers by the people in charge of the workshops are a real treasure-trove that is only now starting to be explored. This is a vital task that is crucial for enhancing the visibility of the workshops and the World Social Forum itself, already thinking about its continuation.

Prompting much interest, the testimonial sessions proved an effective way of presenting the experience built up by people closely identified with the causes of citizenship. They certainly supplemented a preliminary effort to chart who we are and what we are doing, for all the men and women engaged in constructing alternatives to the dominant globalisation. The parallel meetings with mayors and parliamentarians added resonance to the Forum as an innovative event able to spur a steady stream of ideas.

The I World Social Forum sketched out a skeleton framework of issues affecting us all, as well as the initiatives that we are launching and the practices we are developing, the alternative proposals that we can produce, and the networks that we are striving to build up in order to underpin their feasibility. Although this is a coherent framework, nothing here is systematised. One of the risks was precisely that this vast wealth of diversity would disperse into anarchy. This did not occur due to the common principles and values that inspire the broad range of participants in the Forum. These principles and values act like cement for hearts and minds, bringing activists together from all over the world in a wave of enthusiasm.

The first and most important outcome of the Social Forum was the event itself, held at this time. More than any discussion, its existence became a relevant political fact. Few people would have imagined before it took place just how much room it could make, and how much support it could drum up. The second crucial political outcome, which is inseparable from its predecessor, was the production of the World Social Forum as the antithesis of the World Economic Forum in Davos, the Mecca of neo-liberalism, the meeting-point and cross-roads for the elite heading up the economic and financial globalisation drive. Consequently, at its birth, the Social Forum showed that there is a global perspective that we are building up as men and women all seeking human dignity and freedom, rights, citizenship, and sustainability, while on the other hand there is the global standpoint of the World Economic Forum, with its neo-liberalism and the economic and financial stakes held by giant corporations, the law of the strongest in market terms.

It is important to have prompted public discussions and the clash of standpoints. This is a vital element in the identity of the World Social Forum as a specific area. The main objective is not to line behind a single idea able to challenge the dominant mind-set. Despite all the tensions, pressures and misunderstanding in this first version of the Forum, its key objective was preserved, enhancing the diversity of alternatives and ideas based on citizenship and prompted by the lack of alternatives to the single mind-set of neo-liberalism. It did not produce just one official document, but rather issued many different statements drafted by a wide variety of networks and organisations through the many different workshops. Respecting the diversity of view points and contradictions presented in these documents when comparing them, what might be called the document issued by the World Social Forum was finally drawn up. In fact, the visualisation and dissemination of this set of documents is a practical task that has not yet been concluded, due to the way in which everything happened in Porto Alegre.

This attempt to ensure the open and non-deliberative nature of this event was certainly not free of risks, although it enhanced the ideas, initiatives and experiences of civil society. Right from the start, even during the preparatory phases, and during the days in Porto Alegre, tension could be felt between an event calling for mobilisation and direct action and the wish to establish an area for reflection and discussion. The latter finally prevailed, despite everything that happened. Another constant risk was that the Forum would either split up into parties and factions or adopt an official stance. The open discussions with State and Municipal government leaders in parallel to their generous support and the breadth of their understanding of the nature of this event were vital factors in surpassing expectations and growing into what is in fact become: a civil society event with massive social and political density, indicating the possibility to the world of hatching a broad-based movement based on ideas fostering citizenship.

Challenges to Progress through the World Social Forum Initiative

The impact caused by the I World Social Forum prompted high expectations, in the hope of forging ahead with this initiative. This was clear on the faces of almost all the participants. And this driving force was certainly a powerful spur to continue following the signs from Brazil and other corners of the Planet, as well as many of those who were unable to be present but forwarded their wishes to participate and support. The media amplified the Forum and endowed it with echoes, prompting us to accept the public commitment to continue.

It seems that there is today a need for an area that is global in size where we can compare and polish our dreams, utopias, ideas and proposals, experiences and movements. There is a desire and an awareness – usually diffuse – expressed in a wide variety of ways and even contradictory in different societies and cultures, but which all point towards a more humane world that is democratic and sustainable, grounded on the ethical principles and values of freedom, equality, diversity, solidarity and participation. This heritage – entwined with the idea of citizenship and that humankind has strained to produce from its entrails – is jeopardised by the avalanche of economic globalisation.

But in its stubborn persistence, this is the heritage that lays the stepping-stones for initiatives such as this. Activists from all over the Planet have plunged into a wide variety of local struggles whenever they can, engaged in initiatives and processes that allow them to join up with others, to imagine and think about the world they want. The World Social Forum could serve as the yeast that makes a powerful movement of ideas rise steadily.

Some definitions of its continuation seem to cause little dissent: this event should be held on an annual basis on the same dates as the Davos Forum in Switzerland, and should be as global as possible. This is why I will not spend time on these aspects. I take a position on six controversial issues that I feel are true challenges that all of us, both men and women, must face in order to strengthen the World Social Forum.

How to Globalise the Forum

Despite the presence of representatives from 117 countries at the I World Social Forum, it was clear that Africa, Asia and Northern and Eastern Europe were poorly represented, as well as the Caribbean and Central America. This was paralleled by gaps in the global social representation of players from the vast spectrum of men and women, young and old, with widely-varying ethnic, racial and cultural profiles, as well as the mentally and physically challenged, among many others. A more representative audience would not be solved merely through opening up to diversity in full, with clearer summons or urging people to participate. There is a problem of logistics involved here, including the capacity to underwrite the costs of attending. In general, the participants in the World Social

Forum, particularly from most of the Southern countries, lack the funds to finance their own trips. And it is not easy to raise these funds through international cooperation.

At the same time, the experience of Porto Alegre revealed that the place where the Forum is held serves as a power tool for animating and reviving local movements, associations, organisations, groups and networks. This is a highly positive aspect of what the Forum intends to be. But to do so, it must maintain its global dimension, added to the local affairs, moving from the local to the global level and ensuring that they interact. The worst danger would be to "Brazilianise" the Social Forum, binding it to the political logic of a specific country or place.

This prompted the Organising Committee to suggest that the Forum should travel around the world. But how? And when? These positions then began to firm up. Once the pressure eased, I still feel that the most daring idea to globalise the Forum appeared at the last minute, through a consensus among its members: a Multipolar Forum for 2002. But it will be multipolar through initiatives in other regions and countries held at the same time, with the same visibility, creating the same atmosphere of a global citizens meeting, with all of us feeling that we are taking part in a single, uniglobal initiative. The challenge lies in the organisation, but this can surely be done if we dedicate to this the same or greater efforts than we devoted to organising the I World Social Forum in Porto Alegre. Video, audio and internet resources can be used to run real-time discussion sessions in different parts of the world wherever these World Social Forum events are held.

The Nature of the World Social Forum

The innovative factor here is the privileged political and cultural position that the Forum could well hold in the global context, closely linked to extending its quality as a meeting place for discussions. Mobilisation and direct action already have their own global agendas, and no matter how important they may be, they do not need the World Social Forum. This should be preserved as a confluence of networks and movements for thinking strategically, with an eye to action. After all, it was through action that we became established. However, we need this global citizenship university, where we can meet people with many different ideas and practices, in order to fine-tune our proposals for the future.

Outlining the Common Values and Principles that Drive Us

The World Social Forum will be a nursery for ideas and proposals, whose power springs from its social and cultural diversity, grounded in its theoretical and practical consistency. Producing documents, taking up positions, making them public and disseminating them widely are all crucial requirements and a right of all those engaged in an initiative such as the World Social Forum. But any attempt to arrive at a single document would strap us into a homogenising strait-jacket, while removing the legitimacy of criticisms fired at the single-minded approach of globalisation.

So how can we explain what draws us together in the World Social Forum? It is the ethical principles and values clustering together the diversity of who we are. This is why it is an urgent and ongoing task for the political and cultural foundations of the World Social Forum to draw up a Charter of Values and Principles to which the participants adhere. This could provide positive criteria for administering our diversity, without running the risk of allies that are totally undesirable through their ideas and practices.

The Issue of the World Social Forum Agenda

This is a particularly important challenge. There seems to be little dissent on this matter, because the Agenda has not yet clearly emerged. At the Porto Alegre Forum, almost everything could be slotted in – but it must be acknowledged that it was not the consistency of its Agenda that caused an impact, but rather the mere intention of drawing it up, in counterpart to the World Economic Forum in Davos. At least, this was how the media saw us.

In fact, we function as a kind of scale. On the one hand, the organisers proposed the core theme panels for the morning sessions. On the other, the participants were urged to suggest workshops for the afternoons. The idea here was to foster meetings among the proposals in order to draft and validate a working agenda for the future. And this did in fact occur in Porto Alegre, at least to some extent. The core theme panel sessions were quite open and apparently stimulating. In turn, the workshops exceeded all expectations in terms of their wealth and diversity. But what about the future Agenda? Something still to be defined, as the discussions were so varied and abundant that it was almost impossible to identify the Agenda reflecting the new version of the World Social Forum. Here I refer to that

Agenda that called for a closer-knit approach to the many issues inspiring people from all over the world.

The issue of the Agenda is important, insofar as the World Social Forum intends to be pro-active rather than re-active, as is the case with most of the world citizenship events. The Agenda itself – which does not depend on the immediatist agenda of the "owners" of the world – is vital for the Forum in order to build up an identity as the immediate antithesis of the World Economic Forum, in counterpart to the powerful institutions that draw up the globalisation policies, such as G-7, WTO, WB, IMF and many others.

The challenge is to produce an agenda that, as noted by Boaventura Souza Santos in Porto Alegre, is able to "propose something new to maintain the old". Faced with the dismantling of rights by globalisation, their protection demands that a new standpoint be built up that will foster their universalisation through dialog with the multi-culturality that constitutes the emerging planet-wide citizenship. This also seems to be a task that cannot be postponed, under threat of the World Social Forum losing its way.

Upgrading our Practices

The alternative proposal is included under citizen initiatives from all over the world, even if embryonic form. In general they are local and limited, spurred by the urgency of situations, with the experiences of movements and organisations constituting a real laboratory for alternatives. The Forum could function as a "translator", helping acknowledge equality in diversity, spotlighting our similarities and differences. What we need is to build up an exchange of expertise and know-how rooted in action, identifying the nerve-centres of these issues, and proposing a task of systematic political reflection. This is a job that the World Social Forum could recommend to all its participants, right from the preparatory stages, encouraging assessments and analyses of its practices as a condition for their implementation. A task still to be completed after the Porto Alegre Forum is to collect and appreciate what has already been done, prompting so many workshops and enlivening so many panel and testimonial sessions. We may lack capital, but we are rich in citizen practices that guarantee our Forum to develop a standpoint that is radically different from that of the World Economic Forum.

Legitimacy and Operating Capacity in the Organisation of the World Social Forum

In principle, the role of the Organising Committee of the I World Social Forum was over once the event was held. How can the operating conditions required for its continuation be introduced? This challenge has been left open. There is no doubt that the Brazilian entities on the Organising Committee of the I Forum have some very special responsibilities that they cannot shrug off. Equally, the Rio Grande do Sul State and Porto Alegre City Governments remain involved, as well as all those who supported the Forum in some way.

The problem lies in its legitimacy, even though this does not cover its full scope. The invitations to help organise the continuation of the World Social Forum could be issued by a Committee that should be global in both geographical and social terms. This is a delicate and difficult task that can only be carried out by the Organising Committee itself. We will need much generosity and political grandeur. The immediate need is to identify the networks and movements that have most clearly adhered to the World Social Forum and are willing to do their utmost to continue this initiative. Moreover, all those who are eager to globalise the Forum and even to organise simultaneous events in their home region become members of the Committee itself through their efforts.

In order to undertake these efforts to become operational, we should move towards setting up an International Politics Committee, that will be responsible for defining the guidelines for the World Social Forum, together with a representative Organising Committee with operations capacity at every place where the Forum will be held, in addition to an Executive Secretariat that will form the link between the Political Committee and the various Organising Committees, while undertaking the activities needed to network and organise a Multipolar Forum. There is no way of being dogmatic on this issue. But it is better to take a risk – as we did with the I World Social Forum – than wait around for the ideal conditions to appear.

In closing, it should always be borne in mind that the World Social Forum is well worthwhile, although not an immediate space for the exercise of power. Although politics and policies are part of its identity, its higher commitment is to expanding the world public area for the exercise of citizenship. We should do everything to avoid becoming an event that merely struggles for positions, whatever they may be. It is the wave of citizenship that we need to pump up, rather than letting it peter out among the breakers on the beach. This is how we can offer our contribution to making another world possible.

SECTION II
APPROACHES

HUMAN DIGNITY AS A BASIC CONCEPT OF ETHICS AND HUMAN RIGHTS

Paulo César CARBONARI (Brazil)

Introduction

Fostering the promotion and protection of human rights means striving to transfer to the daily routines of humankind, in all its plurality and historical diversity, the conditions needed to ensure that human dignity is understood as an undeniable starting-point and guiding principle for actions. Steadily building up on this basis, with no backsliding, the social and political arrangements and frameworks that pave the way to the effective implementation and realisation of human rights is a basic challenge, ranked among those calling for a world with adequate space and time for affirming humanity. We want to spur a discussion of the importance of human rights, considered from an ethical standpoint and based on the idea of human dignity.

In order to achieve our objective, we begin with the discussion on the nature of the reflection we wish to undertake. This means discussing to what extent ethics – as a philosophical reflection – can indicate elements for establishing human dignity as a cornerstone of human rights. Next we establish dignity as the core issue in the discussion on human rights. Finally, we will draw some conclusions from an historical standpoint.

The Place of Ethics[1]

Initially, as a recently-established unit of reason, philosophy implies acknowledging the intersubjective validity of moral standards as a *requirement* for the exercise of rationality as such, in order to affirm all and any type of knowledge as valid and meaningful. This includes the implicit duty of being rational, as rationality involves the insurmountable need for discussion, always regulated publicly[2]. This clearly indicates that we will

---

1 Part of Chapter III of our Master's Dissertation, defended in March 2000 for a Master's Degree in Philosophy, Goiás Federal University, tutored by Professor José Nicolau Heck.

2 According to Apel: "Among the *indisputable assumptions* (among the *regulatory conditions of possibility)* of the discussion would be that of having already accepted a *fundamental rule* constituting the *rules of an ideal community with unlimited discussion*". See K-O Apel, *Una ética de la responsabilidad en la era de la ciencia,* Buenos Aires (Almagesto), 1990, p. 19.

pursue our objectives along these lines according to the ethics of discourse, as presented by Karl-Otto Apel.

Discussing and participating in the communication-based community is not the result of a subjective decision, an act of faith, or an awareness that is reached empirically. Discussion is the transcendental condition of possibility for both understanding possible future subjective decisions, acts of faith and also considering all and any empirical conditions. The fact that we discuss – an empirical conditioning factor – does not provide the foundations for the rules of discussion. Accepting this freely is a necessary condition, but not sufficient to validate the rules. Consequently, acknowledgement of discussion and well-founded agreement is a condition that is sufficiently confirmed through the process of transcendental reflection. It is not a fact to be demonstrated, but rather to be acknowledged as always present in the rational process[3].

The reconstruction of the conditions of practical reason is an exercise in communication that cannot waive the *a priori* argumentation[4]. Acknowledgement of the *a priori* significance of discussion implies acknowledging the *a priori* practice of participation (taking part) in the process of its establishment, consequently breaking away from the *methodical solipsism* in practical reasoning. The duty of complying with the basic rule consequently does not depend on a decision of will or straightforward wish. It depends on acknowledgement that it is already implied in the act of proposing a rule that is justified. In the final analysis, even the act of refuting the need of the justification for a basic rule is in itself an exercise in argumentation and as such must assume the conditions for the argumentation, including the rule of basic ethics – without which its performance would be contradictory. The question of justifying the rule is not *without sense,* except in case of withdrawing *eo ipso* from argumentation either against or in favour of this – recalling Aristotle, becoming a plant rather than a discussant.

---

3 The in-depth analysis of this issue implies a discussion over the *de factum* understanding *of the reason,* in the Kantian and Humean sense and its reinterpretation by Apel. By Apel, among other texts, check: *La Transformación de la Filosofía,* (translated by Adela Cortina, Joaquin Chamorro & Jesus Conill), Madrid (Taurus), 1985, Tome II. The last text: *La ética de la responsabilidad en la era de la ciencia* (*o.c.*); by Kant, *Fundamentação da Metafísica dos Costumes e Crítica da Razão Prática.*

4 In *Una ética,* Apel says: "In so far as the argumentative discourse in itself is not *contingent* with regard to discussion, unless *this is pre-established a priori (this cannot be transcended in the reflection on the conditions of possibility)* it may be said, in the spirit of transcendental Kantian philosophy: *the rules of cooperation in argumentative discourse are unconditionally mandatory,* meaning *they are categorical",* *o.c.*, p. 21.

The grounds for this process must follow a reflexive foundation model. Initially, it is important to note that the intention is to provide the foundations for *a single* basic moral rule, rather than a system of morals. This is because, as we will show, the rule itself implies the possibility of respect for various different systems, provided that their basic meaning is grounded on the rule that is universally acknowledged. Consequently, here this implies the need for a mandatory foundation of validity for the basic ethical rule, rather than an argument that could force a person to voluntarily strengthen the rule whose validity is already deemed to be beyond discussion. This does not mean providing grounds for the need to follow a basic rule, but rather showing that following any rule, and the basic rule in particular, implies the mandatory need for it to be valid, and consequently properly grounded.

The basic ethical rule establishes that the only human pretensions that are ethically relevant are those that could be made universal through an agreement that is basically founded on rational argument, with the purpose of the supportive formation of the will[5]. Consequently, Apel concludes:

> "The subjective decisions taken by the conscience of each person and required by the Christian tradition, secularised through liberalism and existentialism, are now tempered by the requirement of an *a priori* intersubjective validity – so that each person immediately acknowledges the public argument as an explanation for all possible criteria of validity and consequently for the rational formation of the will"[6].

Immediately, pursuant to this formulation, Apel affirms that: "Understanding the principle presented here doubtlessly implies acknowledging at the same time that little can be achieved through the simple proposal of the principle, if the long-term task proposed together with the principle cannot be achieved"[7]. This issue introduces a constraint on the basic ethical principle (of the rule). This constraint consists of the fact that even someone who fully understands the moral principle cannot immediately participate in a (real) communication community, as this person remains bound to their real position and social status, resulting in the assumption of specific moral responsibilities. However, it must be noted that this lack

---

5 In *Una ética,* Apel formulates the basic rule or *principle of universalisation* as follows: "Acting only according to that maxim that places you in a position to take part in the discourse that provides the grounds for those rules whose consequences for all those affected are able to achieve consensus and take decisions alone or in cooperation with others, according to the spirit of the possible results of the ideal practical discourse" (p. 31).

6 K.-O. Apel, *Estudos de Moral Moderna,* (translated by Beno Dischinger), Petrópolis (Vozes), 1994, p. 151.

7 *Ibid.*, p. 151.

of material grounds that rank the principle within a context of idealism, in fact puts an end to a dialectic (that falls short) of idealism and materialism. In the words of Apel:

> "Consequently, anyone involved in a discussion always assumes two things: initially, a *real community of communication,* of which the person becomes a member through a socialisation process, and second, an *ideal community* of *communication* that in principle would be in a position to adequately extend the meaning of these arguments and definitively assess their truth"[8].

The apparent constraint on the principle consequently includes a dialectic that is constitutive of the transcendental structure of the *a priori* aspect of the argument. Tackling a situation of asymmetry and relativism in the real community is a condition for the possibility of thinking about the principle and attempting to implement it. This means understanding that the principle itself is *a priori* involved with the need for the historic realisation of the conditions of the discourse, of the argument.

It is on the basis of this requirement (historical, we would say) of all the arguments that Apel reaches what are known as the *basic regulatory principles for the long lasting strategy of moral action of each man.* This also involves what is known as the *principle of complementation* of the basic ethical rule. In *Transformation,* Apel explains this as follows: "First of all, for all types of action and refraining from action, steps should be taken to guarantee the *survival* of the human species, as well as the *real* community of communication; and second, to firm up the *ideal* community of communication within the real community"[9]. *The relation between these two implied aspects is the following, according to Apel: "The former objective is the vital condition for the latter: and that latter objective endows the former with its meaning – a meaning that is already anticipated in each argument"*[10]. What initially seems to be conservative in fact ceases to be so, as its meaning lies in allowing the realisation of the ideal community.

This means that it is not through destroying humankind, their historical situation, that the conditions needed to bring about the ideal community will be created; rather that the acknowledgement of the historical situation is the condition for allowing the ideal community. Here Apel clearly explains the *outer* problem, where the technical and scientific consequences indicate the destruction of the conditions needed for the survival of

---

8 *Ibid.*, p. 155.
9 *Ibid.*, p. 157.
10 *Ibid.*, p. 155.

humankind with dignity, as a real threat to the real community. From here it is possible to clearly understand the importance of taking the situation seriously, not as an absolute datum, but rather as a component that should be transformed, striving for better conditions. The condition of equality of the participants in the argumentative discourse required by the ideal community implies acknowledging the moral and historical asymmetry, striving to overcome this through ushering in symmetrical conditions in history as well. Consequently, the ideal community would not be a mere postulate or a store-house of our best intentions as humankind, just as the real community is not the storehouse of resistance to all systematic colonisation in itself. Both are supplemented in dialectic terms, in the sense that a contradiction must be borne from the standpoint of its historical accomplishment as a long path of achievement. The act of bearing here acquires the meaning that no attempt at synthesis is undertaken, unifying them, but rather an attempt to understand, that without taking them into account and without taking them seriously, no change may be attempted, nor may any morally significant action be justified. The validity of any moral action consequently does include the obligation to acknowledge that it may only be meaningful if it could be universalised through a process consisting of the supportive formation of the will, in an intersubjective process of reaching consensus within the communication community.

Human Dignity, Core Concept of Ethics and Human Rights

The establishment of a universally valid standard, an attempt undertaken by ethics and not without major problems, is also to some extent an attempt that proved necessary in order to establish human rights as universal. Consequently, human rights are featured among the regulatory contents of universally valid ethics. It is clear that the topic of human rights does not end with this aspect, which is perhaps the most difficult to establish, but also extends into matters of a juridical and political nature that we merely indicate, as we will not be able to deal with them in any depth here. In our view, and without becoming involved in juridical and political disputes on the universal, indivisible and independent nature of the human rights, we wish to place this issue on ethical grounds. This means that we feel that human dignity is the core foundation that can be converted into ethical rules, in terms of content, which means that human rights – ethically understood as guaranteeing human dignity – form a basic concept of a universally valid system of ethics.

We base this interpretation on the understanding that the concept of human rights is endowed with an inner *regulatory unity* that is grounded on the *equal dignity* of each human being as a moral subject, juridical subject, political subject and social subject. The acknowledgement of this *regulatory unity* finds a reflexive echo, because the construction of any arrangements, whether juridical, political or social, must always be grounded on the guaranteed conditions for human beings to play the leading role, which is not transferable. This *regulatory unity* creates conditions for guiding the construction of the historical arrangements for its implementation, while in contrast, for the critics these arrangements do not firmly reflect the prospects of their implementation.

Disagreeing with liberal or liberalising theses, we affirm that economic, social and cultural human rights are not hierarchically below civil and political human rights. They are at an equal level. We are tired of having to put up with situations where successive governments justify dictatorship by stating that in widely asymmetrical societies, curtailing the fundamental freedoms is justified in order to guarantee social and economic progress. Or else that, although poor, it is better for us to live in an era that guarantees the basic freedoms, offering us a chance to move into the competitive field of liberalism and perhaps cast some of the more sophisticated satisfaction benchmark of human demands, always individually, this means that dealing with human rights is dealing with all human rights, civil, political, economic, social and cultural human rights.

This position implies acknowledging that there is no freedom that may be exercised without a social area of solidarity. As confirmed by Frailing: "Human beings are material beings and need material goods to survive. Without meeting basic economic needs, the existence of the persons in freedom is not possible, shaping their existence"[11]. This means that ensuring that basic human rights are complied requires all-round treatment, which is also in play when we speak of their acknowledgement as universal. This means that all human rights claim to be acknowledged as universal. Obviously, the historical process of acknowledgement for many rights has progressed differently. But assigning privileges to any of them would mean yielding up the basic principle of human dignity.

Universality is a deep-rooted aspiration of more genuine human acts. We act in order for everyone to acknowledge that our action is the best, the most justified. But speaking of universal matters is far more difficult, as this implies a far more complex issue: diversity. Universality implies the thorny

---

11 Frailing, apud Bielefeldt, *Filosofia dos Direitos Humanos*, (translated by Dankwart Bernsmüller), São Leopoldo (Unisinos), 2000, p. 125.

problem of establishing what can effectively be acknowledged as universal, and this necessarily implies yielding on the particular aspects, tackling the problem identified in the ethical aspects, in some way.
Translating this issue into historical terms, a fair number of countries, groups and nations all over the world have taken much time to acknowledge the universal nature of human rights, while others have not yet even acknowledged them, alleging that this represents the ideal of life not for humankind as such, but for the Western capitalistic life-style, and is consequently not appropriate for the life-styles of such groups, countries or nations. With this specific problem, the struggle for human rights has stretched out for many years.

The Conference of Vienna[12] seems to have reached a slightly more satisfactory formula on this matter. This states that the local and historical context should be taken into account, which means that the interpretation and even the application of fundamental rights may differ, on the one hand, but a condition for ensuring them is the need to acknowledge the fundamental rights viewed as the *regulators* of action. According to the United Nations Organisation (UNO), the very idea of human rights embodies the idea of respect for diversity and plurality. Consequently, opposing human in the name of diversity and plurality is to some extent rebutting them. In other words, a basic agreement is required in order to guarantee diversity: at the very least, we should all respect differences.

However, this agreement may not be a mere dovetailing of interests, or a covenant for survival in the Hobbesian style. To the contrary, we rather believe that it should be an agreement grounded on reasons justifying its maintenance and even possibly its future modification, seeking an agreement that is more satisfactory for all. If it fails to cover all the consequences, and if its reasons are not properly grounded, it will be unable to satisfy everyone, and will have to be rewritten. In brief, guaranteeing human rights as universal rights moves away from the essentialist stance, which on the one hand believes in a certain idea of Human Nature to be preserved, while on the other it moves away from the contractualistic

[12] The II World Conference on Human Rights was organised by the United Nations and held in Vienna in 1993. In its Declaration and Programme of Action (UN – Doc. A/CONE 157/23) it states that: “All human rights are universal, indivisible and interdependent, and are related among themselves. The international community should treat human rights in a global manner, as well as in a fair and equitative manner, on an equal footing, giving them all the same weight. The importance of national and regional characteristics should be borne in mind, as well as those of the various historical, cultural and religious heritages, although the states have the duty, regardless of their political, economic and cultural systems, to foster and protect all human rights and fundamental freedoms” (Free translation of § 5).

approach that justifies them through matching up interests. This is where the idea of human dignity enters as the basic content for both establishing ethics as well as the basis of human rights. However, even this idea must be configured as a historical construction, aloof from essentialistic, naturalistic or contractualistic positions.

Within this context, the justification of the right lies within a complex cluster of reasons that should satisfactorily handle many different aspects, and need not be invoked as prior to the act of recognition. Other recognition provides sufficient motivation for common reason, or it will be a mere farce that will collapse when faced with the first clash. In other words, it is only with very serious and justified reasons that we will be able to acknowledge the diversity of others. And these reasons cannot be private. They must be common to the reasons of other people.

Citizenship, the Historical Aspect of Dignity

In his speech to the IV National Conference on Human Rights held in 1999 in Brasília, Brazilian jurist and Chief Justice of the Inter-American Court of Human Rights, Dr. Antônio Augusto Cançado Trindade said: "within this context, the main challenge lies in locating the human *persona* at the heart of the entire development process, which requires a spirit of greater solidarity in each national society and the awareness that the fate of each person is inexorably linked to the fate of all persons"[13]. In other words, this consists of building up an idea of citizenship in the broadest sense of the word, interconnected with the many different aspects of human life, and set against the backdrop of human dignity.

According to this logic, we understand that in addition to this solid foundation that is grounded on human dignity, human rights also require a historical basis underpinning their implementation in social and political areas. Consequently, this is why we open up a dialogue between the idea of the universally valid rule constituted according to the principle of Apel and the idea of human rights, while grounded on human dignity. The historical mechanism that is generally believed to be empowered to foster the development of this process is that of a democratic society. Consequently, according to the rationale of Bielefieldt, democracy and human rights progress arm-in-arm as follows:

---

[13] A.A. Cançado Trindade, 'O Brasil e o Pacto Internacional dos Direitos Econômicos, Sociais e Culturais', in: Lower House, Human Rights Commission, *Report of the IV National Conference on Human Rights,* Brasília (Publications Coordination Unit), 2000.

> "Through the metaphor of the reciprocal embrace, we wish to establish the regulatory unity between human rights and democracy, through which, concomitantly and with no hierarchical structure required, a difference may arise that does not consist of a difference in principles, but rather represents a difference in the *manner of implementing* this and the inalienable principle of supportive freedom. Should this core unity as the principle of human rights and democracy fade away, or one if becomes subordinate to the other, both of them lose"[14].

Through this, we wish to show that human dignity is the ethical foundation of the regulatory unity of human rights and democracy play, which are the historical construction of the conditions for its implementation within a real community that is properly prepared. This means that the specific content of human rights is a historical construction, based on human dignity. This has a historical aspect, the non-transferable nature of any possible content that could add to what should be understood as human rights. The historical bases underpinning the conditions for the further construction of human rights are those of democratic societies in the fullest sense, extending well beyond the mere formality of selecting representatives to fill positions of power.

References

Apel, Karl-Otto, *Estudos de Moral Modern,* (translated by Benno Dischinger), Petrópolis (Vozes), 1994.

- "La ética del discurso como ética de la responsabilidad: una transformación posmetafísica de la ética de Kant", in: K.-O. Apel, E.D. Dussel, & R. Fornet-Betancourt, *Fundamentación de la ética y la Filosofia de la liberación,* (translated by Luis F. Segura), México (Siglo Veintiuno/Iztapalapa), 1992, p. 11-44.
- *La transformación de la Filosofia,* (translated by Adela Cortina, Joaquin Chamorro y Jesus Conill), Madrid (Taurus), 1985. Tomes I & II. In the original: *Transformation der Philosopie,* Frankfurt am Main (Suhrkamp), 1976, 2 vol.

---

[14] Heiner Bielefeldt, *Filosofia dos Direitos Humanos,* (translated by Dankwart Bernsmüller), São Leopoldo (Unisinos), 2000, p. 135. The text continues as follows: "A concept of democracy dissociated from human rights would not only threaten these rights and the fundamental freedom that they represent, but would also threaten its own leanings towards freedom and would certainly degenerate into a simple conformity of the majority. On the other hand, the unilateral primacy of material rights over democracy would not only narrow its area of responsibility, but would also result in the materialisation of the concept of human rights, in which the weight of their emancipationist significance would be lost, for historically open rights to freedom".

– *Una ética de la responsabilidad en la era de la ciência,* Buenos Aires (Almagesto), 1990.

Bielefeldt, Heiner, *Filosofia dos Direitos Humanos,* São Leopoldo (Ed.Unisinos), 2000. In the original: *Philosophie der Menschenrechte,* Darmstadt (Wissenschaftliche Buchgesellschaft), 1998.

Cançado Trindade, Antônio Augusto, 'O Brasil e o Pacto Internacional dos Direitos Econômicos, Sociais e Culturais', in: Lower House, Human Rights Commission, *Report of the IV National Conference on Human Rights,* Brasília (Publications Coordination Unit), 2000.

THE EXPANDING NATURE OF HUMAN RIGHTS AND THE AFFIRMATION OF THEIR INDIVISIBILITY AND ENFORCEABILITY[1]

Jayme BENVENUTO LIMA Jr. (Brazil)

Introduction

In this paper, I intend to discuss the concept of the indivisible nature of human rights, based on their practical significance for those who defend such rights in their daily lives. My purpose is to demonstrate the inadequacy of the generation-based[2] classification of human rights, offering only a limited approach to this issue. According to this traditional view, only civil and political rights are considered as human rights *par excellence* and consequently warrant clearly defined mechanisms for their practical implementation. Meanwhile, economic, social and cultural rights are seen as achievable only through phasing them in over time, apparently not justifying mechanisms for their immediate implementation.

In contrast to this position, I claim that economic, social and cultural rights are just as vital as other human rights, which is why we should strengthen existing mechanisms ensuring their enforceability, while creating others as required.

---

1 Text presented at the Workshop on Economic, Social and Cultural Human Rights, at the World Social Forum, reviewed and expanded for this publication. Held in Porto Alegre in 2001, this Workshop was promoted by Cedar International (The Netherlands), the Latin American Platform for Development and Human Rights (PIDHH) and the National Human Rights Movement (Brazil). Icco (The Netherlands) offered considerable support.

2 First-generation of human rights are civil and political rights, essentially individual, appearing during liberal struggles against classic absolutism (the right to life, freedom, expression of thought and others), once viewed as being against the State. Second-generation human rights are economic, social and cultural human rights that are collective, arising from the socialist struggles of the past century and prompted by criticisms of insufficient liberal rights (right to education, right to work, right to healthcare, right to housing, etc.) which are enforceable through positive State action. Third generation human rights are the rights of peoples in terms of their countries, in order to ensure better distribution of wealth with mutual respect and use of Nature (rights to a healthy environment, international cooperation, development, etc.). Jayme Benvenuto, *Os Direitos Econômicos, Sociais e Culturais como Direitos Humanos. Uma Justificação,* Master's Degree Dissertation, Law Degree, Recife (Computer print-out), 2000, p. 22.

While urging the indivisibility of human rights, I also intend to demonstrate the practical consequences of affirming this concept. However, this is not a discussion of merely theoretical importance with no practical results in peoples' lives, and more particularly for human rights movements and groups. These consequences include the need to establish a standard of enforceability for all human rights, regardless of classification or category. After all, classifications or categories are merely ways of helping us understand phenomena, and should not intervene in the actual existence of these matters. Their existence does not depend on the classifications adopted.

Taking the concept of the indivisible nature of human rights as a condition for their practical implementation, I feel that it is necessary to consider and analyze the notion of the progressive nature of human rights. Economic, social and cultural human rights are particularly significant here, in order to endow them with fresh meanings that are more appropriate and broader-ranging, highlighting progressive aspects that streamline their implementation in today's world.

I will open this discussion with an analysis of the idea of the indivisible nature of human rights.

The Indivisible Nature of Human Rights

"Poverty is just as degrading as torture"[3]. This phrase was spoken by the Representative of Indonesia during the 56th Session of the UN Human Rights Commission. Although uttered by an official representative of a government that is known to violate human rights *en masse,* it nevertheless sums up the meaning of the concept of the indivisible nature of human rights. This concept strives to validate an all-round understanding of human rights.

The affirmation of the indivisible nature of human rights is linked closely to the end of the World War II, when the United Nations Organisation (UNO) was established, together with international systems for protecting human rights under the framework of the Universal Declaration of Human Rights. The Universal Declaration, which was issued in 1948, sought to cover civil, political, economic, social and cultural human rights with no generation-based distinctions. Yet, the subsequent years produced a world

---

[3] Excerpt from the speech by the Representative of Indonesia at the 56th United Nations Human Rights Commission Session, Geneva, March 2000.

that was deeply split into two economic and ideological blocs – capitalism and socialism – that undermined attempts to achieve a full understanding of human rights. As affirmed by Cançado Trindade, the initial idea under the aegis of the United Nations "was to include in a single Covenant all civil, political, economic, social and cultural rights, endowed with *report and petition* systems to implement them (this latter in a separate Protocol)". However, the outbreak of "specific ideological conflicts during the Cold War period and the process of colonies breaking away to declare their independence helped establish the basis for the two Covenants of Human Rights".[4, 5]

With the world split into two political and economic blocs, statements were heard within the liberal capitalist movement claiming that economic, social and cultural human rights were "communist", while left-wing movements called civil and political human rights "bourgeois". Shortsightedly, both statements were designed to undermine the credibility of the rights in question, which clashed with these respective doctrines. This split between liberal and socialist tenets blocked a more rational approach proving that human rights are endowed with such vast scope that they transcend matters of liberal of socialist doctrine.

With the end of the Cold War and the collapse of all these standpoints that divided not only world views but also countries, it become quite clear that human beings have political, civil, economic, social and cultural needs that should be met through defining their rights. After all, rights are social constructions that have historically been shaped by human requirements. This means that there is no way of denying the legitimacy of these rights today, seen from a broad-based standpoint. Overcoming the sterile dichotomy between civil and political human rights, and economic, social and cultural human rights would have been a major step forward in the history of humankind, if it were not merely an attempt to catch up on lost time stretching back at least forty years. This prompted the urgent need to include the idea of indivisible nature of human rights in the practices designed to implement them.

---

4 Antonio Augusto Cançado Trindade, *A Proteção Internacional dos Direitos Humanos e o Brasil,* Brasília (Edições Humanidades, Brasília University Foundation), 1998, p. 26/27.

5 "Despite this worldwide ideological split, the I World Conference on Human Rights, held in Teheran in 1968, proclaimed the indivisible nature of human rights, and praised the common-sense of those who believed in human rights as a concept transcending ideologies. More recently, after the end of the Cold War (1993) the II World Conference on Human Rights reaffirmed the indivisible nature of human rights as a key concept for preserving the progress in the validity of human rights. Jayme Benvenuto, *Os Direitos Econômicos, Sociais e Culturais como Direitos Humanos, o.c.,* p. 23.

However, any understanding of the indivisible nature of human rights requires at least a relative criticism of the generation-based classification that split them into three generations, allegedly keeping pace with the appearance and validation of these rights. The practical constraints of this classification are demonstrated by its inability to establish clear-cut distinctions between many human rights, as follows:

An initial distinction related to *the content of human rights* is intended to demonstrate that some rights are more important than others, due to their significance in the history of humankind, meaning that they require more effective protection mechanisms. A classic example is the right to life (physical) considered – according to this view – as the most fundamental of all rights. However, as stated by Cançado Trindade, taken in its broadest sense, the right to life also includes "the *conditions of life* (the right to live with dignity)". These "belong to a time falling under the domain of civil and political rights, as well as under economic, social and cultural rights", insofar as a definition of life restricted to the existence of physical life is not acceptable.[6] In fact, this same understanding is expressed in a decision handed down in 1999 by the Inter-American Court of Human Rights presided by this Brazilian Jurist, in the case known as *Villagrán Morales versus Guatemala,* involving the extermination of street children in Guatemala by police officers belonging to death squads. This decision was handed down with concurring decisions from Justices Cançado Trindade and Abreu Burelli, in a milestone decision that ushered in a new era for international law on human rights. The official juridical world had began to acknowledge the indivisible nature of human rights in practice, which means viewing and handling specific rights at any one single time as having civil, political, economic, social and cultural repercussions.[7]

The practical outcome of acknowledging the indivisible nature of human rights in the case of the Guatemalan street children is the call by the Inter-

---

[6] Antônio Augusto Cançado Trindade, 'A Proteção Internacional dos Direitos Econômicos, Sociais e Culturais: Evolução, Estado Atual e Perspectivas', in: *Tratado de Direito Internacional dos Direitos Humanos,* p. 396.

[7] "The duty of the State to take positive measures becomes more marked in terms of protecting the lives of people who are vulnerable or defenseless, living in high-risk situations such as street children. The arbitrary loss of the right to life is consequently not limited to unlawful homicides; it also extends equally to depriving people of the right to live with dignity. This view conceptualizes the right to life as belonging at one and the same time to the domain of civil and political rights, in addition to economic, social and cultural rights, while illustrating the inter-relationships and individual nature of all human rights". Organisation of the American States, International Court of Human Rights. Series: *Resolution and Decisions.* Case: Villagrán Morales and Others (Street children case). Decision handed down on November 19, 1999, San José, Costa Rica, 2000, p. 105-109.

American Court on Human Rights for "positive protection measures provided by the State" in order to ensure the right to life. Should this be lacking, it would hold the State liable for the death of the Guatemalan street children, who could well have been Brazilian, Colombian, Peruvian or living in any other country in Latin America that is faced with the tragedy of children being murdered by police officers and death squads. Acknowledging that the loss of life is not only physical but also social, insofar as "the life of these boys was already bereft of any meaning", the Court defined the right to life as "living with dignity". This manner of interpreting the right to life – and human rights as a whole – made a great deal of difference for validating these rights.

Regarding the distinction between the *temporal nature of the validation of human rights,* civil and political human rights would precede their economic, social and cultural counterparts. However, this distinction fails to take into consideration the fact that certain rights – such as the right to ownership (today understood as the supreme economic human right) – arose through liberal struggles and consequently during the validation period for civil and political human rights. It is quite true that the *liberal* understanding of the right to ownership fixed a highly personal and even restrictive meaning for this right (insofar as very few people had access to it); and over time, the right to ownership acquired a social significance that made it far broader-based. However, this shift in meaning over time does not invalidate the essence of the idea of ownership, as it acknowledges the "domain" of humankind over material and immaterial things. The idea here is that right from the start it has meant the *economic* appreciation of human requirements converted into rights.

Similarly, the right to equality – which is constantly identified among civil and political human rights – is grounded on the argument defending economic, social and cultural human rights. In a certain way, this right might be identified as being more closely related to the latter category than to the former. The right to equality that is urged today has expanded, based on the same historical process that extended the right to ownership, and no longer means acknowledging a formal right for citizens, but must rather represent a real possibility of becoming accessible to all citizens. And this is the current meaning, for instance, of calls for universal access to the right to healthcare or education.

The distinction between *the individual or collective nature of human rights* views civil and political human rights as being of an essentially individual nature, insofar as they would be guaranteed to citizens against the power of the

State, in keeping with all liberal theories that strive to curtail State intervention in people's lives as much as possible. In counterpart, it is felt that economic, social and cultural human rights demand effective action on the part of the State in order to validate them.

In the light of this understanding, we also encounter serious difficulties in classifying certain rights as either first or second generation. This is the case of the right to strike and trade union freedom, which may be identified as civil and political human rights because they arise from and are correlated with freedom of expression, requiring individual action in order to curtail State power. However, they are also considered as economic, social and cultural human rights, as they may be demanded from the State and are related to labour rights – public, collective and social rights. The difficulty of classifying them extends to several other rights, such as *civil* human rights to legal aid provided by the State, and electoral rights that – although civil – demand positive effective State action in order to ensure them.

From a different standpoint, it is said that economic, social and cultural human rights would be enforceable only through the definition of the corresponding government policies (economic and social) rather than legal and judicial measures ensuring their enforceability – this is the distinction in terms of the *possibilities of the enforceability of human rights.* This understanding seems unaware that civil and political human rights also require corresponding government policies (civil and political) to validate them, in addition to juridical enforcement mechanisms. In the field of civil and political human rights, government entities and guidelines (such as rights councils, human rights commissions, human rights action programmes, etc.) assign these rights to the field of government policies, without which the practical possibilities of existence for juridical mechanisms would be drastically reduced. Whether civil, political, economic, social or cultural, human rights require the adoption of policies designed to turn the legal definitions of these rights into a reality.

Another distinctive point is related to the *capacity for immediate application of human rights.* Civil and political human rights that are enforceable by individuals against the State would have the possibility of immediate validation. As economic, social and cultural human rights are enforceable through government policies, they would only be validated step by step, paced to the development of an (uncertain) economic future of the States. The mere existence of labour rights that are immediately enforceable demonstrates the lack of consistency in this distinction.

It is important to realize that what makes labour rights immediately enforceable is the existence of a government policy intended to ensure them, allied to the corresponding legislation that is endowed with its own tools, tailored to ensure the application of justice to these matters. The lack of such mechanisms in other areas, extending beyond the mere definition of favourable legislation, often reveals an intention to postpone the validity of economic, social and cultural human rights to an uncertain future, at the same time displaying a lack of commitment to human rights as a whole[8].

The inadequate nature of these attempts to establish absolute distinctions among the categories of rights results in paradoxes that hamper universal access to human rights and their validation. One of these paradoxes is represented by the view that civil and political human rights would have victims where rights are violated by certain agents (individuals and corporate legal entities at the domestic level, and the State at the international level); meanwhile, economic, social and cultural human rights would not be subject to breach as they cannot be assigned to anyone. This is yet another attempt to strip economic, social and cultural human rights of their characteristics as human rights, because both victims and violators are quite clear (basically, individuals, corporate legal entities, and the State). The violation of economic, social and cultural human rights occurs as soon as the State fails to meet its obligations to regulate international commitments or to undertake the alterations covered by the national legislation[9].

---

8 Cançado Trindade clearly sums up the incongruent aspects of fragmented views of human rights. "For governments, the pretext of working towards the "progressive implementation" of certain economic and social rights in an unspecified future systematically violates civil and political rights (eg. Latin America under the dictators, particularly during the 1970s)! How many governments have shielded themselves behind the conquest of civil and political rights in order to deny the validity of economic, social and cultural rights (eg. Latin America today)! How many governments have dared to proclaim themselves to be "promoters" of some economic and social rights, in order to continue minimising civil and political rights (eg. The fundamentalist countries in the works of the II World Conference on Human Rights, in addition to various Asian countries today)! How many governments all over the world still insist on "selecting" the right to which they "give priority", promoting and implementing the others in a future that is completely undefined!" Antônio Augusto Cançado Trindade, 'A Proteção Internacional dos Direitos Econômicos, Sociais e Culturais: Evolução, Estado Atual e Perspectivas', in: *Tratado de Direito Internacional dos Direitos Humanos*, p. 391.

9 "A State that has the means available to reduce infant mortality and fails to do so breaches the provisions guaranteeing the right to life, which is an indisputable right that can be claimed through the Courts, and for which sheltering or protective actions are necessary". Roberto Garretón M., 'La Sociedad Civil como Agente de Promoción de los Derechos Económicos, Sociales y Culturales', in: *Serie Estudios Básicos de Derechos Humanos*, Tome V, San José (Inter-American Institution for Human Rights), 1996, p. 79.

The generation-based classification of human rights has been used to emphasize certain nuances in human rights, as this is a broad-ranging category. Like all classifications, this reduces the understanding of the matters classified, which is why it should be used with caution, as required.

While not denying the existence of differences among human rights, including those related to the specific characteristics of the tools ensuring their enforceability, their indivisible nature spotlights the practical impossibility of compartmentalising human rights. Rights rated as civil and political can be materialized only if other rights – rated as economic, social and cultural – are also respected to at least a minimum level, and vice-versa.

This is why I feel that it is more appropriate to talk about civil and political human rights and economic, social and cultural human rights in order to imbue all human rights with the idea of indivisibility. While acknowledging the existence of the different types of rights, this standpoint clusters them under the mantle of human rights, endowing them with a certain conceptual unity.

The Enforceability of Human Rights

"Hell is full of good intentions"[10]. The popular adage repeated by Bobbio in the context of defending the validation of human rights, says much about the need to ensure enforceability – which is the possibility of the practical existence of rights – and the focus of human rights in today's world. Enforceability (including the right to justice and the possibility of claiming rights through the Courts) is today an imperative in both the theory and practice of human rights. After all, declarations of rights, constitutions and laws in general lose any practical meaning if there is no possibility of their effective application.

Rights defined as having "progressive" applicability cannot be viewed as being genuine rights. Quite correctly, Bobbio wonders whether: "a right whose acknowledgement and effective protection are postponed *sine die* in addition to being dependent on the will of subjects whose obligation to implement the "programme" may be merely a moral (or at the most

[10] "As I have already interpreted the scope that the discussion on human rights is already assuming, as an indication of the moral progress of human kind, it would not be inopportune to repeat that this moral growth cannot be measured by words but rather through facts. Hell is filled with good intentions". Norberto Bobbio, 'A Era dos Direitos', in: *A Era dos Direitos,* Rio de Janeiro (Editora Campus), 1992, p. 64.

political) obligation, can correctly be called a 'right'? (...) The figure of the right is correlated to the figure of the obligation"[11].

In order to progress towards the implementation of human rights from an indivisible standpoint, it is vital to move beyond certain rather limited ideas on the theory of human rights. Today, this initially means paying more attention to economic, social and cultural human rights, due to the gap in terms of the possibilities of their validation, compared to civil and political human rights. For many people, this affirmation may sound biased, as it assigns more weight to economic, social and cultural human rights. It may even sound pointless to defend the indivisible nature of human rights. I answer this in advance by saying that this is a matter of contextual relevance, similar to that justifying affirmative action – with a view to ensuring equality among the classes of rights in the near future.

Moving beyond limited ideas also means that the greater difficulties encountered in implementing economic, social and cultural human rights – caused by economic crises, limited validation of national and international mechanisms, globalisation processes etc. – should not hamper their implementation, but should rather be viewed as challenges. From this standpoint, working with the idea of establishing firm targets to tackle situations breaching these rights could well prove an effective approach. Provided that it is not taken in the limited sense – I would even say with improper intentions – of many governments, which exploit this idea to postpone the validation of rights as much as possible. It is not in a rhetorical sense that these targets should be set.

Dealing with these violations consequently requires a genuine will on the part of the State or government to achieve a certain level of respect for human rights. Many countries with high income concentration levels – like Bangladesh, Ethiopia, Morocco, the Ivory Coast, the Philippines, Paraguay and Swaziland[12] – have been introducing economic and social plans that at least attempt to improve the situation of penury in which most of their people subsist. In order to be effective, plans of this type should set firm targets to be achieved within specified deadlines, in parallel to an efficient monitoring system that ensures the implementation processes and universal access to these rights. Brazil's National Human Rights Programme (PNDH

---

11 Norberto Bobbio, 'Direitos do Homem e Sociedade', in: *A Era dos Direitos, o.c.*, p. 79-80.

12 United Nations Economic and Social Council. Operational Activities of the United Nations for International Development Cooperation, Poverty Eradication, Capacity-Building, Resources and Funding, and the Executive Boards of the United Nations Funds and Programmes, *Report of the Secretary-General,* E/1999/55, Geneva, 1999.

– *Programa Nacional de Direitos Humanos*) is being expanded in order to guarantee economic, social and cultural human rights as well. This review must necessarily include the definition of the targets that can be achieved through various control mechanisms, both juridical and political. I am referring to the need to monitor the definitions included in the programmes, as well as the policies and sets of actions needed to speed up the human rights implementation process. After all, the shortfall in human rights in most societies throughout the world is vast, urging that they should become a reality.

In keeping with the view defended by the United Nations, I think that it is also vital that programmes and actions proposed for inclusion under these plans should be guided by the quest to eradicate poverty. The eradication of poverty worldwide is the main challenge facing the States, the international community and the United Nations at the turn of this century. Programmes related to economic, social and cultural human rights should consequently address the fairer distribution of wealth and the expansion of opportunities. The fact that extreme poverty is growing worse all over the world justifies all and any effort to deal with it[13].

As acknowledged in the United Nations Declaration on the Right to Development (1986) "massive, flagrant violations of human rights" are the outcome of "colonialism, neo-colonialism, *apartheid*, all forms of racism and racial discrimination, foreign domination and occupation, and aggression and threats against national sovereignty, national unity and territorial integrity, as well as threats of war" which are social processes that should be overcome as a condition for seeking peace.

When referring to the need for free, active and significant participation and the distribution of the benefits built up by humankind, this Declaration highlights the old theme of human equality. "The States should take all necessary measures at the national level to implement the right to development and should, *inter alia*, ensure equal opportunities for all, in

---

13 In the words of the World Bank "one half of the world's population lives on some two dollars a day". According to the UN Independent Expert on Human Rights and Extreme Poverty, Anne-Marie Lizin, "one fifth of the population of the globe lives in utter poverty. In 1996, the Assembly-General of the United Nations estimated that over 1.3 billion people in the world, most of them women, live in utter poverty, particularly in the developing countries, and this figure continues to rise". While government rhetoric from representatives all over the world agrees that all human beings deserve decent economic, social and cultural living conditions, the gap between the developed countries on the one hand and the poorer countries and the developing countries on the other is expanding rapidly". Jayme Benvenuto, *Os Direitos Econômicos, Sociais e Culturais como Direitos Humanos, o.c.*, p. 22.

terms of access to basic resources, education, healthcare services, food, housing, employment and fair income distribution". Furthermore: "appropriate social and economic reforms should be implemented in order to eradicate all social injustices". When referring to the right to development in these terms, the UN Declaration on the Right to Development raises this to the status of a "human right".

Bearing in mind the vast gap between firmly implementing civil and political human rights and economic, social and cultural human rights, it is vital to consider practical possibilities for implementing this latter category of rights, through either the right to sue for them through the Courts, or through government policies.

In terms of the *right to claim human rights through the Courts,* the introduction of laws fostering the enjoyment of economic, social and cultural human rights is a step still to be taken. Among the possibilities, I think that it is important to seek procedural mechanisms (including those with constitutional status) that are designed specifically to guarantee economic, social and cultural human rights. On a preliminary basis (and consequently open to in-depth development), I propose that a legal remedy should be introduced, which I would describe as an Action Calling for Compliance with Social Commitments. This legal remedy would be intended to ensure the compliance by government authorities with the social commitments undertaken through government or State programmes or guidelines. Its scope would be far broader-ranging than the traditional legal remedies guaranteeing civil and political rights, such as the writ or court order, for instance. As a tool for ensuring the validation of economic, social and cultural human rights, the Action Calling for Compliance with Social Commitment would hold civil servants liable under both civil and criminal law, if failing to comply (or complying only partially) unjustifiably with the proposals put forth in government or State plans and guidelines.

The purpose behind this idea is obviously to avoid – as occurs today – unjustified failures to implement programmes, plans and guidelines properly, when necessary to social development and with community expectations focused on this compliance. In this case, should there be no plausible justification for non-compliance (such as a severe economic crisis, for instance) the "programme" or "plan" becomes an obligation to be guaranteed by execution through the Courts.

Looking at the implementation of *government policies,* I initially feel that it is vital that they should establish social data-bases in order to ensure efficient implementation, including economic and cultural aspects. In my view, these data-bases should list the many vulnerable aspects found in society, moving beyond merely economic topics. When defining social welfare policies, it should be acknowledged and borne in mind that conditions such as gender, sexual preference, age, race and ethnic origin, among others – which are related to cultural and social inequalities – result in severe tensions that must be eased through social inclusion programmes. With regard to the economic aspects as such, it is vital to explore the poorest parts of the country, for instance, and to an even greater extent develop in-depth knowledge of the mechanisms that hobble social development. With an in-depth knowledge of this reality, it will be possible to establish pro-active mechanisms that could help open up alternative paths to development.

Monitoring targets – which is a vital part of the process of implementing social welfare policies – is part of the assumption that it is possible to speed up the process of implementing human rights, and particularly economic, social and cultural human rights, through State and non-State mechanisms that ensure ongoing discussion of the most appropriate ways to achieve this implementation. Monitoring these targets necessarily requires the will of the State, as well as the participation of society in the process of discussing and implementing these rights.

Just as targets must be established for the State and society in order to deal with difficulties and/or weak points noted in reality, it is also necessary to set up a broad-ranging monitoring system that is tailored to the scope of the targets established. The vital need to establish this monitoring system is justified by the requirement that the target should not become a dead letter in government plans and guidelines.

In order for this monitoring system to function properly, I feel that it would be a good idea to set up councils or commissions, or to include this topic on the agendas of the current human rights councils, with the necessary breakdown into sub-commissions or sub-committees designed specifically to protect economic, social and cultural human rights at the Federal, State and Municipal levels, assigned the duty of examining the real situation and proposing solutions for the violations of these rights, including changes in the law. Their members should blend knowledge, expertise, know-how, representativity and availability, eager to roll up their sleeves in order to guarantee the implementation of the plans at their respective levels, through monitoring activities.

Human rights councils and commissions play a political role that is very important, although they can also handle a significant juridical role, bringing the Judiciary Authorities into action on topics tagged as high priority. In order to become effective, discussion on the allocation of all types of resources required to implement government policies is a crucial factor in the activities of these councils and commissions, which should provide specialized knowledge and expertise, while overseeing government budgets in order to achieve their objectives.

On the other hand, I believe that the experience of the United Nations in appointing Special Theme Rapporteurs, assigned the responsibility of investigating specific situations and proposing solutions, could well be a mechanism that might be successfully replicated nationwide in Brazil. We could think about appointing representatives of organised civil society – accredited by the government entities to be monitored – as Special Rapporteurs. They would be responsible for building up in-depth knowledge on social issues in Brazil, reporting back on an annual basis on these government entities and institutions as a whole, while attempting to introduce sweeping changes into reality in terms of indivisible human rights. This mechanism could constitute – as it does at the international level – an important method for dealing with social problems and finding solutions to matters related to human rights, fostering social changes and results.

As shown, government policies are clearly one way of resolving or reducing social problems through a process of dialogue and clearly-defined actions that are intended to speed up the implementation of economic, social and cultural human rights, although acknowledging that the legal path has not yet exhausted all possibilities of implementing these rights.

When discussing government policies, the word "public" is not intended to establish an absolute distinction, in contrast to "private". Today, the meaning of the word "public" is related to an understanding of life in society, to the common goods, regardless of whether it is the State or other social entities that are involved in achieving the common good. The development of social public policies is consequently not limited to the State – although this is (and should continue to be) their main implementation agency. But non-governmental organisations and business corporations are also able to implement these schemes – in many cases with results that are more than satisfactory.

The intention of public policies is clearly to offset the inequalities caused by differentiated access to economic resources or cultural processes that fail to take the specific characteristics of minority sectors into consideration, through either the actions of the State or the actions of society.

Contrasting with everything that has been built up by the centralised State, today new ways of implementing public policies are now being sought, involving the community. In order to follow this fresh path, much effort is being channelled to cutting costs and simultaneously bringing in better results. However, it is salutary to stress here the importance of community involvement (society) in developing public policies, from the standpoint of extending citizenship and citizens' rights. In addition to democratising the government administration, community participation[14] fosters the development of information and skills within a society where they were not found previously, consequently implying heavier responsibilities with public assets. This means that social participation is required as a way of defining investment priorities while ensuring proper project implementation. The importance of this aspect is so great that the participation of social organisations for promoting economic, social and cultural human rights is viewed today by international assessments on the implementation of the International Covenant on Economic, Social and Cultural Rights as being a step forwards to the implementation of economic, social and cultural human rights.

Phasing in Economic, Social and Cultural Human Rights

The issue of phasing in economic, social and cultural human rights is a core factor in discussions on this matter, for a very simple reason: the lack of funding, although their implementation does not depend exclusively on this type of resource. However, it should be made quite clear that this problem does not only affect economic, social and cultural human rights. Many civil and political human rights as well lack progressive action, with sweeping effects on the behaviour of entire sectors of the population, or most of them.

---

14 "In this sense, there is a tension between what the participation offers in terms of cutting costs, and what this implies in terms of democratisation and the possibilities of social autonomy (...) in addition to reducing costs, community involvement is upgrading project performance and impacts". Carlos M. Hacia Vilas, '¿Dónde va la política social?', in: *Estado y Políticas Sociales después del Ajuste. Debates y Alternativas,* Caracas (National Autonomous University of México/Editorial Nueva Sociedad), 1995, p. 196.

This is why in Brazil today, it is not possible to belief that torture has been banished from police stations, or that death squads no longer kill people just because the Civil and Political Rights Convention and the Brazilian Constitution condemn and ban torture and defend the right to life[15]. This concerns the perception that the law – in terms of the implementation of rights – requires a certain period of time to adapt to reality.

The excessive importance assigned to funding has in fact blocked the implementation of many economic, social and cultural human rights through the acquiescence of many States to their varying levels of vulnerability in many social sectors. The argument that funds are short is frequently used by civil servants, delaying the implementation of economic, social and cultural rights.[16]

However, this is exactly the opposite of the intended outcome for the International Covenant on Economic, Social and Cultural Rights, through adopting the idea of phasing in these rights. The proper interpretation of the progressive implementation mentioned in this international document is not the "lack of definition" of periods and deadlines for ensuring their economic, social and cultural human rights. To the contrary, this Covenant seeks to drive its own implementation schedule. This discussion was also noted during the preparation of the International Covenant on Economic, Social and Cultural Rights. Fears arose that the concept of progressive implementation might result in endless delays in terms of implementing these rights, and even the deliberate avoidance of the obligations accepted under this Covenant by the States[17].

---

15 "An obligation to take "steps" or establish "measures" is found in Article 2(2) of the International Covenant on Civil and Political Rights, and in Article 2 (1) of the Convention on Torture and Other Forms of Cruel, Inhuman or Degrading Punishment or Treatment. As both these tools require immediate implementation, the phrase itself may not contain connotations of progressive implementation". Matthew Craven, *The International Covenant on Economic, Social and Cultural Rights. A Perspective on its Development*, Oxford/New York (Oxford University Press), 1995, p. 109.

16 "The dominant characteristics of obligations related to economic, social and cultural rights should be "progressive" in nature (...) as they are generally rated as unsuitable for immediate implementation, due to the considerable expenses involved in this process". Matthew Craven, *The International Covenant on Economic, Social and Cultural Rights, o.c.*, p. 130.

17 "This concern was expressed during the preparation of the International Covenant on Economic, Social and Cultural Rights, noting that the reference to progressive implementation would allow the States to delay the implementation of these rights indefinitely, or even refute their obligations completely. However, most people did not agree with this view, arguing that implementation should be sought "without delay", so that the full implementation could be achieved 'as soon as possible'". Craven, Matthew, *The International Covenant on Economic, Social and Cultural Rights, o.c.*, p. 130.

This issue reflects the fears of those who drafted the Covenant, which had a marked effect through establishing obligations and monitoring systems that are completely different from those of other international agreements. Indeed, the International Agreement on Civil and Political Rights establishes the clear obligation to "respect and implement" the rights contained in this regulatory document and stipulates the structures that support the implementation of these rights. The International Covenant on Economic, Social and Cultural Rights merely indicates that these rights should be phased in.

However, there is no way that this Covenant was to leave the future uncertain in terms of economic, social and cultural human rights, following the interpretation of the Limburg Principles.[18] Concern over limited funding was taken under consideration from a realistic standpoint, but with the idea that the States should use as much funding as possible to implement these rights.

In other words, the expression "phased-in implementation" in the Covenant is related directly to the recognition that economic, social and cultural human rights can be implemented over a short period of time. Consequently, the concept of "time" has a special meaning for economic, social and cultural human rights, as they are meaningless if their implementation is postponed indefinitely.

As interpreted by the Covenant, the lead-time for implementing these rights should be "reasonable". In terms of the Covenant, "moving towards the implementation of economic, social and cultural rights" does not mean handing their implementation over to God. To the contrary, this reflects a general principle of international law that requires the States to undertake the actions needed to comply with international standards that are freely signed[19].

---

18 On the progressive implementation of Economic, Social and Cultural Human Rights: "Under no circumstances whatsoever may this be interpreted as an indication for States of Law to postpone indefinitely their efforts to achieve full implementation". United Nations. Document E/CN.4, 'The Limburg Principles on the Implementation of the International Covenant on Economic, Social and Cultural Rights', in: *Human Rights Quarterly*, Vol. 9, No 2, Cincinnati (John Hopkins University Press), 1987, p. 125.

19 "The basic obligation of the International Covenant on Economic, Social and Cultural Human Rights is that the States Parties should 'take steps' towards implementing the rights contained therein. However, the phrase 'impelled to take steps' in itself merely reflects the general rule of international law that requires the States to take the necessary actions needed to implement the provisions of the Covenant". Matthew Craven, *The International Covenant on Economic, Social and Cultural Rights, o.c.*, p. 109.

Consequently, defining a basic core[20] of economic social and cultural rights can be handled correctly only within this broad-ranging idea of "progressive implementation", but never as a way of curtailing the identification or recognition of new economic, social and cultural human rights. This follows in the footsteps of the progress of human and civil rights.

---

[20] "It is significant that a start is being made today on considering what would constitute a "fundamental core" of economic, social and cultural rights. Some, like the Inter-American Commission on Human Rights, argue that this core would consists of labor, healthcare and education rights (...) while mention has also been made of the possible components of this core including what are known as the "subsistence rights" (meaning the right to food, housing, medical care and education)". Antônio Augusto Cançado Trindade, 'A Proteção Internacional dos Direitos Econômicos, Sociais e Culturais: Evolução, Estado Atual e Perspectivas', in: *Tratado de Direito Internacional dos Direitos Humanos*, p. 395.

PRIORITY ISSUES AND IMPEDIMENTS TO REALIZING THE RIGHT TO ADEQUATE HOUSING[1]

Miloon KOTHARI (India), UN Special Rapporteur on the Right to Adequate Housing

Globalization and the Right to Adequate Housing

The Sub-Commission resolutions on trade, investment and finance (1998/12, 1999/30 and 2000/7), the study of the Special Rapporteurs on globalization and its impact on the full enjoyment of all human rights (E/CN.4/Sub.2/1999/11 and E/CN.4/Sub.2/2000/13) and the work of CESCR, including its statements on globalization in 1988 and to the third Ministerial Conference of the World Trade Organization in 1999 (E/C.12/1999/9), as well as its days of general discussion and informal workshops with civil society alliances such as INCHRITI, are evidence of the increasing interest in and invaluable contribution to the understanding of globalization issues.

It is well established that the benefits of globalization vary with the level of development of countries and also, to a large degree, the ability of people to take advantage of the opportunities offered by it. For the homeless and the poor, the benefits of globalization have been hardly significant. The findings from the UNCHS Urban Indicator Database reveal that there is a wide gap between income groups, within countries and across countries, in terms of the availability, affordability and habitability of housing and access to utilities, which has resulted in an increase in the number of people in inadequate and insecure housing and living conditions.

Nearly all countries at all levels of development have undertaken macroeconomic reform programmes during the past two decades, strongly influenced by market forces and policies of international financial institutions (IFIs). These reforms and domestic policy decisions regarding liberalization, deregulation and privatization have, to varying extents, constrained

[1] Report of the Special Rapporteur on adequate housing as a component of the right to an adequate standard of living, Mr. Miloon Kothari, submitted pursuant to Commission resolution 2000/9. Ecosoc. Commission on Human Rights. Fifty-seventh session. Item 10 of the provisional agenda. Distr. General, Chapter II, n.56-86.

the exercise of monetary and fiscal policy options for social purposes, including provision of adequate housing. In addition, the United Nations Conference on Trade and Development (UNCTAD) reports that, despite these economic reforms, the expectant economic growth has been too slow, particularly in the least developed countries (LDCs), to make a significant improvement in living or social conditions.[2] The drawbacks of the growing reliance on narrow macroeconomic considerations that drive the availability of resources to social sectors have been a growing concern in a number of United Nations treaty bodies.

Where developing countries have successfully attracted a large increase of private capital flows, the rapid growth of cities typically outpaces the provision of adequate housing, resulting in an increased number of the poor living in squatter settlements with no security or civic services. This situation is further aggravated when urban authorities or private operators clear such settlements for commercial use or high-income housing. Moreover, increasing trends towards privatization of housing services and markets also typically result in land speculation, the commodification of housing, the application of user fees for housing resources such as water, sanitation and electricity, and the repeal or amendment of land ceiling and rent control legislation. The result is the increased marginalization of the poor.

The intention of the Special Rapporteur is to establish linkages between the processes of globalization and the realization of the right to adequate housing through, *inter alia*, collection of empirical data and analysis and assessment of the impact of macroeconomic adjustment and debt service on national housing and land policies. There is also a need to ascertain whether the current global social policy prescriptions, under the rubric of "good governance" (World Bank, United Nations Development Programme, UNCHS) and "poverty reduction" (World Bank, International Monetary Fund) are compatible with housing rights principles and State obligations.

There is an urgent need to define a research agenda to determine the impact of economic globalization on housing and land rights. The Special Rapporteur will seek the advice of and hopes to collaborate with relevant mechanisms of the United Nations including interested treaty bodies and the Special Rapporteurs on globalization and its impact on human rights, structural adjustment and debt and the right to food, possibly through

---

2 See UNCTAD, *The Least Developed Countries 2000 Report*, UNCTAD/LDC/2000.

convening an expert seminar. The Special Rapporteur would appreciate assistance from Governments and civil society in providing him with information and support in conducting such exercise, including facilitating his country visits.

Drinking Water as a Human Right

Access to safe drinking water and sanitation is intrinsically linked to full realization of the right to adequate housing. Globally, 1.7 billion persons lack access to clean water and 3.3 billion are without proper sanitation facilities.[3] The Special Rapporteur is aware of the inspiring work of the Sub-Commission on this subject, exemplified in the working paper by Mr. El Hadji Guissé on the right to access of everyone to drinking water supply and sanitation services (E/CN.4/Sub.2/1998/7). In this paper, Mr. Guissé mentions specifically paragraph 8 of CESCR General Comment No. 4, which states that "all beneficiaries of the right to adequate housing should have sustainable access to ... safe drinking water". He also highlights impediments to access, including macroeconomic issues such as the effects of external debt, structural adjustment programmes, the privatization of State enterprises and inadequate planning that results in the unequal distribution, both socio-economic and geographical, of water. To this list the Special Rapporteur would like to add the impediments to the realization of the right to housing that come from the application of "user fees" to water, especially when this is done without regard to the capacity of the poor to spend the meagre funds they have for this life-giving resource. In light of the need to enhance the human rights-based work on access to potable water and sanitation, and consistent with Sub-Commission resolution 2000/8 which stress the "international cooperation" aspects of the work, the Special Rapporteur will ensure that this issue remains a central component of his mandate and intends fully to support and complement, from a housing and land rights perspective, the mandate and important work of Mr. Guissé.

Poverty and its Impact on Housing Rights

The Special Rapporteur intends, through analysis and case studies, to elaborate further on the nexus between poverty and housing rights, and highlight several issues for the attention of the Commission and the United Nations system. Recognizing that any policy recommendations made during

---

[3] Santosh Mehrotra, Jan Vandermoortele & Enrike Delamonica, *Basic Services for All? Public Spending and the Social Dimensions of Poverty*, Florence (UNICEF Innocenti Research Centre), 2000.

his mandate must consider as participants the people and communities living in insecure and inadequate housing and living conditions, and incorporate their views, the Special Rapporteur intends to examine, *inter alia:*

The impact of growing income disparity among and within countries;

The impact of economic globalization;

Non-compliance with the international human rights instruments; and

The overemphasis at the national level with wealth per se and a lack of strategies for distributive justice, including land reform and increases in social spending.

Faced with this reality, it is urgent to challenge the misconception that the poor, especially those living in slums and other marginal areas, are responsible for social violence and environmental degradation. Indeed, they are the primary victims of such phenomena. A new form of discrimination, not yet addressed in existing human rights instruments, has emerged and people are increasingly marginalized and discriminated against not merely on the grounds of race, class or gender, but because they are poor. The Special Rapporteur will attempt to ensure that this form of discrimination is taken into account in preparations for the World Conference against Racism, Racial Discrimination, Xenophobia and Related Intolerance.

The Special Rapporteur would also like to draw attention to the housing situation of LDCs in view of the increasing poverty, inadequate civic services and other environmental and social factors that have affected LDCs during the last decade. The Third United Nations Conference on the Least Developed Countries (LDC-III), to be held in Brussels in May 2001, provides an opportunity for both LDCs and developed countries to reaffirm their obligations under ICESCR and renew their commitments in the new Programme of Action to be adopted. The Special Rapporteur notes with regret that, despite the recognition of housing issues in the 1990 Programme of Action, the current draft Programme of Action for LDC-III (A/CONF.191/IPC/L.4) does not contain any reference to housing as a component of an adequate standard of living, which is essential in building the human capacities of LDCs. The Special Rapporteur urges the Conference to recognize and to institute mechanisms for integrating economic, social and cultural rights in the implementation and follow-up of the Conference outcomes.

Gender Discrimination in Housing and Land Rights

The Special Rapporteur recognizes that there is a gender dimension to every human rights violation and that this is especially true in respect of housing rights violations. Access to and control over land, property and housing are determinative of women's overall living conditions and are necessary to the development of sustainable human settlements in the world today. These entitlements are essential for women's economic and physical security and to the struggle for equality in gender relations.

Pursuant to the Commission resolution 2000/13, and in order that women's critical role is recognized and their rights advanced, the Special Rapporteur will encourage the international community to ensure that the strategies and objectives envisioned in numerous legal instruments are realized and that women are accorded substantive rather than illusory rights as they pertain to housing. He will encourage and support the necessary structural transformation in respect of women's empowerment and, to this end, will endeavour to promote awareness of, and accountability to the commitments and responsibilities of Governments and the international community.

Of grave concern to the Special Rapporteur is the situation of women whose lives are governed by both constitutional and personal status laws. Of special import to women in countries with such laws is that the equal right to inherit land and property is either precluded by customary law or mediated by a male relative. The Special Rapporteur stresses the right of women to be "free from all forms of discriminatory conduct", as enunciated in resolution 2000/13, and, in accordance with this conviction and the resolution, intends to investigate this issue throughout his mandate. The Special Rapporteur intends to collaborate on this issue with the relevant units and programmes of UNCHS, relevant treaty bodies and related mandates, especially the Special Rapporteur on violence against women.

Children and Housing Rights

Article 6.2 of the Convention on the Rights of the Child states that "States Parties shall ensure to the maximum extent possible the survival and development of the child," to which children's housing rights and living conditions are integrally linked. These human rights are essential to their cognitive, physical, cultural, emotional and social development, particularly as children are disproportionately vulnerable to the negative effects of inadequate and insecure living conditions.

The Sub-Commission, in its resolution 1994/8 on children and the right to adequate housing, stressed the adverse impact of poverty, and in particular of inadequate housing and living conditions, on the basic rights of children. This draws the link between poverty and the absence of conditions conducive to development, namely, clean water, sanitation facilities, food, health and education. Throughout his mandate, the Special Rapporteur intends to devote special attention to the impact that violations of the right to adequate housing have on the basic rights of children, especially the girl child and others having special needs and/or subject to discrimination.[4]

Moreover, the Special Rapporteur encourages States and United Nations bodies, the World Bank and the International Monetary Fund, to take a proactive approach to realizing children's rights to housing and, in accordance with resolution 1994/8, to develop sustainable poverty reduction solutions with a view to ensuring that the housing and living conditions are improved for the world's half a billion children living in abject poverty. The Special Rapporteur recognizes as well that solutions must necessarily include the participation of children.

The Special Rapporteur will attempt to ensure that these issues are given due consideration at the forthcoming Special Session of the General Assembly on Children, September 2001, which will include a review of the progress made since the World Summit for Children in 1990.

Forced Evictions

The issue of forced evictions has been mentioned briefly in various sections of this report. In his next report, the Special Rapporteur will devote attention to the phenomenon of forced evictions which are, as recognized in Commission resolution 1993/77, gross violations of human rights. Specifically, he will conduct an in-depth review of the legal definition of forced eviction as enunciated in international human rights and humanitarian legal instruments and various resolutions of the Commission and Sub-Commission. He will explore documents that have expanded the legal definition, including CESCR General Comments Nos. 4 and 7; the expert seminars on housing rights (1996) and forced evictions (1997); concluding observations under treaty bodies; United Nations guidelines on development-based displacement and on internal displacement; the human

4 The Special Rapporteur takes note of several important reports by UNICEF such as *Poverty Reduction Begins with Children* and *the State of the World's Children 2001*, which have embraced a human rights approach.

rights dimensions of population transfer; and principles on restitution, compensation and rehabilitation of victims. Moreover, it is the intention of the Special Rapporteur to look at forced evictions that are the result of, *inter alia,* ethnic cleansing, civil conflict, development projects and the denial of the right to self-determination. He will devote particular attention to the disparate effects of forced eviction on women and children.

Indigenous and Tribal Peoples' Housing and Land Rights

The Special Rapporteur takes note that the pursuance of the right of every woman, man, youth and child to gain and sustain a secure home and community in which to live in peace and dignity becomes most strikingly clear in the case of indigenous and tribal peoples' right to adequate housing, especially in respect of land claims and rights. This question has been one of the most contentious issues for States in their relationship with indigenous peoples, and has been central to the consideration of the United Nations of the human rights of indigenous and tribal populations since 1987 when it was noted in the conclusions and recommendations of José R Martínez-Cobo.[5] The special relationship of indigenous people to their lands is not only made clear by their conduct and articulation of their way of life, but by the fatal consequences of their historical dispossession of them.

The Sub-Commission's Special Rapporteur on the subject, Ms. Erica-Irene A. Daes, has pointed out that, for indigenous peoples, survival rights involve at least four key elements related to their place to live: (a) that a profound relationship exists with their lands, territories and resources; (b) that this relationship has various social, cultural, spiritual, economic and political dimensions and responsibilities; (c) that there is a collective dimension to this relationship; and (d) that the intergenerational aspect of such a relationship is crucial to indigenous peoples' identity, survival and cultural viability (see E/CN.4/Sub.2/2000/25). Each of these elements has corresponding dimensions strengthened by the holistic conception and widespread legal recognition of the right to adequate housing.

The Special Rapporteur intends to examine these links and the housing dimensions that emerge from the explicit standards found in international instruments such as ILO Convention No. 169 concerning Indigenous and Tribal Peoples in Independent Countries and the draft United Nations

---

5 *Study of the Problem of Discrimination against Indigenous Populations,* Volume V. *Conclusions, Proposals and Recommendations,* United Nations publication (Sales No. E.86.XIV.3), paras. 196-197.

declaration on the rights of indigenous peoples. He will seek to address the United Nations Working Group on Indigenous Populations and develop a working relationship with the Permanent Forum on Indigenous Issues with a view to understanding the many obstacles that remain for the enjoyment of legally recognized indigenous housing and land rights.

Domestic Applicability and Justiciability

More than 30 countries currently include housing rights in their constitutional framework, in addition to specific legislation. For the 145 States that have ratified the ICESCR, ensuring the domestic status and application of the constituent rights remains an important priority. Consequently, justiciability of the right to adequate housing in courts at all levels is needed in order for States effectively to respect, protect, promote and fulfil the right to housing. Facing that enduring challenge, it is important to take note of some significant developments, both encouraging and regressive.

One of the most significant of these developments has been the recognition accorded to the right to housing in the Constitution of South Africa:

"Section 26 (1) Everyone has the right to have access to adequate housing. (2) The State must take reasonable legislative and other measures, within its available resources, to achieve the progressive realization of this right. (3) No one may be evicted from their home, or have their home demolished, without an order of court made after considering all the relevant circumstances. No legislation may permit arbitrary evictions."

This far-reaching provision has already had legislative impact. On 4 October 2000 the Constitutional Court of South Africa delivered a decision in respect of the housing rights of persons forced to live in deplorable conditions while waiting for their turn to be allocated low-cost housing.[6] The judgement significantly advanced the right to adequate housing domestically as well as internationally by resting on section 39 of the Constitution of South Africa,[7] article 11.1 of the ICESCR[8] and the

---

6 See *The Government of the Republic of South Africa et al. v. Irene Grootboom et al.*, Case CCT 11/00, heard on 11 May 2000 and decided on 4 October 2000.

7 Section 39 states that courts must: "Promote the values that underlie an open and democratic society based on human dignity, equality and freedom [and] must consider international law".

8 South Africa became a signatory on 3 October 1994, but has not yet ratified the Covenant.

minimum core obligations for States parties to the Covenant set out in General Comment No. 3.[9]

The Court held that relevant international law must provide guidance to domestic courts, but more importantly, that as a signatory to the Covenant, South Africa was bound to uphold the principles therein. The Court also held that the State was obligated to abide by its commitments in proactive and practical ways, despite financial constraints, and that the programmes and policies necessary to meet these commitments are matters appropriate for judicial review.

In stark contrast, two recent judgements from India can be considered significant setbacks. In the same month as the case in South Africa, the Supreme Court of India *in Narmada Bachao Andolan v. Union of India and Others*[10] revealed a regressive attitude towards housing rights and disregard for both fundamental human rights and India's obligations under the ICESCR.[11] At issue was the continued construction of the Narmada Dam and its significant impact on both the environment and the hundreds of thousands of tribal people in the Narmada Valley, who have been displaced with inadequate resettlement and rehabilitation plans.[12]

The Special Rapporteur is concerned that, despite detailed knowledge of the inability of the authorities to determine the total number of people to be displaced and to find adequate land for their resettlement, and the incomplete resettlement for those already displaced, the Supreme Court ruled that "... displacement of the tribals and other persons would not per se result in the violation of their fundamental or other rights..."[13] and held that the construction of the dam would continue. The judgement contra-

---

9 Justice Yacoob of the Constitutional Court of South Africa described the meaning of minimum core obligation: "It is the floor beneath which the conduct of the State must not drop if there is to be compliance with the obligation. Each right is a 'minimum essential level' that must be satisfied by the States parties".

10 *Narmada Bachao Andolan v. Union of India and Others*, 18 October 2000 [hereinafter *Narmada*].<

11 The Supreme Court of India has held on numerous occasions that international law can be read into the domestic law of the country. *Gramophone Co. of India v. B.B. Pandey*, 1984 (2) SCC 534; *PUCL v. Union of India*, 1997 (3) SCC 433; *and CERC v. Union of India*, 1995 (3) SCC 42 are cases that support this assertion. In adition, article 51 of the Constitution of India states: "The State shall endeavour to ... (c) foster respect for international law and treaty obligations in the dealings of organized people with one another ...". Accordingly, the courts and the legislature are encouraged to maintain harmony with international law in their decision-making.

12 According to official figures, the Sardar Sarovar Project will displace 40,827 families, mostly from tribal communities. The unofficial total is estimated to be as high as half a million.

13 Narmada, at para. 61.

dicts previous Supreme Court rulings that have upheld the right to shelter as related to the right to life[14] as well as the Narmada Water Disputes Tribunal decisions. It is also dismissive of the legitimate struggle of the people of the Narmada Valley led by the Narmada Bachao Andolan (Save the Narmada Campaign), petitioner in the case.

In another case, the Bombay High Court heard a petition filed in 1995 by the Bombay Environmental Action Group (BEAG) to "remove forthwith" informal settlement dwellers (as "encroachers") adjacent to the Sanjay Gandhi National Park so as to ensure the protection of "the environment and all its aspects". Subsequent to the petition, the Bombay High Court of 7 May 1997 directed the relevant authorities to evict persons from their homes, pursuant to various wildlife protection and conservation laws, effectively depriving them of their livelihood.

The Indian Peoples Human Rights Tribunal on Sanjay Gandhi National Park, determined that the BEAG petition was clear evidence that its vision of a "clean environment" excludes vast sections of the population who were *unpropertied* and living in abject poverty. As well, the Court's summary eviction order will eventually affect half a million slum-dwellers. Particularly disturbing was the fact that the Court not only ordered this mass eviction, but it explicitly ordered the demolition of homes and the destruction of all belongings and construction materials which, in the first wave of evictions, were gathered and burnt by the demolition squad.

The recognition of the indivisibility and interdependence of human rights is essential to their full realization. It is therefore a matter of concern that judgements across the world are unfortunately providing a legal basis for a growing conflict between proponents of the right to a healthy environment and the right to housing and livelihood. These judgements not only create disharmony among complementary human rights, but in doing so violate the human rights of the very people the courts are charged with protecting.

In both cases cited above, the Special Rapporteur has received communications from affected parties. He will continue to monitor these and other

---

[14] See *Francis Coralie v. The Union Territory of Delhi,* (1981) 1 SCC 608*; R. Francis Mullin v. Administrator of Union Territory of Delhi* (1982) 2 SCR 516; *Olga Tellis v. Bombay Municipal Corp.,* (1985) 3 SCC 545; *Shantistar Builders v. Narayan Khimalal Totame and Others* (1990) 1 SCC 520; *Keshavananda Bharti v. State of Kerala* [as reported *in Unnikrishnan v. State of Andhra Pradesh,* p. 2229]; and *Chamelli Singh and Other v. State of Uttar Pradesh* (JT 1995 (9) SC 380. Excerpts from this judgement will be available on the OHCHR Web site on housing.

such cases and take action to expose the inconsistencies of such judicial decisions with the international provisions concerning housing rights and forced evictions. Under the theme of "Justiciability of the right to housing" he will dedicate a section of his next report to both the progressive and regressive developments in respect of the human right to housing in domestic courts, and would appreciate receiving information on developments such as those highlighted above.

ECONOMIC, SOCIAL AND CULTURAL RIGHTS IN SOUTH AFRICA: ENTITLEMENTS, NOT MERE POLICY OPTIONS

Venitia GOVENDER (South Africa)

Introduction

The Constitutional vision of South Africa post apartheid is characterised by the establishment of a society based on "social justice" and the improvement of the "quality of life of all citizens" so as "to free the potential of each person"[1]. Issues of inequality and discrimination are certainly not new in South Africa. Thus the "new" Constitution is historic and has very clear social objectives for transformation and justice. However, the actual possibility of realising the goals enshrined in the Constitution and Bill of Rights are dependent on the realities on the ground. Much will depend not only on the written texts of the Constitution and laws, but also on the institutional structures, general public awareness and the culture of how society uses law in practice. No law enforces itself. Thus the role, will and commitment of all the actors in society dictate the level to which implementation of these noble goals are achieved.

For the majority of South Africans 1994 marked a starting point, not the destination, of the journey to reclaim their political and legal rights and their social, economic and cultural citizenship. Thereby re-asserting the view that social, economic and cultural rights are key to transforming the lives of South Africans beyond meeting basic needs. Economic, social and cultural rights are more than mere policy directives or goals; they are guarantees and entitlements without which the realisation of civil and political rights would be superficial and severely constrained.

Constitutional Provisions and Foundation for the Realisation of Economic, Social and Cultural Rights

In the pre-1994 dispensations the majority of South Africans were stripped of their land, and denied access to decent housing, health care services, food, water, social security and education. Consequently South Africa remains one of the most inequitable countries in the world with the

---

1 *Constitution of the Republic of South Africa*, 1996 Act-preamble.

wealthiest 10 percent of the population accounting for 60 percent of the country's wealth.[2]

South Africa – Post Apartheid

The inclusion of social, economic and cultural rights in South Africa's 1996 Constitution reflects the understanding that the core values of dignity, freedom and equality are not just about the absence of civil and political violations. Violations of the majority of South Africans civil and political rights have been well documented and acknowledged. The legacy of Apartheid, however, and its contribution to the impoverishment of the majority, particularly rural people continues to be felt. Economic and social rights are especially important to poor people and communities still suffering from the disadvantages of the apartheid system.

Turning briefly to the subject of cultural rights, it is important to note that the debate on these issues has largely been absent when considering economic and social rights.[3] When it has been addressed it has been done so as distinct and isolated concepts, focusing on issues such as language, traditional leadership, and customary law. This is somewhat ironic, given the emphasis some South Africans have placed on separate identities and minority rights. But perhaps this is understandable in the context of the overarching mission to build a new country which, in the words of the Constitution's preamble, is *"united in our diversity"*. The relationship between dominant and subjugated cultures has moulded the history of South Africa and there remains great sensitivity about aspects of cultural rights, such as the issues of self-determination and traditional leadership. The relationship between these issues and economic and social rights, however, remain critical, particularly in terms of identifying and prioritising key issues in the broader debate on the inter-relatedness of these rights, and programmes of action to protect or fulfil these rights. How, for example, does customary law positively or negatively affect the protection or realisation of economic and social rights? In short, we in South Africa have a long way to go in terms of working out how these issues relate. This

---

2 'Healthcare is still far from equitable', in: *Reconstruct, The Sunday Independent*, 12 December 1999. The poorest 40% of households account for only 11% of total income, while the richest 10% of households, equivalent to 7% of the population, accure over 40% of total income. See Julian May, *Poverty and Inequality in South Africa,* Natal (Centre for Social and Development Studies, University of Natal), 1998, p. 2.

3 This appears to be reinforced by the Constitution itself, which tasks the South African Human Rights Commission to monitor the realisation of seven key areas relating to economic and social rights. – Section 184(3). This is complimented by the academic debate on economic and social rights, which also tends to exclude debate on its relationship with cultural rights.

remains a crucial challenge and will remain a critical area for future debate and intervention. To date the Chapter 9 Institution focussing on the Promotion and Protection of the Rights of Cultural, Religious and Linguistic Communities has not been established. Extensive debate around the specific role and function of this Commission is still being engaged in. The Constitution however does recognise 11 official languages and customary marriages are regarded as legal.

South Africa is frequently lauded as having one of the most progressive Constitutions in the world. There was, however, considerable opposition from some quarters to the inclusion of economic and social rights in the final Constitution, and arguments that it was simply not practical for the country to make undertakings that it would struggle to live up to. Conversely hundreds of submissions from civil society to the Constitutional Assembly, (which was responsible for drafting the final Constitution) called for inclusion of these rights as pivotal to the task of addressing the inherited inequalities of the colonial and apartheid dispensations. From a human rights perspective, therefore, it is commendable that legislators opted for the inclusion of a panoply of rights relating to (a) education (b) health (c) social security (d) environment (e) water (f) food, and (g) housing.

The first thing to note about these social and economic rights is the manner in which they are expressed. The writers of the Constitution were careful enough not to frame the rights in a way that would place an absolute and unambiguous obligation on the government to fulfil. The Constitution does not say that everyone has a right to land or adequate housing.

According to the Bill of Rights, the government may fulfil some of these economic and social rights "progressively" and "within its available resources". In effect, this means that the full enjoyment of the rights by everyone will take time, and recognition that the government may not have the resources to ensure that everyone has these rights immediately. It infers, however, that at the very least, the government should draw up and follow a plan of action, which focuses on both the immediate and long term for achieving the full realisation of these rights.

Other rights require more immediate implementation. These include the right to basic education, emergency medical treatment, the right of every child to basic nutrition, shelter, basic healthcare services and social services, as well as the socio-economic rights of prisoners.

The Bill of Rights also commits government to taking "reasonable legislative and other measures" to realise its Constitutional responsibilities. Since

1994, and in particular since February 1997 and the introduction of the final Constitution, South Africa has begun to build a body of laws around the Bill of Rights and Constitution. In six and a half years Parliament has repealed and amended a plethora of old laws. It has also introduced a range of laws rooted in constitutional protections. Specific emphasis has been given to the development of a gender friendly policy context and there have also been substantial shifts at a policy level and legislative level.

In addition, South Africa has signed and ratified a number of international treaties and conventions, which contain specific and inferred economic and social rights components. These include the UN Conventions on the Rights of the Child and on the Elimination of All Forms of Discrimination Against Women. It is, however, of some concern that despite signing the International Covenant on Economic, Social and Cultural Rights in 1994, South Africa has yet to ratify the Covenant. No reason has been publicly offered for the delay in this process. South Africa is also party to the African Charter to human and peoples' rights.

Democracy Building Institutions – Chapter 9

In addition to the Bill of Rights, the plethora of laws and legislation, and the Constitutional Court Chapter 9 of the South African Constitution establishes six Democracy Building Institutions, designed to act as checks and balances against the abuse of power and for monitoring and assessing the realisation of the economic and social rights. Section 184(3) of the Constitution empowers the South African Human Rights Commission to require relevant organs of State to provide the Commission with measures that they have taken towards the realisation of the rights in the Bill of Rights concerning housing, health care, food, water, social security, education and the environment. This provision has the capacity to ensure not only the monitoring of the implementation of these rights, but also the accountability.

And finally this legal and policy foundation is backed up in terms of the Constitution, the responsibility of enforcing rights lies not only with the courts, but with the independent Commissions, parliament, the executive, provincial legislatures, local government and all organs of State.
The South African Constitution makes it clear that constitutional rights are to be judicially protected and enforced. The courts are given the widest possible powers to develop and forge new remedies for the enforcement of Constitutional rights (Section 172(1)(b) and 167(7)).

Economic, social and cultural rights, unlike civil and political rights, have not had the benefit of a long tradition of interpretation by judicial and quasi-judicial bodies. Their content and scope are therefore somewhat under-developed and are in a process of evolution.
However, we should be cautious about focussing exclusively on the courts as the primary mechanism for enforcing economic, social and cultural rights. Litigation is but one of the many strategies. Ideally courts should be seen as the last option, especially in light of the fact that access to courts in South Africa is almost impossible to the most vulnerable (in terms of procedure and costs). To date only two cases focussing on socio-economic rights have been brought before the Constitutional Court (Soobramoney, Grootboom).

At this stage I would like to provide some insight into three of the individual socio-economic rights and to highlight fundamental challenges in terms of the sheer extent of the need that exists in South Africa.

Education

Section 29(1)(a) of the South African Constitution, guarantees everyone the right to basic education and adult basic education.
In order for this right to be realised, the State has to build schools with the necessary amenities and also ensure there is proper management of these schools- Schools Act (No 84 of 96). Furthermore, the right in s29 (1)(a) is not limited to ensuring that everyone gets to go to school, once they are at school, they must also receive quality education.

Education is perhaps the one social area that was subject to the greatest degree of fragmentation on racial and ethnic grounds in the apartheid era. The proliferation of departments and institutions and the duplication of bureaucracies and consequent inefficiencies were notorious.
Other problems that the education system faced under apartheid were the poor quality of instruction due to poor training of teachers, irrelevant learning materials and language difficulties, the collapse of the culture of learning and teaching in schools due to political and labour disputes, and the lack of adequate facilities and learning resources, especially in township and rural schools. A survey conducted by the Human Science Research Council in 1996 found that:

- 51% of South African schools suffered from a shortage of textbooks
- 69% had no materials
- 73% had no learning equipment

- 61% had no access to telephones
- 83% had no libraries
- 24% were without water within walking distance
- 12% had no toilet facilities
- 57% had no electricity[4].

It is widely recognised that the Department of Education has managed to put in place a comprehensive new policy framework through a series of White Papers and policy initiatives. These include policies with regard to further education, higher education, governance, management, finance, teacher training, curriculum, and language. This is an impressive achievement in that the Department is covering systematically area after area, and is seeking to translate its overall vision into concrete policies to address all aspects of the system.

Education, however, continues to be a source of serious concern in South Africa and remains the largest budgetary line item. September 1997, some R8 billion had been spent on addressing backlogs in the education system. Spending in this area continues. Although budgetary commitments to education have improved slightly, the pass rate of matriculants (final year exams) has dropped from 57,4% from 1988 to 47,1% in 1998. The 1997 results were the worst since 1979. The racial differences in achievement remain as high as ever, with very high pass rates among white and Indian students (over 95%), high rates among coloreds (85-90%) and very low rates among Africans (way below 50%). In some of the more rural and African provinces, such as the Northern Province, the pass rate is below 40%. Given that many African and rural students do not attempt to take the examinations, the actual pass rate among the entire cohort is lower[5]. Some analysts, however, have dismissed statistics provided by the Department of Education and Training as unreliable.

Inequity within the schooling system remains one of the country's toughest challenges. Although there have been moves to address these issues, it will take a continuous concerted effort to ensure that this is the case. Financial restrictions remain central and undoubtedly do impact on performance rates. On all accounts, schools in the Northern Province and Eastern Cape are worst off, followed by KwaZulu Natal. The enactment of the National Norms and Standards on School Funding Act during the course of next year and beyond is a further attempt to redress inequalities between

---

4 'The Voluntary Sector and Development in South Africa 1997/8', in: *Development Update, Quarterly Journal of the South African National NGO Coalition and Interfund*, Vol. 2 No. 3, 1999.

5 *Ibid.*

affluent and poor schools. The Act introduces a new subsidy scheme for public (i.e government) and independent (i.e. private) schools.
Improvements in education must be accompanied by a restoring of a "culture of learning". In February 1997, the government launched a three-year Culture of Learning and Teaching (COLT) campaign in a bid to tackle the issue. Though conditions have improved since the 1980s, the education system is still struggling with a range of misconduct ranging from absenteeism among students, teachers and management, to drug and alcohol abuse, vandalism, violence and school closures. The "integration" process has also been marred in some communities by racial incidents, such as the furore that erupted in the North West Province town of Vryburg during 1998 and 1999.
With the deepening and development of the democratic dispensation, so came the need to develop a new curriculum to teach the future youth of the country. Curriculum reform remains a crucial area of education provision. A number of problems have been picked up during the piloting phase of the "Curriculum 2005" process which remains ongoing. Concerns have been raised by some monitors that Curriculum 2005 "tended to exacerbate differences between privileged and under-privileged – or mostly white and black – schools, in spite of its aim to achieve the opposite"[6].

The Higher Education Act of 1997 aims to establish a single co-ordinated higher education system, and to restructure and transform tertiary institutions to make them more responsive to the country's human resource, economic and development needs, and with a specific mandate to redress past discrimination. South Africa has 21 university level institutions – "too many for a country of its population and size and very costly given the duplication of disciplines and faculties. At least half of these universities produce graduates with sub-standard qualifications"[7]. Inequity between the institutions, in terms of resources and facilities remains acute. Under-representation of Africans in tertiary institutions continues, although enrolment statistics show that they are increasing. By 1997, over 50% of university entrants were African. Developments at universities are hampered by the huge student debts that have accumulated, particularly in traditionally "African" universities.

The financial situation and limited access to sustained student funding continues to undermine access to tertiary education. Since 1994 the State has cut funding to the tertiary sector in favour of primary and secondary

---

6 'The Voluntary Sector and Development in South Africa 1997/8', in: *Development Update, Quarterly Journal of the South African National NGO Coalition and Interfund*, Vol. 2 No. 3, 1999.

7 *Ibid.*

education. State funding has been reduced from 80 to 100 percent of institutional budgets to about 50 percent over the past few years, even though there has been an increase in the number of students.[8]

The situation also remains problematic in the field of adult education. "Adult basic education and training (ABET) is going through one of its darkest hours", says Bohlale Nong, director of the Adult Educators and Trainers Association of South Africa. In 1994 there were over 200 NGOs and CBOs involved in adult basic education. Funding has since been reduced and the number of NGOs has dropped to 38.[9] Approximately 30% of the adult population in South Africa remains functionally illiterate. State support for ABET remains negligible, with over 98% of the education budget going to formal sector education. Most ABET projects are financed by private corporation, foreign and domestic donors.

Poverty and Human Rights, Report of the National "Speak Out on Poverty Hearings"

The new Minister of Education Prof. Kader Asmal, during his first address as the new Minister of Education, identified a number of areas where the government has failed in its obligation to realise the right to education:

- *Failures of governance and management.* He highlighted the serious lack of leadership, governance, management and administration in many parts of the education system. Many of the provincial departments are unable to perform the tasks laid down in the legislation, the results have been fraud, corruption and a lack of discipline in the institutions of learning.
- *Continued inequality in access to educational institutions.* The majority of the poor (who are mostly rural black people) continue to attend schools that are decrepit and with no basic amenities.
- *Poor quality of learning.* This has contributed to South African students faring badly in the international standardised test. The shocking Matric results of 1998 highlighted the deepening education crisis.

Social Security

Section 27(1)(c) of the Constitution provides that "Everyone has the right to have access to social security, including, if they are unable to support themselves and their dependants, appropriate social assistance." Subsection (2) provides that "the State

---

8 *Ibid.*

9 'Adult education in dire straits', in: *Reconstruct, The Sunday Independent,* 5 September 1999.

must take reasonable legislative and other measures, within its available resources, to achieve the progressive realisation of each of these rights."

South Africa is one of very few nations in Africa (and elsewhere in the developing world) that provides social security and social assistance, in the form of pensions, grants and services, to the elderly, disabled, indigent families with children and other needy categories.

Under the apartheid dispensation benefits were skewed in favour of particularly white, but also coloured and Indian recipients. The Black African population received the lowest levels of benefits, and millions relocated to so-called independent homelands and self-governing territories fared even worse.

Over 2,8 million people were recipients of such assistance in 1998-1999.[10] The number of people accessing this support, however, does not mean that the needs of the poor are adequately addressed. Indeed, there are approximately 18 million living in the poorest 40% of households and about half of these live on less than US$1 a day.[11] Consequently, many needy people are either unable (because they are unaware, or unable to access available services) or being refused access to such services. The situation is particularly acute in rural areas, where most poor households are headed by women. Over 70% of our rural population are living in poverty.[12]

In addition, few specific provisions are made for the homeless and South Africa's towns and cities have seen a marked increase in the number of people 'sleeping rough' on the streets. Many having replaced the poverty of their rural circumstances for an equally, if not more precarious existence in urban and metropolitan settings.

Although government commitment to this right is demonstrated in a budgetary allocation of over R16 billion per annum, there is general agreement that this amount is woefully inadequate and that needs will continue to outstrip the government's capacity to support. This has forced them to make some hard and unpopular decisions. In 1998 the government replaced the existing maintenance grant which provided support for

---

10 South African Human Rights Commission, *2nd Economic and Social Rights Report – 1998 – 1999,* p. 209. This includes over 1,76 million old age pensions and 620,000 disability grants (see p. 222).

11 Julian May, *Poverty and Inequality in South Africa,* Natal (Centre for Social and Development Studies, University of Natal), 1998, p. 2.

12 *2nd Economic and Social Rights Report, o.c.,* p. 214.

indigent families with children. As with so many other aspects of South African society, the minority racial groups (and especially the white community) benefited disproportionately. The new government simply could not afford to extend this service to all needy indigents. He replaced the system with the Child Support Grant which radically reduced the amount of money allocated and restricted eligibility[13] with the intention of addressing the acute inequalities by spreading assistance to a greater number of recipients. With limited infrastructure and other related problems of accessibility we have yet to see the expected increase in the number of beneficiaries.

The problems, however, do not relate exclusively to budgetary restrictions. Huge difficulties remain in the administration of this budget. Although many of these problems relate to the ongoing transformation and restructuring of the departments, there is ample evidence that mal-administration, incompetence (as well as corruption) have all adversely affected delivery.[14]

Consequently hundreds of thousands of people have been adversely affected in some provinces, where pensions have been arbitrarily suspended and services cut. There is also considerable concern regarding the apparent lack of bureaucratic and political accountability. Last year, for example, the government admitted it had failed to spend its US$70 million Poverty Relief Fund, despite numerous worthy applications for disbursements to the fund. No one was held accountable and the Minister responsible was simply shifted to another portfolio.

Water

Section 27(1)(b) provides for the right of access to sufficient food and water.

The provision of clean water in sufficient quantity is important in its own right, as well in its implications for health, food security and overall economic development. While the water programme over the past four years has been heralded by many as the government's most successful initiative, there is concern about the methods that have been used, consultation processes, the use of privatisation schemes, and most

---

13 A standard grant of approximately US$15 per month, per child up to the age of 7 years is now provided.

14 See, for example the Human Rights Committee's Quarterly Review, *Social and Economic Rights in the Western Cape,* November 2000, p. 54-63.

importantly the sustainability of operation and maintenance of completed projects which are dependent on the principle of cost recovery.

Government legislation and RDP standards have laid the framework for what 'access' to water entails, and what government obligations must be. The definition of access as being 25 litres of clean water daily, available 90% of the time within 200 metres of the dwelling, has been for the most part accepted, as it is in keeping with international standards and World Health Organisation guidelines. Realising this access for all South Africans in the short term, and realising access of 50-60 litres daily per individual in the long term, are goals that form the foundation for minimum governmental obligations.

Upon coming to power in 1994, government estimated that there were approximately 12 million people without access to proper water supply. This appears to have been an underestimate, and NGOs are generally in agreement that current backlogs are closer to 17-20 million individuals.[15]

Race and area differentiate service provision. Tapped water inside the house is available to 47% of the population overall, with an additional 20% who access it on their property but outside the house. As with electricity, water is nearly universally available for whites and Indians, widespread among coloureds (83%), but only available to about a third of Africans (32%, with an additional 24% who get it on the property).

In rural areas only 12% have tapped water at home, and an additional 11% on the property. In informal settlements 16% have tapped water on the grounds but none at home. Most rural people use tapped water from outside their property (34%), from rivers or streams (14%), and from boreholes (14%).[16]

The Department of Water Affairs (DWAF) operates at a national level with no provincial counterparts. The removal of a tier of bureaucracy seems to have enabled DWAF to deliver better than most other departments. At the same time, as in all service sectors, the amalgamation of the various administrations into one structure, and the subsequent freeze on retrenchments, has led to human resources and restructuring problems as well as a drain on resources. While consolidation has led to uniformity in policy, it has impacted negatively on capacity and delivery.

---

15 Government of National Unity, *Mid-term report to the nation,* Pretoria, 1996, p. 38.

16 Piers Pigou, Ran Greenstein, Nahla Valji & David Everatt, *Monitoring socio-economic rights in South Africa: Public Perceptions,* CASE, June 1998.

Positive legislative steps have been made, however, in giving DWAF regulation over any project that pollutes water resources, repealing the previously biased 'riparian rights', and recalling water resources as belonging to the State or nation at large. Water Committees have been established at a local level to run individual projects and maintain them after completion; however, these have been somewhat controversial. They are for the most part government-appointed structures, and are therefore top-down and non-representative. Tensions between appointed Committees and traditional structures have erupted in some communities.[17]

Many assessments of the previous government's water projects have concluded that the top-down approach of benevolent giving cultivated a disjuncture between the service structure and the community it was intended to benefit. Although water provision under the new government has demonstrated rapid progress, this has been done at the expense of sound developmental strategies involving community participation. Policy development has involved consultation with NGO's, and DWAF has exhibited perhaps the highest willingness of all line departments to work co-operatively with the NGO community. Little effort has been made, however, to extend this consultation process to a community level. There has been little evidence of participatory approaches, carrying out of needs assessments, or educating communities in operations and maintenance.

In the absence of community participation and inclusion in water development projects, sustainability is an illusory goal. Non-consultation means that dynamics unique to a region cannot be taken into consideration, often the very dynamics that impact most heavily on the success of projects. For instance, concerns raised in the course of the Poverty Hearings in the Northern Province brought to light the fact that water projects often fall under the authority of a headman or chief who regulates how water is used.

Food

Malnutrition continues to be a cause of considerable concern, particularly amongst South Africa's poor and its children. According to the Johannesburg-based African Children's Feeding Scheme, they feed 11,000 children daily throughout Gauteng. But these may be the lucky ones. Health experts estimated in 1998 that 25% of the country's children between the age of 6 months and 6 years suffer from some form of malnutrition. The causes of malnutrition are multi-sectoral: households

---

17 *Ibid.*

without adequate food supplies, lack of child-care, poor diet and a lack of water and sanitation. Virtually every variable is underpinned by social and economic factors.

Since 1994 government has developed policy to create an integrated nutrition programme addressing health issues such as early detection, development to improve food security and improving nutrition knowledge. Implementation of the policy has been more difficult and is often blamed on an inadequate understanding of the importance and multi-faceted nature of nutrition problems.[18] Food security remains a major concern, with 20% of the urban population and 60% of people living below minimum subsistence levels. Widespread poverty, hunger and malnutrition plague the rural environment. Many rural children are particularly vulnerable with 72% of the farm population living below the poverty line.[19]

The latest cholera epidemic has focussed much attention on the need and breakdown in water and sanitation delivery. The current increasing cholera epidemic has exposed serious fault lines within water and sanitation provision to the rural poor. The cholera epidemic is fast gaining a stranglehold in Africa, with levels this year higher than those recorded since the early 1900s.

Challenges that Impact on the Realisation of Social and Economic Rights

The Constitution provides an excellent framework for the realisation of economic, social and cultural rights. However, the practical realisation of economic, social and cultural rights has not emulated the expanse of the Constitution. The question is why? The reasons for the ever-increasing gap between policy and implementation are manifold. To begin with an understanding of how human rights became enmeshed within the broader framework of South Africa's negotiated settlement. Human rights emerged as the unifying language to cement the two main protagonists in the conflict, the African National Congress and the National Party. Human rights became the language of compromise as opposed to the language of principle.

---

18 'Malnutrition affects 25% of young children', in: *Reconstruct, The Sunday Independent,* 7 March 1999.

19 'Most South Africans do not have food security', in: *NGO Matters,* Vol. 3, No. 12, December 1998, p. 14.

This approach to human rights is amplified in the contradictions between the Constitutional provisions and the macro-economic policy (Gear), which is based on cost recovery and limiting State social spending. Both these objectives of the economic policy runs counter to improving the basic quality of peoples lives, within the stark reality of high unemployment, high illiteracy, high HIV/AIDS infection rate and low infant mortality rates. Moving away from being the most unequal country in the world, South Africa is expected to invest in its people as a matter of priority and not delegate its responsibility through privatisation, to private companies, where accountability to the population is scant. The challenges of transformation of the civil service, in terms of purpose, focus, skill and capacity are central to narrowing the gap.

Inter-relation Between State Departments

This idea of working together, sharing information is based on the fact that it is impossible and impractical to develop policy around one right alone. There has to be a firm understanding and appreciation for the inter-relatedness and indivisibility of rights. An attempt was made in South Africa to establish a National Consultative Forum on Human Rights. This forum was to provide the formal linkages between the departments and to provide capacity in terms of integrating human rights into their programme plans, budget etc. This forum has all but become defunct. Human rights are still viewed by departments as appendix to the work processes and relegated to a desk (human rights desk) in departments. In addition to a lack of co-ordination between State departments, consultants who are drawn in to develop and draft policies are completely unfamiliar with the way government departments work. Thus the policies are almost out of sync with the realities of the implementing mechanism (State department).

Definition of Rights

Establishing and agreeing on the minimum core contents and parameters of social and economic rights is in fact defining the very essence of the rights. Unfortunately the current status of defining these core minimum standards is far from conclusive. These standards could serve as useful indicators and immediate target for monitoring the implementation of social and economic rights. These standards could also be used to measure in a broad sense (short, medium and long term) the States compliance to the notion of progressive realisation.

The human rights debates in South Africa are centred on academia. We engage in discussions in abstract, process oriented, and in a sometimes sterile and intangible manner. This has contributed to the notion that human rights are alien concepts. The language and phraseology we use is indicative of the difficulty of correlating daily life to rights. This weakness in the NGO sector has had the effect of alienating the recipients and weakening the lobby for the realisation of rights.

The Realisation of Economic, Social and Cultural Rights

Just administrative action is central to the realisation of economic and social rights. Its inclusion in the final Constitution reflect a recognition of the importance of service delivery mechanisms and the need for fair and transparent processes. Despite the enormous amount of work undertaken to amalgamate the plethora of administrations, service delivery through the civil service continues to be severely criticised.

Knowledge and Awareness

Understanding of and attitudes towards rights (a) amongst service delivery / implementing agencies (State and non-State actors) and (b) the general population. According to the survey conducted by a research organisation – CASE –, most South Africans don't understand day to day experiences within the rights paradigm even though many are involved in rights related issues on a daily basis.

South Africans must be educated about their rights and the mechanisms to access them, as part of broader initiatives to eradicate poverty and realise socio-economic rights.[20]

Economic, Social and Cultural Rights as Transformative Rights

The South African Constitution does more than just create a set of formal rules and entitlements. One of the envisaged effects of the South African Constitution is the transformation of South African society to a society based on democracy, equality, dignity and freedom from fear and want. Recognition of the transformative nature of our Bill of Rights is central to our ability to move beyond the vestiges of apartheid and its effects.

Economic, social and cultural rights are rights which aim at transforming and improving the standards and quality of peoples lives in a real sense, not only as an end in themselves, but as a means to preserving the dignity of the person. Thus the very core of economic, social and cultural rights is human dignity and equality.

---

[20] 'Report on socio-economic rights out soon', in: *NGO Matters*, Vol. 4, No. 1, January 1999, p. 2.

Understanding economic, social and cultural rights as transformative necessitates an understanding and acceptance that human rights, human development and humanity are parts of a trilogy that cannot be divided. Thus placing an enormous challenge on us to move beyond the process and interact with the reality. The mere provision of a house, water, education etc, is not enough in terms of the realisation of economic, social and cultural rights. The methodologies used, the resources made available for delivery, education, the standard and quality of the service, the sustainability of the service, the timeousness of the intervention, the development of basic infrastructure, the involvement of the recipients, the creation of accessible mechanisms etc have to be met, for us to agree that the right has been realised. In other words, the human being as a holistic individual is the central focus and not the act of delivering a service or product.

South Africa needs to move beyond regarding human rights as the language of pragmatic political compromise rather than the language of principle and accountability. This remains the key disjuncture between policy and implementation and of recognising that economic, social and cultural rights are guarantees and entitlements and not only policy goals.

SEARCHING FOR THE RIGHT(S) APPROACH

Wieteke BEERNINK & Harry DERKSEN (The Netherlands)

Introduction

As a church-related co-financing organisation in the Netherlands, ICCO has the broad aim of working on poverty eradication. For ICCO poverty is not a natural phenomenon, but directly related to injustice. Our view on the universality of human rights is strongly rooted in the values of the great world religions. As a Christian organization, ICCO has adopted equality, justice and human dignity as the core-values that guide us in our work.

The experience of the past 30 years has shown the close interrelation and interaction between human rights, stability and security, development potentials and democratization. At the conference "From Needs to Rights" organized by ICCO in cooperation with the Institute of Social Studies in The Hague in November 1998, this interrelation was further clarified. Indeed, sustainable development and stability seem to be possible only when they are concurrent with clear improvements in democratization, good governance and human rights and vice versa.

Much has been achieved since the adoption of the Universal Declaration of Human Rights in 1948. At the same time, there is a growing concern that economic, social and cultural rights have by and large been ignored by human rights organizations and development NGOs alike. Human Rights organizations were primarily concerned with only civil and political rights, while development NGOs took a needs-based approach towards poverty.

In recent years some work has been done to develop alternative approaches to respond to violations of Economic, Social and Cultural Rights.[1] Quite a number of northern and southern development NGOs as well as governmental and inter-governmental institutions, now adopt a rights-based approach. Although the conceptual base of such a rights-based approach has been clarified by these and other authors, much work still needs to be done before for northern and southern NGOs to can really put a rights-based approach to work. For many NGOs, this will require not only a

---

1 See for instance Berma Klein Goldewijk & Bas de Gaay Fortman, *Where Needs Meet Rights – Economic, Social and Cultural Rights in a New Perspective*, Geneva (WCC Publications), 1999.

rethinking of their policies, but also a change in attitudes, approaches and strategies, a change in their core-practice, development of their learning abilities and a resetting of their agenda's. This entails a fundamental change in many NGOs and will require time. In this paper a few elements of this change are elaborated.

Change of Attitude

In many southern countries, a debate is ongoing about the *ethnocentric* or *Eurocentric* attitude of the West that tries to sell western values and western models for development in the south. This Eurocentric attitude not only exists within western governments, but also in western NGOs and donor agencies. One result can be the adoption of northern models that do not fit the southern context. Sometimes one sees the total rejection in the south of whatever comes from the west or what is perceived as western, including a rejection of human rights and democratisation.

A change in attitude by northern NGOs is needed, to an attitude based on equality and true partnership. From its own cultural and religious background, ICCO promotes universal values such as equality, justice and dignity, and cooperates with those from other cultures and religions that promote these same values. In this recognition of common values and principles we find solidarity and the attitude of listening to each other, learning from each other and jointly engaging in action to protect and promote these values.

Approaches and Strategies

A change in development approach is needed both in the south and the north. The traditional development approach is still very North-to-South and welfare- oriented. It is often not more than a set of projects. Development assistance is to a large extent still used to address only some of the most obvious manifestations of poverty. As development aid funds are only marginal compared to the extent of the problems of poverty, they can at best create *little islands of happiness* of limited outreach, limited sustainability and low replicability.

As indicated above, the root causes of poverty are often manifold, and situated at different levels. To address these root causes, it is first of all necessary to make a proper analysis of the manifestations and causes of poverty and injustice. This analysis should include an inventarization of the strengths and weaknesses of both state and non-state actors and of instituional factors, which have a positive or negative influence on this situation of poverty and injustice. This obviously requires in-depth knowledge and understanding of the historical, socio-economic, cultural and political developments in the country.

Secondly adopting a rights-based approach will require the development of strategies that truly address the root causes of the problems. Such strategies need to be *process-oriented* rather than a collection of individual projects.

Strategy is often confused with the planning of a set of activities. While planning is a process of breaking down goals and activities into different components, making a strategy is a more creative process of synthesis; a process where components are put together in such a way that together they form one coherent approach to attaining the goals that have been set.

Depending on the context in which the NGO operates, process-oriented strategies should take into account the following considerations:

- Working at different levels – the causes of poverty and injustice are found at different levels: grassroots, regional, national and international, and these are interlinked; the struggle will have to tackle them all.
- Working with different approaches -legal, political, socio-economic, cultural, and religious.
- Working with different actors – state- (at various levels) and non-state actors of many types.
- The combination of working at different levels, using different approaches, and simultaneously making horizontal and vertical linkages is a key to a strong strategy.
- The greatest challenge for NGOs is to mobilise people, and to remain accountable to people. This means that at a grassroots level people should be aware of and approve the work that is being done, for instance at international level.
- Finding a right balance between addressing immediate needs of people and addressing the more structural and long-term issues. Both need to be done simultaneously for people to survive and for people to be able to engage in the far longer-term struggle for their rights.
- Maintaining an independent position is essential. NGOs should take care not to accept funding or other support from sources, which might compromise them or impose conditions that conflict with the core aims of the NGO.
- No single actor can make such an in-depth analysis as indicated above, and can adopt and implement a comprehensive and holistic strategy

containing all the elements mentioned here. Strategies therefore should include the formation of a rights-movement with like-minded actors who are able and prepared to overcome narrow-minded and short-term institutional interests.
- NGOs have a wide variety of instruments to choose from. This includes study and research, documentation, public action, education and awareness raising, monitoring, networking, media, lobby and advocacy, litigation and giving legal advice.
- Often people whose rights are being violated are portrayed as victims who are helpless and who need our assistance. This, in a way, disempowers them for the second time. Enhancing the claim-making capacities of people and communities themselves should therefore be adopted as a guiding principle.

Adopting a rights-based approach and strategy often implies a shift from operating within safe and accepted spaces within society to action-oriented approaches that challenge the existing power structures, both in the national society and internationally. Development NGOs have been put under pressure, both by foreign donors or backdonors, to 'show results', i.e. to show that money for projects was spent in an efficient and in an effective way. As rights-based approaches are much more process- and action-oriented, easily visible results cannot be expected.

Monitoring & Evaluation

Human rights are a conglomerate of more than sixty rights, which are not comparable with each other. It is already difficult to establish evaluation parameters applicable to two rights, let alone to sixty. The causes for human rights violations can be manifold, and it is often a complex of different factors, including insufficient legal protection, incompetent or corrupt implementation and cultural attitudes, that allow these violations to take place. How could it ever be possible in such cases to evaluate the effects of one single activity in this complexity of interdependent forces? Even if the situation of the people improves, the question as to whether this has a clear relation to the activity of this particular Human Rights Organisation can never be answered.

In spite of such difficulties, it is important for NGOs to find ways of obtaining reasonably reliable indications of the effects and impact of their strategies. If continuous analysis of the overall context and the influence of actors is combined with continuous efforts to establish the impact of one's own strategies, it is likely that reasonably accurate indicators for impact can be obtained. This is important since all NGOs should strive for optimum performance.[2]

North-South Agenda

In adopting a rights-based approach, northern NGOs acknowledge that problems of poverty and injustice are indeed global problems, which need to be addressed in the South and in the North. The consequences of adopting a rights-based approach for northern NGOs is therefore to accept that funding of southern initiatives to address poverty and injustice should be matched by northern initiatives to address problems related to the negative consequences of economic globalisation and existing global power balances. Both national northern institutions and international institutions with northern dominance play a crucial role in setting the economic and political boundary conditions for development in the South; addressing these constraints is clearly a prime task for the northern NGOs. Realizing that problems of poverty and injustice need to be addressed in a joint campaign for the 'globalisation of decency', northern and southern NGOs need to move towards establishing a common agenda and finding complementary strategies.

Networking

As argued above, a rights-based approach requires establishing linkages between several levels and many different actors. Linking serves to render the work more effective. But linking is also essential in order to learn together. No single NGO or institution can reasonably claim to have *the* answer to any existing problem of poverty and injustice. It is therefore of paramount importance to form local, regional, national and international networks aimed at the exchange of our experiences and aimed at a collective development of our knowledge.

---

2 See also *Measuring the Impossible? – A preliminary study on impact assessment of human rights activities*, ICCO, December 2000.

SECTION III
INSTRUMENTS

INTER-AMERICAN TOOLS FOR THE ENFORCEABILITY OF ECONOMIC, SOCIAL AND CULTURAL RIGHTS

Adalid CONTRERAS BASPINEIRO (Bolivia)

Enforceability of Economic, Social and Cultural Rights

To an increasing extent, human rights in Latin America and the Caribbean are forming part of political decisions and the claims put forth by citizens, as well as academic concerns, government policies and everyday conversation. Nevertheless, their knowledge, appropriation and implementation are still incipient, subject to just as many questions and guesses as answers, with discussions over their nature, content, universal scope, interdependence and indivisibility constituting concerns that are no longer restricted to just the academic world, because they are beginning to spread throughout the web of the many different forms of power relationships.

The ways of exercising power on this Continent have ascribed a role to human rights making reparations for inequities, in their dual juridical and social dimensions. In juridical terms, this is supported by the international rules and tools established by both the Universal and International System, and socially through the demands, claims, proposals and struggles of citizen organisations who know that the human condition rightfully endows them with this status. At both levels, human rights are an area of political construction and collective inventiveness, linked indissolubly with democracy, development and culture. Consequently, any mention of tools ensuring the enforceability of economic, social and cultural rights in Latin America always refers to historic processes, juridical instruments, social mobilisation and everyday claims: in fact, political actions.

Nevertheless, a situation prevails here where knowledge, appropriation and implementation of economic, social and cultural rights remains sparse, in parallel to the application of contemporary concepts such as the proposal for Sustainable Human Development, defined as "a cultural option for change focused on the final objectives of development itself, meaning the fulfilment of the aspirations of the people"[1], where human rights are viewed as integral rights that are being called for to an increasing extent by both

[1] Mahbub Ul Haq, *El desarrollo humano sostenible. Nuevo enfoque del desarrollo*, UNDP, 1995, p. 3.

individual and social players, in various areas and disciplines – not only juridical – and with many different motivations, ranging from very specific through to broad-based policies.

Actions promoting progress grounded on the concept of human development are now being enriched through an emphasis on human rights. This means that development, economic, social and cultural rights, as well as human rights in general are inherent to human dignity. Consequently, the international community and the States are bound and committed to promote, respect and comply with matters established through binding international agreements and covenants. These rights are also legitimised by the customs of the peoples and the relationships among the States. This requires us to understand that the universal scope of these rights endows the peoples with specific ways of implementing them, shaped by their own cultures and customs.

In the dynamics of this historic process, the enforceability of economic, social and cultural rights becomes a key factor in building links between philosophy and practice, between the juridical and the political, between demands and the active implementation of rights, between immediate needs and government policies. This dynamism calls for even greater vigour within a historical context where the results of applying structural adjustment policies throughout a decade of firm and systematic restructuring throughout the region are showing obvious signs of depletion. The limited feasibility of this model is reflected in rising poverty and utter poverty rates, even questioning the legitimacy of the Washington Consensus that provided ideological support, with spreading unemployment and citizen reactions expressed through the resistance to the Millennium Round of talks held by the World Trade Organisation in Seattle, or the crowds flocking to the Peoples Summit, held in parallel to the Americas Summit in Quebec, as areas where civil society is emerging and calling for the primacy of human rights over any treaty or agreement.

The tension between the effects of adjustment policies and the upsurge in citizen demands has strengthened the trend towards the enforceability of all human rights, opening up fresh fields of demands for settling accounts, in the field of trade, integration and capital investment, for instance, as well as free flows of capital and their impact on the crises assailing the global financial system, in parallel to rising demand to introduce regulation and social development mechanisms, tackling the foreign debt, utter poverty and exclusion, severe environmental deterioration, habitats and natural resources, flows of migrants with attempts to control them at all costs, cultural identities jeopardised by homogenisation processes, the right to self-determination for the indigenous peoples and their inclusion in national projects and pluri-cultural States, hemisphere-wide security, the social agenda and democratic governance in a region characterised by the precarious footing of its regimes and authoritarian culture.

Finally, the existence of common problems and issues within the framework of globalisation has prompted the appearance of players with new identities and fresh demands, well able to deploy the existing mechanisms to the advantage of the peoples. To do so, it is necessary to redeem critical thought and interconnect these new players, creating new accounting mechanisms and making better use of the existing facilities, in order to bring out the full potential of the emergence of citizenship in national, social and political processes, as well as international fora.

Under these conditions, the process currently under way offers fertile ground for the conceptual, juridical, political and social development of human rights. Similarly, the deployment of the tools ensuring the enforceability of economic, social and cultural rights is one of the most encouraging ways of rebuilding societies with greater equity and better opportunities for all.

The Standing of Economic, Social and Cultural Rights in the Region[2]

The right to protection of the family, mothers, children and adolescents, the family – which is the natural key element in society – warrants the broadest possible protection, with all possible assistance, particularly for the care and education of the children in the family, obviously protected by tangibly solid relationships between their parents. This standard is not always accepted in the Latin American countries, where increasing numbers of families are breaking down due to the lack of jobs for heads of families, with children leaving home to become "street kids".

The case of Brazil is eloquent: with 20 million young people aged 12 to 17 years, only 22,000 are sheltered by some type of social or educational measures, and among them, 0.94% are involved in homicides and 0.5% in robberies. In plain figures, this means that 10% of the crimes in Brazil are committed by juveniles under 18 years old. Peru is not immune to this

---

[2] Based on Hugo Rodríguez, *Derechos Económicos, Sociales y Culturales. Balance en Siete Países Latinoamericanos*, Lima, Peru (PIDHDD/CEDAL), November 2000.

problem of family breakdowns: 100,000 families live in utter poverty, and without the presence of a spouse to care for the children, with at least 356,000 single mothers, in addition to one million children with no documentation. These are extreme situations that are becoming common throughout the Continent, with fewer jobs and a lack of decent living standards. There is a shortage of special measures for protecting and assisting all marginalised children and adolescents, in addition to mothers abandoned by the institutions – whether State-run or civil – that are responsible for safeguarding this social heritage. The Inter-American Platform for Human Rights, Democracy and Development is working towards these ends.

Respect for the Right to Health, which is a priority for all but a benefit for only a few, shows that the health of the population of Latin America is undermined by a lack of care and attention from government institutions entrusted with this responsibility. In parallel to rapidly-deteriorating infant mortality and morbidity rates, the spread of epidemic, endemic and occupational diseases constitutes an explosive clinical situation. The apocalyptic plague of AIDS – with no respect for social status – is spreading mercilessly over the Continent, fuelled by promiscuity: there are 13,798 people infected in Argentina, with 4,598 in Peru, while 4,000 people die each year in Mexico, just as an example. Another disease affecting large numbers of people is tuberculosis: there are 22,500 people suffering from this disease in Mexico, with some 27,700 in Peru. Due to limited government attention, infant morbidity and mortality rates provide crude birth control by decimating the population under the age of 5 years. There are 37.4 deaths per 1,000 births in Brazil, 7.6 per 1,000 in Argentina and 52 for 1,000 in Peru.

The right to an adequate standard of living: food and housing are affected by the rural exodus, with peasants flocking into the cities where they subsist in shanties and tenements under a renting system that eats away people's savings, leaving Latin America homes far too tightly-packed for comfort. Contrasting with the modernity of leading cities such as Buenos Aires (Argentina), Santiago (Chile) and Rio de Janeiro (Brazil), the slums known as *villas miseria, callampas* and *favelas* are home to huge numbers of people. The housing shortage in Argentina tops three million homes, equivalent to 33% of the nation's populace; Brazil has 30 million homeless and jobless, while 73.5% of Mexicans live in homes with no piped water or sewage services. Nutritional standards are linked closely to national poverty levels, hovering close to utter poverty in Latin America. In 1997, the number of Peruvians living in utter poverty reached 12.34 million.

Initially covering limited aspects such as personal savings, family safety and social welfare, social security facilities are making progress, moving ahead over the years towards mandatory national systems and helped by private insurance schemes and mutual funds. The unceasing assault on human rights in the field of social security in Latin America is due largely to abusive practices by governments that on the one hand claim a shortage of funding for underwriting the "security" of the people, in order to justify their non-compliance with this right, while on the other these services are being individualised and delegated to private institutions that have taken over the pension fund systems. This leads to the assumption that the vast majority of the population is excluded from this right.

Charting the social security systems of Latin America indicates that these countries are more similar than different. The private pension fund systems in Peru, Chile and Bolivia are quite comparable in terms of both definition of their names and tools: these schemes seek higher profitability on amounts paid in, and provide the following services: retirement pensions, disability pensions, survivor pensions, all benefiting increasingly smaller portions of the population, due to the effects of so-called labour flexibilisation. Argentina has a government-run pension scheme based on mandatory State payments, financed through a share-out system: this is one of the few countries where a glimpse of solidarity still remains, for workers joining the AFJP, thanks to this government-run system. In Colombia, the insurance system clearly reflects the gap between those who pay in more (private insurance) and those who pay in less (public insurance).

The social security system in Latin America (and more specifically its government-run pension schemes) is threatened by neo-liberal reforms on two fronts: lower government premiums and the promotion of privately-run options, which means that – like everything touched by the magic wand of neo-liberalism – there are few beneficiaries and many disadvantaged.

Classifying the Tools for Ensuring the Enforceability of Rights

In the usual language of the defenders of human rights, instruments are taken to be the regulations and jurisprudence covering the various types of human rights. Following this principle and focusing on the Inter-American instruments, we should turn to the documents generated by the regional organisation policies. From this standpoint, we start out from an understanding of economic, social and cultural rights in the region: the origins of the Inter-American system in 1948, the Charter of the Organisation of American States, the American Declaration on the Rights and Duties of Man, and the Inter-American Charter for Social Guarantees. The various chapters of these documents enshrine the standards and rules for education, science, culture and labour. Later, the Additional Protocol to the Inter-American Convention on Economic, Social and Cultural Rights was adopted, and in 1999, the optional San Salvador Protocol came into force, which "acknowledges the close links between the effectiveness of economic, social and cultural rights, and that of civil and political rights, as such constituting an indissoluble whole that is grounded on the acknowledgement of the dignity of the human person, requiring permanent care and promotion in order to achieve full effectiveness, without which there can never be any justification of the violation of some of them for the sake of the implementation of others."[3]

These Inter-American instruments underpin the enforceability of economic, social and cultural rights, together with international tools and regulations such as the International Covenant on Economic, Social and Cultural Rights and others, including the Universal Declaration of Human Rights itself, the Convention on Children's Rights, the Convention Against All Forms of Discrimination Against Women, the Agreements of the International Labour Organisation covering the Fundamental Rights of the Worker, the Agreement of the International Labour Organisation on Indigenous and Tribal Peoples, the Declaration of the UN Assembly-General on the Right to Development, and the Declaration of Teheran, Vienna, Copenhagen, Rio and Beijing, among others.

Furthermore, grassroots actions throughout the region have been drafting other documents inspired by the enforceability, and the indivisible and universal nature of economic, social and cultural rights, subject to enforcement through the courts, which guide the actions of organisations and civil society. These documents include the Declaration of Quito, signed in July 1998 by various regional human rights organisations.[4] Another important document is the Social Charter of the Americas, drafted by the Inter-American Platform Human Rights, Democracy and Development and the Continental Social Alliance (ASC – *Alianza Social Continental*).[5]

---

3 IIDH/CEPAL, *Igualdad de los modernos. Reflexiones acerca de la realización de los derechos económicos, sociales y culturales en América Latina*, San José, Costa Rica, 1997, p. 21.

4 The organisations signing the Declaration of Quito are the Inter-American Platform for Human Rights (PIDHDD), the Latin American Association of Promotion Organisations (ALOP), the Regional International Workers Organisation (ORIT), the Economic and Social Rights Centre (CDES) and the Federal International Human Rights Federation (FIDH).

5 ASC/CEDAL/PIDHDD, *Carta Social Americana*, Lima, Peru, January 2000.

Without ignoring the existing regulations and mechanisms as tools, in this paper we intend to analyse these instruments as strategies and actions undertaken by citizens, calling for the enforceability of their economic, social and cultural rights from the standpoint of their integration and indivisibility with the other rights, and based on existing universal, regional and national regulations. Having explained this, we affirm that within the context analyzed, the construction and implementation of instruments for the enforceability of the economic, social and cultural rights respond to the many different challenges[6] at the conceptual level, within the field of government policies, as well as grassroots movements and the ways rebuilding the social fabric and strategic alliances. Consequently, there is no single option for instruments that ensure the enforceability of human rights. Among their many different expressions, we stress the Alternative Reports and Political Actions, whose separation is more practical and conceptual, as both are grounded on similar standards and objectives.

The Alternative Reports offer an area for revealing the true development status of economic, social and cultural rights, at the same time as they indicate the possible lines for resolving the many different aspects of various economic, social and cultural rights. On the one hand, this includes preparing Alternative Reports, written from the standpoint of civil society and presented in parallel to the Official Reports to the UN Commission on Economic, Social and Cultural Rights in Geneva.

We also stress Political Actions, which are practical expressions of grassroots organisations and mobilisation calling for the implementation of very specific rights, with the possibility of ensuring that they are enforceable through the courts, in order to endow them with concepts, standards, regulations, indicators and social activities, effective at the international and national management levels, with government implementations. These actions include campaigns; actions providing support for the mechanism for citizen calls demanding their legally established rights; and the use of statistical indicators analysing their political scope.[7] These actions may also arise from the preparation of specific case studies presented to the governments and the Commission, in addition to the Inter-American Court or the OAS System.

---

6 See *Desafíos para la Exigibilidad de los derechos Económicos, Sociales y Culturales. Balance de la estrategia de la Plataforma Sudamericana de Derechos Humanos, Democracia y Desarrollo*, Lima (CEDAL), July 1999.

7 For examples of these types of enforceability, see Wola, *El camino al Siglo XXI: desafíos y estrategias de la comunidad latinoamericana de derechos humanos*, Washington and Lima, December 1999.

The Alternative Report as an Instrument for Enforceability

The Alternative Report includes many different and even conflicting contributions. For aspects related to human rights in general and economic, social and cultural rights in particular, the Alternative Report was broad-ranging. It has an ethical foundation, objectively describing the true situation of the economy, social organisations and culture which the Official Report normally attempts to mask by presenting data attempting to justify government policies neither based on nor acknowledging the basic postulate of human rights for a decent quality of life. In contrast, the Alternative Report strives to portray the true reality and its subjects. It also has a positive aspect, indicating ways of resolving the effects on citizenship as well as the mandatory obligations of the States and the complicity of the multilateral agencies in the deployment of international standards for human rights.

The basic purpose of the Reports is to reshape government policies through highlighting different aspects of enforceability through lawsuits filed with national courts and international entities protecting human rights, basically the Commission on Economic, Social and Cultural Rights of the United Nations Development Program (UNDP), pressuring governments to meet their commitments accepting the primacy of human rights.

In order to avoid the Alternative Report becoming merely an exercise in description or simply an action in response, it is necessary to consider the impacts and define the results expected at specific levels and over given periods. Examples of these results or accomplishments might include rewording or else respecting certain juridical standards; other examples of achievements are decisions handed down that constitute jurisprudence and extend the field of the enforceability of human rights through the courts; still other examples can be implemented, such as the approval of national human rights plans as State policies, or setting up joint committees with State sectors in order to oversee, investigate or sanction certain types of violation or define specific government policies focused on human rights and gender equity.

The drafting process for these Reports is occurring to an increasing extent in many different countries, but with similar motivations: 1) to demonstrate the real status of economic, social and cultural rights, normally concealed by the Official Reports; 2) to include a grassroots perspective (citizen demands, interests and proposals) in these Reports; 3) to spotlight the topics and problems of economic, social and cultural rights for citizenship, urging their protection; 4) to enhance visibility with international entities, encouraging them to include citizen viewpoints when defining their policies; 5) to prompt changes on government policies incited to by citizens as well by international organisations; 6) to build up strategic responses in many different sectors in order to implement social policies; and 7) to strengthen the capacities of human rights organisations in their attempts to help shape development policies and buttress democracy from a human rights standpoint.

In methodological terms, a common concern among the many different experiences noted is the need to interlink four types of actions: 1) strict, systematic investigation with data, checking the effects of the application or violations of economic, social and cultural rights; 2) citizen participation; 3) efforts shared out among many different organisations, in parallel to the development of strategic responses; and 4) lobbying or working closely with international organisations in order to ensure a favourable reception for the reports, while pressuring governments to comply with their recommendations. It should be noted that an aspect which is lacking in practice but well to the fore among the concerns is following up on the resolutions issued by the Commission on Economic, Social and Cultural Rights.

There are many outstanding efforts and experiences at the regional level, striving to ensure grassroots participation, sometimes in consultation processes for drawing up the Reports, and in most cases with the broad-ranging dissemination of the Reports for analysis and enrichment; in the case of Brazil, the presentation of the Report was accompanied by activities that included press conferences, seminars, and demonstrations on the day it was presented in Geneva.

Challenges for the Enforceability of Economic, Social and Cultural Rights

The experience of presenting the Reports and the enforceability actions in general offers lessons that the Inter-American Platform on Human Rights, Democracy and Development defines as challenges[8], and that we recapitulate in order to shape the tasks required to deploy the regional tools for ensuring the enforceability of economic, social and cultural rights.

---

8 PIDHDD, *Plan regional 2000 – 2002 de la Plataforma Interamericana de Derechos Humanos, Democracia y Desarrollo*, Lima, 2000.

One of these challenges lies in the conceptual output needed to strengthen the doctrine and jurisprudence, in order to affirm the integrative links and enforceability of all human rights. It is clearly necessary to legitimate the economic, social and cultural rights of human rights, grounded on their collective nature and procedural implementation, together with their links to development over the medium and long term. Consequently, it is necessary to move ahead with the enforceability through the courts of these economic, social and cultural rights, through applying the current regulatory structure as well as building up new legal tools. Moreover, at the methodological level, it is necessary to work with indicators for measuring and implementing the various types of rights, without losing sight of their integrative links.

Another challenge that has become more significant through the alternative concepts in these Reports consists of not forgetting the importance of a vital and strengthened State that can ensure fully effective human rights. However, this challenge is set against a backdrop where State obligations are tending to shrink in relative terms[9] through the privatisation of rights, due to the increasing weight of private agents and their effective take-over or even violation of these rights. This is occurring with multilateral organisations and banks opting for macro-economic policies that assign high priority to economic growth targets, trespassing on national sovereignty. The responsibility of the States is expressed in the Declaration of Quito: *"The States have the duty of preventing and sanctioning the occurrence of breaches of economic, social and cultural rights by private agents. The State is responsible for omissions in its duty of protecting them, but such agents shall be held liable for their own acts and the consequence thereof before the courts, under domestic law"* (N° 22). Additionally, Section I of the American Social Charter on the Basic Obligations of the States stresses the obligation of non-discrimination; the obligation of adopting measures up to the maximum amount of resources available; the obligation to adopt provisions under domestic law; the rebuttal of constraints, and the right to citizen participation and consultation, with the States guaranteeing safeguards for the principles of inclusion, representativity, transparency and legitimacy.[10]

---

9 "The legal grounds on which the economic, social and cultural rights are based assumes the presence of a *strong* State as the driving force behind the implementation of these rights, together with a national guideline fostering them." Alirio Uribe, in: *Vigencia de los Derechos Humanos Integrales: un Reto para la Humanidad a 50 años de la Declaración Universal y a las puertas del tercer milenio,* (Presentation by the Corporación Collective de Avocados 'José Laver Restroom' to the World Congress on FID), Dakar, Senegal, November 20 1997, p. 38.

10 PIDHDD/CEDAL/ASC, *American Social Charter,* Section I, Articles 1-6.

A third challenge is related to building up a national scenario that fosters human rights, backed by the international community, so that the scope of the scrutiny and sanctioning capacity of the international community should be truly effective and non-discriminatory on the one hand, while on the other these do not become acts that jeopardise the peace and rights of the civil population. The concepts of national sovereignty and interventionism are under review. To an increasing extent, there is a clash between the legitimate intervention of the international community to protect human rights and the risk of interventions prompted by political interests that may affect the rights of the civil population, frequently breaching the right to life and decent living conditions.

We also note the significant challenge of strengthening the social fabric, protagonism, legitimacy and networking among the social players and the new scenarios for citizenship. This involves identifying the players in a broad range of roles, together with collective demands and agendas, and above all opportunities for establishing areas of interaction and dialog among the many different organisations and civil society, based on their own nature and capacity, assessing the possibilities of grassroots organisations, academic entities, State authorities, private enterprise and the true effects of the NGOs in their attempts to represent and intermediate actions benefiting civil society.[11] These networks should be built up at the local, national, regional and international levels, with different levels of enforceability, but grounded on their integrative links and with the intention to enshrine decent living conditions.

In today's world, the basic challenge of the tools for ensuring enforceability consists of building up links among human rights, democracy and development. These links could well pave the way for a new paradigm that would eliminate the possibility of our countries losing their viability, enmired in their *sui generis* condition of non-development as described by Oswaldo de Rivero[12], through the widespread generalisation of discriminatory, assistentialist policies.

Taking all these challenges into account, we feel that the Reports must support the objective of enforceability, with the possibility of shaping government policies. To do so, it is necessary to foster the creation of new

---

11 Speech by the President to the countries in the Andean Community, Peru, June 2000 and the Peruvian Chancellor at the XXX Assembly-General of the USA, held recently, Windsor, Canada.

12 Oswaldo de Rivero, *El Mito del Desarrollo: los Países Enviable en el silo XXI*, Lima, Peru (Muscat Ault Editors), 1998.

institutional mechanisms for the exercise of participative democracy, through which links, alliances and networks are built up among many different organisations in different regions, as well as between South and North. In order to ensure effective results for the Reports submitted to the Commission for Economic, Social and Cultural Rights, a permanent presence is required, with lobbying and follow-up involving the supportive entities of the European Community.

The enforceability of economic, social and cultural rights cannot be left within this sphere of civil society, as their complementarity must be urged in the public sphere, establishing intervention strategies at many different levels. At the local level, mechanisms should be explored for increasing the availability of legal remedies for economic, social and cultural rights at the local government levels, fostering grassroots participation in parallel to monitoring municipal policies. At the national level, better use of the existing administrative and legal mechanisms is needed, in addition to follow-up of national budgets and investment policies. At the international level, more effective use is required for regional and international protection systems, while strengthening regional and international human rights structures.[13]

[13] Based on Wola, *En camino al Siglo XXI, o.c.*, p. 54.

THE IMPLEMENTATION OF ECONOMIC, SOCIAL AND CULTURAL RIGHTS: PRACTICES AND EXPERIENCES

Flavia PIOVESAN (Brazil)

Introduction

The purpose of this paper is to analyze the implementation of economic, social and cultural rights, presenting practices and cases drawn from the Brazilian experience. This study is undertaken on the basis of the contemporary concept of human rights, stressing the challenges thrown up by the effects of economic globalisation.

This essay proposes three main topics for reflection: a) What is the scope of the instruments for implementing economic, social and cultural rights within the Latin American context? b) What is the balance of experiences in terms of implementing these rights in the case of Brazil? and c) What are the strategies and prospects for moving ahead with the implementation of economic, social and cultural rights, taking into account the excludatory impacts of the era of economic globalisation?

Initially, an analysis will be undertaken of the contemporary concept of human rights, and the manner in which this includes economic, social and cultural rights, stressing their implementation mechanisms. Second, a balance will be drawn up of experiences in implementing these rights, in the case of Brazil. Finally, an assessment will be made of the strategies and prospects for moving ahead with the implementation of economic, social and cultural rights, taking into account the excludatory impacts of the era of economic globalisation.

Tools for Implementing

What is the scope of the tools for implementing economic, social and cultural rights within the context of Latin America?
In the words of Hannah Arendt, human rights are not a given fact, but a construction, a human invention, a work in process that is constantly being constructed and reconstructed[1]. Looking at the historical track-record of

---

1 Hannah Arendt, *As Origens do Totalitarismo,* (translated by Roberto Raposo), Rio de Janeiro, 1979. In this respect, see also Celso Lafer, *A Reconstrução dos Direitos Humanos: Um diálogo com o pensamento de Hannah Arendt,* São Paulo (Cia das Letras), 1988, p. 134. Similarly, Ignacy

these rights, it can be affirmed that the definition of human rights has run through many different meanings. In view of this plurality, this study highlights what is known as the contemporary concept of human rights, introduced through the advent of the Universal Declaration of Human Rights (1948) and reiterated through the Declaration of Human Rights in Vienna (1993).

This concept is the result of a drive to internationalize human rights, which is extremely recent in historical terms, appearing only after World War II in response to the atrocities and horrors of Nazism. Presenting the State as the main violator of human rights, the Hitler years were characterised by a logic of destruction and the discardable status of human beings, which resulted in 18 million people imprisoned in concentration camps, where 11 million of them died, including 6 million Jews, as well as communists, homosexuals, gypsies... The legacy of Nazism was to shape the ownership of rights, meaning the condition of the subject of the rights to the facts of belonging to a specific race – the pure Aryan race. In the words of Ignacy Sachs, the XX century was scarred by two World Wars and the absolute horror of genocide conceived as a political and industrial project[2].

It is within this scenario that the effort to rebuild human rights is placed, as an ethical benchmark and paradigm guiding the contemporary international order. If World War II saw the breakdown of human rights, the post-War years were to see their reconstruction.

On December 10, 1948, the Universal Declaration of Human Rights was approved as a major stepping-stone in the process of reconstructing human rights. It introduced the contemporary concept of human rights, characterised by their indivisible and universal nature. They are universal because they call for the universal extension of human rights, believing that human status is the sole requirement for dignity as a holder of these rights. They are indivisible because the guarantee of civil and political rights is a

Sachs affirms: "There can never be sufficient stress on the fact that the appearance of rights is the outcome of struggles, that rights are sometimes won at the barricades through a historical process packed with vicissitudes through which needs and aspirations are linked through claims and to banners of struggle, before being acknowledged as rights". (Ignacy Sachs, 'Desenvolvimento, Direitos Humanos e Cidadania', in: *Direitos Humanos no Século XXI*, 1998, p. 156). For Allan Rosas: "The concept of human rights is always progressive (...) Discussions on what are human rights and how they should be defined are part and parcel of our history, our past and our present." Quotation from Allan Rosas, 'So-Called Rights of the Third Generation', in: Asbjorn Eide, Catarina Krause & Allan Rosas, *Economic, Social and Cultural Rights*, Dordrecht, Boston and London (Martinus Nijhoff Publishers), 1995, p. 243.

2 Ignacy Sachs, 'O Desenvolvimento enquanto apropriação dos direitos humanos', in: *Estudos Avançados* 12 (33), 1998, p. 149.

condition for ensuring economic, social and cultural rights, and vice-versa. When one of them is violated, the others are also breached. Consequently, human rights constitute an indivisible, interdependent and interrelated unit that links the catalogue of civil and political rights to the listings of economic, social and cultural rights.

When examining the indivisibility of the interdependence of human rights, Hector Gros Espiell teaches: "Only the full acknowledgement of all these rights can ensure the real existence of each of them, as without effectively enjoying economic, social and cultural rights, civil and political rights are reduced to mere formal categories. In contrast, without the reality of civil and political rights, and lacking the effects of freedom in its broadest sense, economic, social and cultural rights in turn lack any real meaning. This idea of the necessary integrality, interdependence and indivisibility in terms of the concept and the reality of the content of human rights – which is implicit in the United Nations Charter to a certain extent – was compiled, extended and systematised in 1948 through the Universal Declaration of Human Rights, and definitively reaffirmed in the Universal Covenants on Human Rights approved by the Assembly-General in 1966, in effect since 1976, with the Proclamation of Teheran (1968) and the Resolution adopted by the Assembly-General on December 16, 1977 on the criteria and means for improving the effective enjoyment of the rights and fundamental freedoms (Resolution n. 32/130)".[3]

In view of the indivisible nature of human rights, the mistaken notion should be definitively rejected that there is a class of rights (civil and political rights) warranting full acknowledgement and respect, while another class of rights (economic, social and cultural rights) in turn do not merit compliance. From the international regulatory standpoint, the idea that economic, social and cultural rights are not legal rights is completely outdated. The idea that social rights are non-enforceable is merely ideological rather than scientific[4]. These are true, authentic fundamental

---

3 Hector Gros Espiell, *Los derechos económicos, sociales y culturales en el sistema interamericano*, San José (Libro Libre), 1986, p. 16-17.

4 As Jack Donnelly explains: "Many philosophers and a large number of contemporary conservatives and liberals have claimed that economic and social rights are not true rights, suggesting that the traditional dichotomy reflects not only the genesis of contemporary standards for human rights but also an order of priority among these rights. Maurice Cranston offers the most widely quoted version of the philosophical argument against economic and social rights. He affirms that the traditional civil and political rights to life, freedom and property are "universal, supreme and moral rights". However, economic and social rights are not universal or concrete, nor are they of supreme importance "belonging to a different logical category" meaning that they are not true human rights (...) The

rights, that are enforceable through the Courts, and demand dedicated, responsible compliance. This is why they should be claimed as rights, rather than as charity or generosity.

As the benchmark event in the drive to internationalize human rights, the Universal Declaration (1948) fostered the conversion of these rights into matters of legitimate interest for the international community. As noted by Kathryn Sikkink: "The International Law of Human Rights assumes as legitimate and necessary the concern of State and non-State players regarding the manner in which the inhabitants of other States are treated. The safety net provided by international human rights strives to redefine what matters fall within the exclusively domestic jurisdiction of the States."[5]

This strengthens the idea that the protection of human rights should not be relegated to the exclusive domain of the State, meaning that it should not be limited solely to the national or domestic jurisdiction on an exclusive basis, because it is a matter of legitimate international interest. In turn, this innovative concept indicates two significant consequences:

1) revising the traditional idea of the absolute sovereignty of the State, which is passing through a process of relativisation, insofar as interventions are accepted at the national level when intended to protect human rights, meaning that types of international monitoring and acceptance of responsibility are accepted, when human rights are being violated[6];

---

stumbling-blocks preventing the implementation of most economic and social rights are more political than physical. For instance, there is more than enough food in the world to feed everyone, widespread hunger and malnutrition exist not because of a physical lack of food, but due to political decisions on its distribution" (*Universal Human Rights in Theory and Practice*, Ithaca (Cornell University Press), 1989, p. 31-32).

5 Kathryn Sikkink, 'Human Rights, Principled issue-networks, and Sovereignty in Latin America', in: *International Organizations*. Massachusetts (IO Foundation and Massachusetts Institute of Technology), 1993, p. 413. The same author adds: 'Basic individual rights are not the exclusive domain of the State, but constitute a legitimate concern of the international community' (*o.c.*, p. 441).

6 Particularly outstanding is the affirmation by the Secretary General of the United Nations in late 1992: "Although respect for the sovereignty and integrity of the State remains a core issue, there is no denying that the old doctrine of exclusive and absolute sovereignty is no longer applicable, and that this sovereignty was never absolute, as it was formally conceived at the theoretical level. One of the main intellectual demands of our times is to rethink the issue of sovereignty (...). Stressing the rights of individuals and the rights of peoples is an aspect of universal sovereignty that resides with all humankind, and which allows the peoples to become legitimately involved in issues affecting the world as a whole. This is a movement that to increasing extent is being expressed in the gradual expansion of international law" (Boutros-Ghali, 'Empowering the United Nations', in: *Foreign Affairs*, vol. 89, 1992/1993, p. 98-99, apud Henkin et. al., *International Law – Cases and Materials*, p. 18).

2) the establishment of the idea that the rights of the individual should be protected at the international level, as a condition of being subject to the Law.

Consequently, this indicates that the era is drawing to an end when the manner in which the State treated its citizens was viewed as a problem falling within the domestic jurisdiction, based on national sovereignty.

The process of universalising human rights has in turn resulted in the formation of an international regulatory system protecting these rights. As taught by André Gonçalves Pereira and Fausto de Quadros: "In terms of Political Science, this meant merely transposing and adapting to International Law the progress that has already taken place in Domestic Law at the start of the century, shifting from the Police State to the Social Security State. But this was sufficient for International Law to move away from the classic phase, such as the right of peace and war, progressing into a new or modern era in its development, where International Law fosters cooperation and solidarity".[7]

Based on the adoption of the Universal Declaration of Human Rights (1948) and the contemporary concept of human rights that it introduced, the International Law of Human Rights began to develop through the adoption of countless international treaties designed to protect fundamental rights. As taught by Norberto Bobbio, human rights arose as natural universal rights and developed as positive private rights (when each Constitution includes Declarations of Rights) and were finally fully implemented as positive Universal Rights[8]. Based on the expanding consolidation of this universal positivism with regard to human rights, it may be affirmed that international treaties protecting human rights reflect a contemporary ethical awareness that is shared by the States, insofar as

---

[7] André Gonçalves Pereira & Fausto Quadros, *Manual de Direito Internacional Público,* IId Edition, Coimbra (Livraria Almedina), 1993, p. 661. The authors add: "The new matters that international law has been absorbing under the conditions mentioned are widely varied: political, economic, social, cultural, scientific, technical etc. But among them the book shows that three should be stressed: protection and guarantees for the rights of man, development and economic and political integration" (*o.c.,* p. 661). In the view of Hector Fix-Zamudio: "(...) setting up international entities to safeguard human rights, which well known Italian treatise-writer Mauro Cappelleti has qualified as transnational constitutional jurisdiction, while court control of the constitutional nature of legislative provisions and concrete acts of authority have affected Internal Law, particularly the sphere of human rights and extended into the international and even community spheres" (Comisión Nacional de Derechos Humanos, *Protección Jurídica de los Derechos Humanos,* México, 1991, p. 184).

[8] Norberto Bobbio, *Era dos Direitos,* (translated by Carlos Nelson Coutinho), Rio de Janeiro (Campus), 1988, p. 30.

they invoke international consensus on topics such as civil and political rights, in addition to economic, social and cultural rights, bans on torture, combating racial discrimination, the elimination of discrimination against women, and the protection of children's rights, among other topics. It should also be stressed that through to June 2000, the International Covenant on Civil and Political Rights had been signed by 144 States Parties; the International Covenant on Economic, Social and Cultural Rights had been signed by 142 States Parties; the Convention Against Torture had been signed by 119 States Parties; the Convention on the Elimination of Racial Discrimination had been signed by 155 States Parties; the Convention on the Elimination of Discrimination Against Women had been signed by 165 States Parties; and the Convention on Children's Rights topped them all, signed by 191 States Parties.[9] The high number of States Parties signing these treaties reflects high levels of international consensus on core issues related to human rights. It is stressed that these international instruments always express the minimum protection parameters, which should be blended with national parameters, with the most beneficial standard prevailing, providing the most protection for human rights.

The contemporary concept of human rights is characterised by the processes of their universalisation and internationalisation, viewed from the standpoint of their indivisibility[10]. It is stressed that the Declaration of Human Rights issued in Vienna in 1993 reiterates the concept of the 1948 Declaration which affirms in its Paragraph 5: "All human rights are universal, interdependent and interrelated. The international community should ensure human rights globally, fairly and justly, on an equal footing, and with the same emphasis."

The Declaration of Vienna (1993) was signed by 171 States Parties, endorsing the universality and indivisibility of human rights and reviving the grounds of legitimacy for the contemporary concept of human rights introduced by the 1948 Declaration. It is noted that the "post-War" consensus is reflected in the 1948 Declaration being adopted by 48 States, with eight abstentions, while the Declaration of Vienna (1993) extends, renews and expands the consensus on the universality and indivisibility of human rights.

---

9 On this matter, consult the *UNDP Human Development Report 2000*, New York/Oxford (Oxford University Press), 2000, p. 51.

10 It should be noted that the Convention on the Eliminations of All Forms of Racial Discrimination, the Convention on the Elimination and Discrimination Against Women and the Convention on Children's Rights cover not only civil and political rights, but also social, economic and cultural rights, endorsing the idea of the indivisibility of human rights.

With regard to tools providing protection for economic, social and cultural rights in Latin America, two instruments warrant particularly attention: the International Covenant on Economic, Social and Cultural Rights and the San Salvador Protocol, in terms of economic, social and cultural rights.

The International Covenant on Economic, Social and Cultural Rights has been signed by 142 States Parties, including many countries in Latin America. Most of the Latin American countries have ratified this Covenant after the democratisation process spread through this region – for instance, Brazil ratified it in 1992.

This International Covenant lists a lengthy catalogue of rights, including the right to work and fair pay, the right to establish and join trade unions, the right to an adequate standard of living, the right to housing, the right to education, social security, healthcare, etc.

If civil and political rights should be promptly ensured by the State, with no excuse or delay – they are backed by what is known as automatic applicability – social, economic and cultural rights are to be phased in, under the concepts of this Covenant. It is worthwhile noting that these rights depend on the actions of the State, which should take all steps to phase in the full implementation of the rights covered by the Covenant in Article 2, Paragraph 1, using all available resources. However, it should be stressed that social, civil and political rights all require both positive and negative input from the State, as the idea that social rights require only positive support while civil and political rights require negative input is both mistaken and overly simplistic. As an example, the costs of the security apparatus ensuring classic civil rights – such as the right to freedom and the right to ownership – could be analysed, or the cost of the electoral apparatus that ensures the feasibility of political rights, or the justice apparatus that guarantees the right of access to the Courts. This means that civil and political rights are not limited to merely demanding omission on the part of the State, as their implementation requires directed government policies that also incur costs.

In addition to a critical assessment of the "cost" of social rights (which are also necessary for civil and political rights, as shown) it is also vital to reflect on what is known as the "progressive application" of economic, social and cultural rights, as a way of extracting their effects. It should be reaffirmed that the Covenant on Economic, Social and Cultural Rights establishes the obligation of the States to acknowledge and progressively implement these rights, using all available resources.

As affirmed by Professor David Trubek: "Social rights seen as social welfare rights imply the view that government has an obligation to guarantee these conditions adequately for all individuals. The idea that welfare is a social construct and that welfare conditions are the responsibility of the government is grounded on the rights listed by the various international instruments, particularly the International Covenant on Economic, Social and Cultural Rights. This also states a universal precept in this field, as it involves an idea that is accepted by almost every nation in the world, although there is still much disagreement on the appropriate scope of government responsibility and action, and the manner in which social welfare can be implemented under specific economic and political systems".[11]

The phase-in of economic, social and cultural rights prompted the clause banning any social backsliding in terms of social rights. For J.J. Gomes Canotilho: "The principle of banning any social backsliding may be formulated as follows: the essential core of social rights already effectively implemented through legislative measures should be deemed as guaranteed by the Constitution, with any measures being unconstitutional that result in the practical annulment, repeal or pure and simply annihilation of this essential core, without introducing any alternative or compensatory scheme. The freedom of the legislator is limited by the essential core already implemented"[12].

Consequently, under the International Covenant on Economic, Social and Cultural Rights that the States Parties (including Brazil) have ratified through the free, full exercise of their sovereignty, it should be noted that the phase-in principle of social rights in itself implies the principle of a ban on any social backsliding.

In addition to the International Covenant on Economic, Social and Cultural Rights, Brazil and most of the Latin American countries have also ratified the San Salvador Protocol on economic, social and cultural rights, which came into effect in November 1999. Just like the International Covenant on Economic, Social and Cultural Rights, this OAS Treaty

11 David Trubek, 'Economic, social and cultural rights in the third world: human rights law and human needs programmes', in: Theodor Meron (ed.), *Human Rights in International Law: Legal and Policy Issues*, Oxford (Clarendon Press), 1984, p. 207. On this matter, David Trubek also affirms that: "I believe that international law is being slanted towards creating obligations that oblige the States to adopt programmes able to ensure a minimum level of economic, social and cultural wellbeing for all citizens on the Planet, in a manner that will progressively upgrade this wellbeing" (*o.c.*, p. 207).

12 José Joaquim Gomes Canotilho, *Direito Constitucional e Teoria da Constituição*, Coimbra (Livraria Almedina), 1998.

strengthens the juridical duties of the States Parties with regard to social rights, that should be introduced steadily with no halts or backsliding, in order to become fully effective. The San Salvador Protocol stipulates a lengthy list of economic, social and cultural rights, including the right to work, trade union rights, the right to healthcare, the right to social security, the right to education, the right to culture ... Just like the Covenant, this Protocol includes the concept that the States should invest all available resources in phasing-in fully effective economic, social and cultural rights. This Protocol allows recourse to the right of petition, submitted to international entities (in this case, the Inter-American Commission on Human Rights) in order to defend two of the stipulated rights: the right to education and trade union rights.

International protection for social rights is added to the national protection mechanisms for these same rights.
With the democratisation process spreading steadily throughout Latin America, most of these countries adopted new constitutions that served as the juridical framework for the transition to democracy and the institutional establishment of human rights. Like Brazil's 1988 Constitution, most Latin American Constitutions endorse the universal and indivisible status of human rights, assigning ample constitutional protection to social rights, which are viewed as truly fundamental rights and subjective public rights (requiring proper compliance) rather than as charity, compassion or generosity by some State.

Consequently, national parameters should be added to international parameters in order to ensure the best and most effective protection for economic, social and cultural rights. This means that politics are no longer viewed as a domain that is juridically free and not bound in constitutional terms. The domain of politics is now subject to constraints and impositions through a binding material project designed to protect human rights, particularly economic, social and cultural rights. In the light of this context, the following question arises.

Experiences, Strategies and Projects

What is the balance of experiences in terms of implementing economic, social and cultural rights in the case of Brazil? What are the strategies and prospects needed to forge ahead with the implementation of economic, social and cultural rights, taking into account the excludatory effects of the era of economic globalisation?

Any reply to this question requires an analysis of litigation involving economic, social and cultural rights in four different arenas: a) local (judiciary authority) and international courts; b) legislative authority; c) executive authority; d) the private sector.

The experience of litigation involving economic, social and cultural rights is still incipient in both the Brazilian and international courts, reflecting: 1) the still-timid acceptance by civil society of economic, social and cultural rights as legal rights that can be claimed through the courts; 2) the limited familiarity of the juridical agents when litigating on these rights (for instance, lawyers are more familiar with the guarantees offered by *habeas corpus* for protecting freedom of movement than with the public civil action defending diffuse rights such as the right to healthcare, education, housing (...); 3) the largely conservative profile of people implementing the Law, insofar as the law is viewed more as a tool for conserving the social order than as a springboard for social transformation.

In the case of Brazil, in general the human rights movement (in the broadest sense, including women's movements, black movements etc.) is seen to be focusing its efforts – with the transition to democracy – far more on demands submitted to the Legislative Authority (changing laws) and the Executive Authority (government policies) than towards the Judiciary Authority as such.

In contrast to the Legislative and Executive Authorities, each of which have established their own human rights agendas (such as by establishing human rights commissions in the Legislative Authority; setting up the National Human Rights Bureau; adopting the National Human Rights Programme...) and even in response to the demands of civil society, no institutional policy focused on protecting human rights has yet been adopted by the Brazilian Judiciary.

This gap reflects not only the still-incipient awareness of this issue among judges in general, but also the low level of involvement of this Authority in terms of the demands put forward by civil society calling for the protection of human rights. In terms of this latter factor, a "reciprocal estrangement" is noted between the population and the Judiciary, with both of them indicating this gap as one of the main obstacles to providing court services. According to a survey carried out by IUPERJ/ABM, 79.5% of the Judges feel that one of the main difficulties facing the Judiciary lies in the fact that it is aloof from the vast majority of the population. Similarly, surveys conducted not only in Brazil, but also Argentina, Peru and Ecuador indicate that 55% to 75% of the population mention the problem of the inaccessibility of the Judiciary.

This "reciprocal estrangement" implies a lower number of claims submitted to the courts calling for human rights. In order to build up jurisprudence protecting human rights as well as consolidating the Judiciary as a centre for affirming these rights, it is vital that civil society should bring the Judiciary into action through its many organisations and movements, fine-tuning the transformatory and emancipatory potential with which the Law should be endowed. Only thus will a more open Judiciary Authority be built up, closer to the people and with greater social and political responsibility.

Additionally, this diagnosis becomes even more complex when witnessing the effects of the economic globalisation process on human rights, and in particular the redefinition of the role of the State. Inspired by the Washington Consensus, the economic globalisation process is grounded on the platform of neo-liberalism, lower government expenditures, privatisation, more flexible social rights, fiscal discipline to eliminate government debt, tax reform, and deregulation opening up domestic markets to foreign trade. In the words of Jurgen Habermas: "Today it is the States that feel they are included in the market, rather than political economy being included within State borders."[13] Economic globalisation has deepened social inequalities and unemployment, worsening utter poverty and social exclusion.

It is within this framework, for instance, that Judiciary Reforms are being urged in Latin America. The proposed reforms for the Brazilian Judiciary seek mainly to respond to the challenges thrown up by economic globalisation, that demand greater "stability" and "foreseeability" from the court system at lower costs, in order to attract international capital. The excluded masses are not included as a focus for high-priority attention in this discussion. As affirmed by Jorge Correa Sutil: "A general description may be given of the most important reforms of court systems in Latin America, analysing their causes and objectives, with no mention being made of the excluded sectors of the population as a relevant player. A preliminary conclusion that is not very optimistic would be that court reform in Latin America is definitively related more to market deregulation than any other factor. It has not been prompted by the dispossessed, and these groups will certainly not be its beneficiaries"[14].

---

13 Jurgen Habermas, 'Nos Limites do Estado', in: *Folha de São Paulo, Caderno Mais!*, July 18 1999, p. 5.

14 See Jorge Correa Sutil, 'Judicial Reforms in Latin America: Good news for the Underprivileged?', in: Juan E. Méndez, Guillermo O'Donnel & Paulo Sérgio Pinheiro (orgs), *The (Un)rule of Law & the Underprivileged in Latin America,* Notre Dame (University of Notre Dame Press), 1999, p. 268. It must be added here that court reform should be placed in context, under

Within this scenario, it is worthwhile asking how the social movements themselves have deployed the law as a tool for social change, which is a highly significant question in terms of safeguarding human rights in Brazil, as well as turning the judicial arena into a strategic forum for achieving social progress and defending the public interest.

In the case of Brazil, court protection for economic, social and cultural rights has focused mainly in the field of healthcare, land and the environment.

In the field of healthcare, the progress of jurisprudence is particularly outstanding in terms of protecting the rights of HIV-positive patients (for instance, supplying medications where this progress in case law was later universalised through promulgating a law making the supplies of medications mandatory) as well as combating abusive, restrictive clauses in medical aid schemes (such as the recent decision handed down by the Supreme Court of Justice on this issue; however, this affects only the middle class, and more from the standpoint of consumer rights than healthcare rights). No court decisions are noted in terms of protecting the right to healthcare on a broader basis covering any significant portion of the excluded sectors of the population (such as the case filed by CELS, in Argentina, and the human rights clinic run by UBA, which managed to annul an Executive Decree suspending the free distribution of vaccines in rural areas due to rising costs and the need for budget adjustments).

In the case of land ownership, decisions handed down in reinstatement cases are of vital importance, as they are based on the principle of the social

---

the aegis of State reform which, according to Luis Carlos Bresser Pereira, consists of four macro-topics: a) an economic and political problem – outlining the size of the State (which involves outsourcing, privatisation, disclosure and the transfer to the non-State public sector of tasks that formerly were assigned to the State); b) a problem that is also economic and political but merits special treatment, which is redefining the regulatory role of the State (which involves problems such as the level of regulation and related strategies); c) an economic and administrative problem – the recovery of governance or the financial and administrative capacity to implement political decisions taken by the government (which involves problems of a financial nature – tackling the financial crisis; strategic – redefining forms of intervention at the economic and social level; administrative, dealing with the bureaucratic manner of administering the State); d) a political problem – the increase in governability or the political capacity of the government to intermediate interest, guaranteeing legitimacy and govern (which involves problems such as the legitimacy of the government in the view of society, the adaptation of political institutions for intermediating interests). (In: *A Reforma do Estado dos anos 90: Lógica e mecanismos de controle*, p. 7/8, apud Ronaldo Porto Macedo & Ana Cristina Braga Martes, *A Reforma do Judiciário e suas Propostas*, paper presented at the XXIV Annual Meeting of ANPOCS, October 2000).

function of ownership, guaranteeing the right to settlement or housing for dozens of landless families, rather than supporting the right of the proprietor to own assets.

The defence of the environment by the Brazilian Judiciary has in turn been sponsored largely by the Department of Justice, although the Civil Public Action Act also empowers associations to file suit as plaintiffs. The Department of Justice is generally brought into action by people in the more privileged classes, with a better understanding of environmental rights and the functions of the Department of Justice. In urban areas, claims are often submitted by the upper middle class, concerned with local environmental issues related to property devaluation, sound pollution caused by recreational activities and religious entities, as well as organisations concerned with the degradation of natural resources in environmental protection areas. Consequently, it is vital to prepare strategies that will allow flagship lawsuits to be filed, preferably collective actions that spotlight environmental aspects as a theme running through many other issues, particularly by selecting cases from underprivileged communities related to environmental violations and involving the right to healthcare, the right to housing and reproductive rights (such as the cases involving poor women victimised by environmental degradation in Cubatão, whose reproductive rights were violated, as they could no longer have children).

In brief, looking at this scenario, it is vital that the human rights movement should redefine and extend its strategies in order to include the strategy of litigating in defence of economic, social and cultural rights.

This inclusion could take place in two different ways: through either introducing a specific juridical programme focused on this type of litigation, or through partnerships with public or private institutions that could bring these demands before the courts.

As examples of this first option, the experience of the Legal and Social Studies Centre (CELS – *Centro de Estudios Legales y Sociales*) in Argentina is particularly noteworthy, as well as FORJA in Chile. These landmark entities in terms of the struggle for human rights were initially established as centres of resistance fighting violations of human rights during the dictatorship years, defending political prisoners, denouncing torture, murder and forced disappearances, which empowered them to redefine and expand their action agendas to include projects spurring litigation claiming economic, social and cultural rights. In Brazil, the competent activities of the National Network of People's Lawyers is also particularly noteworthy, working mainly on issues related to the right to land and housing as well as the National Counsel Network against Racism and Racial Inequality, established in August 2000.

As examples of the second type, the experiences of the Public Interest Law Clinics are particularly noteworthy, such as that run by the University of Palermo in Argentina or the Diego Portales University in Chile, or the *pro bono* legal services starting to appear in Argentina and Chile. Working closely with grassroots movements and social entities, they encourage litigation suing in the public interest and to protect economic, social and cultural rights.

Suing to protect economic, social and cultural rights must be based on careful selection of flagship cases, preferably collective actions with the potential for high social impact, that pave the way for social advances, particularly favouring the excluded sectors of the population. Strategic planning should be encouraged, in order to assess the risks and potential of this new type of litigation. In fact, relationships with the Judiciary must be reinvented, increasing the number of spokespersons and expanding the universe of claims in order to turn this Authority into a centre of affirmation for human rights.

At the international level, the use of the international system must be fine-tuned (United Nations and the Organisation of American States) to protect economic, social and cultural rights through:

a) preparing parallel reports (that allow close networking on human rights movements; diagnosing the status of economic, social and cultural rights, and the prospects for their promotion);
b) the presence of Special Rapporteurs who focus the attention of the human rights movements on specific topics, spotlighting violations and proposals for tackling them – see the positive effects of the visits to Brazil by the UN Rapporteur on Torture;
c) the systematic use of petitions submitted to international entities denouncing the violation of economic, social and cultural rights (for instance, based on the San Salvador Protocol, the right to education and trade union rights could be covered by a petition submitted to the Inter-American Commission on Human Rights);
d) international networking urging the adoption of the Optional Protocol to the International Covenant on Economic, Social and Cultural Rights, introducing the petition system to safeguard economic, social and cultural rights. Particularly noteworthy here is the successful precedent

related to the Optional Protocol to the Convention on the Elimination of Discrimination Against Women, adopted by the United Nations in 2000, as well as the preparation of technical and scientific indicators assessing compliance with these rights, as recommended by the Declaration of Vienna in 1993. These measures would ensure easier access to the courts and greater enforceability for economic, social and cultural rights.

It should also be noted that litigation claiming economic, social and cultural rights requires that juridical strategies should be blended with political strategies, including the development of media strategies that could effectively help consolidate the progress achieved through court cases defending the rights of socially vulnerable sectors of the population.

Finally, the implementation of economic, social and cultural rights should also include other strategies, in addition to litigation strategies for national and international entities, which should be addressed to the Legislative and Executive Authorities, as well as the private sector.

In the Brazilian experience, significant progress has been noted by the Legislative Authority in terms of protecting economic, social and cultural rights, particularly through the transition to democracy, reflected in the gains enshrined in Brazil's 1988 Constitution. The period since 1998 is also characterised by the adoption of vast amounts of legislation designed to protect human rights. It may be stated that 90% of the human rights regulations were adopted in the course of the 1990s, although with greater stress placed on civil rights (for instance, the 1995 Act acknowledging vanished political prisoners as dead in order to pay compensation to their relatives; the 1989 Act punishing racial discrimination; the Children's and Adolescents Statute, promulgated in 1990; the National Human Rights Programme issued in 1997; the 1997 Act against Torture; the 1999 Act covering the Witness Protection Programme...). Furthermore, it is important to stress two significant recent advances in safeguards protecting economic, social and cultural rights based on two Constitutional Amendments issued in 2000, one including the right to housing in Article 6 (Social Rights – Constitutional Amendment 26 dated February 14, 2000) and the other establishing a specific budget allocation for public health (Constitutional Amendment 29 dated September 13, 2000).

With regard to the Executive Authority at the Federal Level, a dramatic drop has been noted in government funding channelled to economic, social and cultural rights, dismantling basic social welfare policies in parallel to a trend towards more flexible labour regulations, alleging that guarantees of social rights (such as the right to work, healthcare and education) would hamper the smooth functioning of the market, free flows of capital and international competitiveness.

Regardless of this scenario at the Federal level, in some States and Municipal Districts, successful government policies have been adopted to protect economic, social and cultural rights, such as the Minimum Wage Programme, the School Grant Programme, Participative Budgets, Supportive Saving Programmes guaranteeing access to loans for low income sectors of the population, Affirmative Action Policies on the labour market favouring socially vulnerable groups; and programmes building plazas and other public areas designed for recreation and culture, particularly in less privileged areas. The adoption of these successful policies is vital for all Federal entities, noting racial and ethnic differences, as well as discrimination based on gender, age and social class, as claimed and stressed by civil society in its proposals to update the National Human Rights Programme, urging that it be extended to include economic, social and cultural rights.

In terms of the private sector, the social responsibility of the business sector should be stressed particularly of the multinational corporations, which are the major beneficiaries of economic globalisation. One of the leading players in international economic relationships has been the private sector. The top 100 multinational corporations post annual revenues that outstrip the GDP of one half of the world's nations. Among the world's 100 largest economies, 51 are multinational corporations and 45 are Nation States. In order to implement economic, social and cultural rights, strategies addressing the private sector are required, such as: a) requiring international loans to be conditional on commitments to human rights; b) demanding commercial sanctions imposed on companies violating economic, social and cultural rights; c) encouraging companies to adopt human rights codes covering commercial or investment activities. It is thus vital to stress the responsibilities of the private sector in the field of human rights.

At the same time, in view of the severe risks offered by the process of dismantling government policies in the social welfare sphere, the role of the State must be redefined, under the impact of economic globalisation. The responsibilities of the State should be buttressed, in terms of implementing economic, social and cultural rights through actions that foster social equality, tackling social inequalities and offsetting the imbalance caused by the markets, in order to ensure sustainable human development.

Summing up, in order to implement economic, social and cultural rights, the challenge emerges of building up a new paradigm, guided by an agenda of inclusion that will be able to ensure sustainable development that is fairer and more democratic at the local, regional and global levels. The imperative of economic efficacy should be matched to the ethical demands for social justice, inspired by a democratic order that guarantees the full exercise of human rights.

If the world is not in order, as arrangements are always a complex problem that remains open to change, the establishment of a new order should celebrate the match between the values of democracy and development, inspired by a belief of the absolute prevalence of human dignity.

THE MEXICAN EXPERIENCE OF ELABORATING AND LOBBYING THE ALTERNATIVE REPORT ON ECONOMIC, SOCIAL AND CULTURAL RIGHTS

Areli SANDOVAL TERÁN (Mexico)

Introduction

Mexico is a Latin-American country with a population of around 100 million, of whom – according to figures acknowledged by the Government – 44 million live in poverty, with 26 million of them living in extreme poverty. The economic model followed by Mexico over the past eighteen years has proven its inability to foster all-round social development: legislative, economic policy and social measures, government plans and programmes following the logic of the structural adjustment have all failed to achieve their objectives, but have rather hastened the deterioration of living standards, affecting the enjoyment of economic, social and cultural rights. To date, protecting major economic, financial and commercial interests has ranked high among government priorities, at the cost of the well-being of the population. Some data document this serious situation:

- Using conservative government figures, in 1992, 44% of the population lived in poverty, with 16% of this sector living in extreme poverty. In 1999, the government affirmed that poverty dropped 1%; notwithstanding, the proportion of people living in utter poverty has risen from 28% of this 43%.[1]
- Out of 32 million children living in Mexico, 12 million live in a situation of poverty.[2]
- In December 1994, the daily minimum wage was 15.27 pesos, and the Constitutional Food Basket cost 8.5 times more, namely 130.76 pesos a day. In April 1998 the minimum wage was 30.20 pesos a day, while the

[1] Social Studies Department of Banacci, with data issued by the National Statistics, Geography and Information Technology (INEGI – *Instituto Nacional de Estadística, Geografía e Informática*), the Economic Commission for Latin America and the Caribbean (ECLAC) and the 1999–2000 Social Development Programme, mentioned in the Alternative Report on Economic, Social and Cultural Rights (Article 2 on the obligations of the Party State).

[2] United Nations Fund for Childhood (UNICEF) mentioned in 'La tragedia de los niños mexicanos... según el gobierno', Masiosare, special supplement, *La Jornada*, May 2 1999, p. 10-11; *Alternative Report on Economic, Social and Cultural Rights* (Article 6 on the Right to Work).

Constitutional Staples Basket cost 281.30 pesos a day, meaning around 9.3 times more.[3]

- The state of Chiapas has a population of around 4,362,000 inhabitants, with 27.5% consisting of indigenous communities divided among twelve ethnic groups. It posts the highest number of municipal districts with high marginalisation rates. Of the 111 municipal districts in this state, 34.23% have a very high marginalisation rate, with 50.45% rated as high marginalisation, 10.81% medium, and only 4.5% of these municipal districts with higher levels of urbanisation post low marginalisation levels. There is not one single municipal district in Chiapas whose rates would define it as having a *very low marginalisation rate*.[4]

The International Covenant on Economic, Social and Cultural Rights

The International Covenant on Economic, Social and Cultural Rights has been in effect in since June 23, 1981. This international instrument establishes a wide variety of legal obligations for the States-Parties related to the following Human Rights furthering social development: free will, gender equality, employment, equitable and satisfactory working conditions, establishing and joining trade unions and the strikes, social security, protection and care for motherhood, childhood and adolescence, food, housing, healthcare, education and culture, as well as the obligation of the States to assign as much funding as possible in order to gradually ensure the full efficacy of these rights through all appropriate means, *including the adoption of legal measures.*

The States Parties to the International Covenant on Economic, Social and Cultural Rights are called upon periodically to appear before the UN Commission on Economic, Social and Cultural Rights in order to present their Reports on the status of these human rights in their countries and explain the measures adopted to ensure their respect, protection and promotion. In turn, this Commission issues comments and recommenda-

[3] The Constitutional Basket of Staples (CBC) is based on the amounts required by a five-person Mexican family consisting of two adults, one young person and two children for food, housing, communications, transportation, education, healthcare, clothing, footwear, personal cleanliness and home care, recreation and culture, consisting of 312 goods and services for use and consumption. Multidisciplinary Analysis Centre (Centro de Análisis Multidisciplinario) & School of Economics, National Autonomous University of Mexico (UNAM – Universidad Nacional Autónoma de México), *Los Hogares Mexicanos,* Survey Report 50, November 1998, using data provided by the bank of Mexico and the National Minimum Wage Commission, mentioned in the Alternative Report on Economic, Social and Cultural Rights (Article 7 on fair and satisfactory working conditions).

[4] CONAPO, *Indicadores socioeconómicos e índice de marginación municipal 1990,* Mexico (Dirección General de Estudios de Población), 1993, p. 15; *Alternative Report on Economic, Social and Cultural Rights* (special chapter on Chiapas).

tions to the Government under examination in order to foster compliance with this Covenant.

Examination of the Government Report

The 21st Period of Sessions for the UN Commission on Economic, Social and Cultural Rights was held in Geneva, Switzerland, from November 15 through to December 3, 1999, when this Commission examined Government Reports from Mexico, Bulgaria, Armenia, Cameron, Argentina and the Solomon Islands. Mexico presented its III Regular Report, covering the status of Economic, Social and Cultural Rights from 1992 through 1996, in addition to additional details, corrections and updating information through to 1999 that the Commission requested from the Mexican Government, through a list of questions forwarded in advance.
The Mexican Report was examined on November 25 and 26. The Federal Executive Authority sent a large delegation of thirteen members, headed by Ambassador Miguel Ángel González Félix (SRE), consisting of civil servants from various departments, including: Governance Bureaus, Public Education Bureaus, Labour and Social Welfare Bureaus and the National Indigenous Studies Institute, with the striking absence of the Social Development Bureau and the Public Credit and Housing Bureau, particularly as this meant that information required for the assessment could not be provided to the Commission.

The Participation of the NGOs in the Alternative Report

The participation of the non-governmental organisations (NGO) in the United Nations System and other International Fora helps build up citizen control mechanisms through monitoring and following up on government administration, including enforceability and rendering accounts, fostering the appearance of areas for consultation, analysis and proposals put forward by civil society.

The Commission opened the afternoon session on November 15 for the presentation of the Report prepared by Non-Governmental Organisations (NGOs) from the countries that were to be examined from the next day onwards. Five participants attended from civil organisations and networks[5] in Mexico, representing the group of entities that drew up the *Alternative Report on the Status of Economic, Social and Cultural Rights in Mexico,* and

[5] Areli Sandoval (*DECA Equipo Pueblo*), Luz Lozoya (*Frente por el Derecho a Alimentarse*), Leticia Salinas (*Casa y Ciudad-Coalición Habitat México*), Javier de la Rosa (*Convergencia de Organismos Civiles por la Democracia*), Marcos Arana (*Defensoría del Derecho a la Salud*).

reflecting concern over the severe deterioration of living conditions in our country. We gave a verbal presentation of the Report, stressing: economic policies and their social impacts; social welfare policies; budgets; the precarious employment situation, social security; working conditions, wages and loss of buying power; problems with food and housing, underscoring the particularly severe situation of women and children. A representative of FIAN International also outlined his concerns over the severe situation of Economic, Social and Cultural Rights in Mexico, stressing the right to food.

Constant contact was maintained with our colleagues in Mexico from other organisations in the Coordination Area (team in Mexico), who presented this Alternative Report at a Press Conference held in Mexico City on November 15, which was covered in three nationwide daily newspapers: *La Jornada, Reforma* and *El Universal.* We also maintained contact with the national and foreign press.

We got as close as possible to the members of the Commission on Economic, Social and Cultural Rights in order to learn about their main areas of interest and focus their attention on the sections and paragraphs in our Report that covered them, while providing them with additional information on these matters. We held daily meetings with the Special Rapporteur from Mexico, Ambassador Jaime Marchand Romero, with whom we built up an interesting and constructive dialogue. We also prepared theme datasheets for the meetings with some experts.

A special presentation was arranged on the situation of armed conflict in Chiapas, addressed to certain experts of the Commission on Economic, Social and Cultural Rights who showed more interest in this matter.

At the end of the session held on November 26, once the examination was completed, Mexico prepared a document and delivered it to the Special Rapporteur for Mexico, listing our comments and explaining our main reasons for concern.

Coordination Area for Civil Organisations Preparing the Alternative Report

In mid-1998, some civil organisations and networks began to build up the coordination area for citizen control – Economic, Social and Cultural Rights, which was an initiative of the *DECA Equipo Pueblo*, under the Citizen Control Project, urging compliance with the commitments of the World

Summit on Social Development held in Copenhagen in 1995, and the convergence of civil entities for democracy through a project on Economic, Social and Cultural Rights, in order to develop the efforts through networking undertaken by many different organisations on matters related to Social Development and Human Rights.[6] The purpose was to establish a monitoring and follow-up process examining the implementation of commitments and obligations undertaken by the Mexican government through international instruments related to Economic, Social and Cultural Rights, in order to ensure compliance, with a view to upgrading the living standards of the Mexican people.

In November 1998, the organisations sharing this coordination area drew up a document with pre-session questions for the Commission on Economic, Social and Cultural Rights, grounded on information other than that provided by the Mexican government in its III Report. The Commission met in Geneva from December 7 through 11, 1998, and accepted the document prepared by the representatives of this coordination area[7], remaining open to receive further information.

During 1999, we decided to include in the Alternative Report our views on the status of Economic, Social and Cultural Rights; since the Citizen Diplomacy Programme run by *DECA Equipo Pueblo*, we had been coordinating all research and analysis efforts, as well as systematising information and drafting the Alternative Report. The Alternative Report on Economic, Social and Cultural Rights in Mexico offers a broad-ranging analysis of the various rights, together with proposals, in addition to case studies on violations of these Economic, Social and Cultural Rights, together with specific sections on Chiapas, the North American Free Trade Treaty (NAFTA) and the Federal Budget. One of the main strengths of this document is the fact that its information is grounded on official sources, and examinations and analysis undertaken by well-known academics, in

---

6 At the moment, the organisations constituting this area are: Casa y Ciudad, A.C. – Coalición Hábitat México, a member of the Habitat International Coalition, Centro de Derechos Humanos Miguel Agustín Pro (PRODH), Centro de Derechos Humanos Económicos, Sociales y Culturales (CeDHESCu), Centro de Reflexión y Acción Laboral (CEREAL), Comisión Mexicana de Defensa y Promoción de Derechos Humanos, A.C. (CMDPDHAC), Colectivo Mexicano de Apoyo a la Niñez (COMEXANI), Convergencia de Organismos Civiles por la Democracia, DECA – Equipo Pueblo, A.C., Defensoría por el Derecho a la Salud, Frente por el Derecho a Alimentarse (FDA – FIAN), Liga Mexicana de Defensa de los Derechos Humanos (LIMEDDH), and the Red de Jóvenes por los Derechos Sexuales y Reproductivos ELIGE. Other organisations have cooperated on a temporary basis, and there is a trend for this group to expand.

7 Paulina Vega (Mexican Commission for the Defence and Promotion of Human Rights), and Leticia Salinas (Home and City – International habitat Coalition).

addition to the documentation on case studies of violations of the Economic, Social and Cultural Rights. The preparation of this Alternative Report produced a vital tool for lobbying and applying political pressure.

Although drafting of the Alternative Report was an office job handled by a few people (drawn from both the organisations and the academic world) the preparation of the Report was a far more participative process in terms of research, analysis and interpretation of the articles of the International Covenant on Economic, Social and Cultural Rights within the Mexican context, discussing the content and its guidelines, and even the language that should be used; there were thirteen organisations participating at this level that also signed the Report. In addition to this key group, an even larger number of civil and social organisations and networks took part, providing valuable information and documentation for case studies. Finally, the Report was signed by 105 institutions, including eight organisations with consultative status before the UN Economic and Social Council (ECOSOC). The backing of international organisations with this status was extremely important, including the International Federation of Human Rights Leagues, the International Habitat Coalition, the *Terre des Hommes* International Federation and the Information and Action Network for the Right to Food (FIAN International), as their signatures on the Alternative Report reflected acknowledgement of the problems and confirmed the validity and legitimacy of the information that we provided to the Commission on Economic, Social and Cultural Rights.

The Alternative Report and a compendium of annexes containing the case study documentation on violations of Economic, Social and Cultural Rights was forwarded to the Commission Secretariat and its eighteen Expert Members in mid-October 1999, in Spanish and English. A package containing the various theme reports and videos on the severe situation of certain economic and social rights was also forwarded to the Commission Secretariat as additional materials available to its Members during the period of sessions. We also prepared and forwarded a summary of the Alternative Report in Spanish and English prior to the meeting, which was published as an official UN document.[8]

Results

The Alternative Report was very well accepted by the members of the Commission on Economic, Social and Cultural Rights, who publicly

[8] This documentation was handed out during the period of sessions of the Commission on Economic, Social and Cultural Rights and can be consulted on the web page of the United Nations High Commissioner for Human Rights: www.unhchr.ch under: E/C.12/1999/NGO/3 dated November 18, 1999.

indicated their appreciation of the coordinated efforts of a large number of non-governmental organisations. This strengthened the document still more, as a tool providing leverage at the national level.
During the sessions devoted to examining the official report on Mexico, the Commission on Economic, Social and Cultural Rights constantly alluded to the contents of the Alternative Report and the documentation on case studies of violation of these Economic, Social and Cultural Rights, as the basis for its questions and reasons for concerns. On many occasions, experts on the Commission drew the attention of the official delegation to certain issues, requesting effective replies to their questions. The experts requested input on definitive government actions and their results, instead of reiterated mentions of plans, programmes, and articles in the Constitution that merely reflected formal rather than practical compliance in terms of respect and promotion of Economic, Social and Cultural Rights in Mexico.
We were able to note immediate results from our lobbying during the preceding days and during the sessions themselves, as some of the experts on the Commission on Economic, Social and Cultural Rights highlighted points causing concern with specific questions on which we insisted. Some experts on this Commission mentioned to us that the information provided by the NGOs would be very useful for the document presenting the final conclusions on the government Reports.
Attending the Commission meetings and lobbying the experts, listening to their opinions and following up on the activities of the delegation sent by the Mexican delegation showed us that there is still much to be desired. Although the government delegation consisted of highly qualified senior civil servants, its performance was not excellent as it did not provide sufficient information for the Commission to carry out a more complete assessment of progress and backsliding in terms of Economic, Social and Cultural Rights in Mexico. For instance, the government delegation avoided answering questions on public outlays on programmes, which would immediately reflect the gap between outlays on social welfare and the amounts allocated to servicing debts.

The matter causing the most concern was that we realised the government delegation was providing false information to the Commission on certain topics, such as the drop in the buying power of wages, insufficient pensions and allowances, the conditions imposed by international financing institutions, and constraints on the main programme for combating poverty (PROGRESA – *Programa de Educación, Salud y Alimentación*). This government refusal to acknowledge certain economic and social problems indicates a lack of political will to solve them.

The period of sessions of this Commission ended with the issue of a document containing the Final Comments and Recommendations to the States Parties to the Covenant (E/C.12/1/Add.41). For Mexico, the Commission drew the attention of the State to the urgent need to tackle the structural causes of poverty, listing a series of specific recommendations designed to resolve serious specific problems such as: the loss of the buying power of wages, discrimination against women workers, the lack of trade union democracy, forced displacement, the consequences of structural adjustment programmes, high mortality levels due to illegal abortions, corruption, military and paramilitary actions in Chiapas and other states, street children, the negative impacts of NAFTA, and others. This document is the main indication that there are many reasons for concern, with the recommendations that we put forward being acknowledged and taken under consideration by this Commission.

Concluding Observations and Comments by the Commission on Economic, Social and Cultural Rights: Mexico, December 8, 1999 (E/C.12/1/Add.41.)

The document containing the concluding observations of the Commission on Mexico lists the positive aspects of compliance with the covenant, including some comments on factors that are hampering its application, while also listing the *main reasons for concern* and concluding with a series of recommendations. Some of these concerns are listed below, together with the measures recommended to the Mexican State by the Commission:

Main Reasons for Concern

- The Commission manifested its concern over the lack-lustre performance by the Party State in complying with the closing comments adopted after examining the previous Report, where the Commission issued some specific recommendations.
- In fact, the Commission is concerned because the Party State made very little progress during the period under examination, despite its struggle against poverty. The Commission is worried because more people are living in poverty or extreme poverty. The Commission also feels that unless the structural causes of poverty are dealt with effectively, it will not be possible to usher in more equitable distribution of wealth among the sectors of society, among States, nor between rural and urban areas.
- The Commission is also concerned by persistent penalties imposed on the indigenous communities, particularly in Chiapas, Guerrero,

Veracruz and Oaxaca, which lack access to healthcare, education, jobs, proper nutrition and housing, among other aspects.

- The Commission also regretted that despite the improvement in the macro-economic indicators for Mexico, particularly the strikingly low level of inflation, the National Minimum Wage Commission has not adjusted the minimum wage appropriately. At times like these, it is necessary to earn some five times the minimum wage in order to purchase the Constitutional Basic Basket of Staples, violating item II of paragraph a) of Article 7 of the Covenant, which is reflected in the National Legislation (Article 123. VI of the Constitution).
- The Commission is also deeply concerned about the situation of women workers in the *maquiladoras*, some of whom are subjected to pre-hiring pregnancy tests, and are usually fired if they become pregnant.
- The Commission also regrets that there is no intention of lifting the reservations of the Party State on Article 8 of the Covenant, despite the fact that the right to set up trade unions and the right to strike are enshrined in the Constitution and the corresponding regulations in Mexico. In particular, the Commission regrets that trade unionism in the government section is not pluralistic, as trade union leaders are not elected through direct balloting.
- The Commission was concerned over the privatisation of the social welfare system, which could have adverse effect on certain services for those unable to pay into a private pension fund, such as the unemployed, the under-employed, low-income workers, and workers in the informal sector.
- The Commission was concerned over the presence of large military and paramilitary forces in the Chiapas indigenous lands and in other parts of the region, particularly the allegations put forward by organisations and civil societies that these squads are intervening in the supervision and application of development programmes and the distribution of economic and social aid, as well as the lack of consultation with the communities in question.
- The Commission was also disturbed to note that the fourth-highest cause of death among women is illegal abortion.

Suggestions and Recommendations

- The Commission exhorts the Party State to tackle the structural causes of poverty in Mexico adjusting its social problems appropriately. Furthermore, the Commission asks the Party State to include civil society in general and assisted groups in particular in the participation, application and assessment of these programmes.

- The Commission requests the Party State to bear in mind the consequences, in terms of effects on Economic, Social and Cultural Rights when negotiating with international financial institutions and applying structural adjustment programmes, as well as macro-economic policies affecting the service on the foreign debt, integration in the free market global economy, etc., particularly for the more vulnerable sectors of society.
- The Commission recommends that the Party State should step up its efforts to lighten any negative effects of the North American Free Trade Agreement (NAFTA) on certain vulnerable sectors of its population.
- The Commission asks the Party State to implement effective measures guaranteeing compliance with item ii of section a) of Article 7 of the International Convention on Civil, Economic, Social and Cultural Rights, reflected in Article 123. VI of the Mexican Constitution, in terms of the official basic basket of staples.
- The Commission also exhorts the Party State to implement immediate measures designed to protect women workers in *maquiladoras*, including banning the requirement of a medical certificate ensuring that these workers are not pregnant when hired, and taking measures through the Courts against employers failing to comply with this ban.
- The Commission recommends that the Party State should consider the possibility of ratifying the Convention on the Minimum Working Age (Agreement N° 138) issued by the International Labour Organisation.
- The Commission asks the Party State to comply with its obligations under Article 8 of the Covenant, and remove the reservations that it has put forward on this Article.
- The Commission exhorts the Party State to do more to provide adequate housing at affordable prices, particularly among the poorer sectors of society. The Commission wishes to receive more detailed information on the number of displaced people forced out of their homes and the manner in which this is handled. It recommends that the Party State should establish mechanisms recording these displacements and their consequences, taking immediate steps against forced displacement and advising the Commission on this issue in its fourth regular Report.
- The Commission exhorts the Party State to continue to implement effective measures that ensure basic healthcare for all children, while combating malnutrition, particularly among children belonging to indigenous groups or living in remote rural areas.
- The Commission recommends that the Party State should supervise and regulate the functions of the military and paramilitary forces in the state of Chiapas and other states, in order to guarantee the application of development and social welfare programmes with the active participa-

tion of the affected communities and with no intervention from the armed forces.
- The Commission recommends that the Party State should take the steps needed to ensure broad-ranging dissemination of the provisions of the Covenant, including classes in human rights at all levels of education that address all sectors of society, particularly the Judiciary and Administrative Authorities.

Lessons Learned

It is noted that the coordinated efforts of many different civil organisations with experience in human rights and matters related to social development strengthen capacities and open up paths for playing a more significant political role. It is considered vital that the next step should be to strengthen the efforts at both the national and local level, for which a strategic plan is needed, striving to make good use of the international success of this process.

Conclusions

The topics of human rights and social development *per se* on the Mexican government agenda are rated as marginal in importance, as there is a trend that has been noted – even with the new government[9] – to stress an economic policy that strikes them from their list of priorities, and consequently has a negative effect on them. The stress on ballot-box politics and financial and commercial issues mean that the coordinated efforts of civil organisations and networks are becoming increasingly important for promoting and defending social rights.

The Alternative Report was produced through broad-based collective efforts that have not yet been completed. Nevertheless, these efforts imply and demand corresponding responses from other governmental and non-governmental players. In terms of following up and complying with the recommendations of the Commission on Economic, Social and Cultural Rights, the Mexican government should also involve the Legislative and Judiciary Authorities, in order to achieve all-round social development that ensures the full and effective implementation of human rights.

---

[9] During the recent federal elections held on July 2, 2000, the Institutional Revolution Party (PRI – Partido Revolucionario Institucional) which remained in power for 71 years, was overthrown through broad-ranging grassroots dissatisfaction, manifested through the ballot-box. However, its economic policies have been continued by the Right-Wing National Action Party (PAN – Partido de Derecha Acción Nacional).

THE BRAZILIAN EXPERIENCE OF THE CIVIL SOCIETY REPORT ON STATE COMPLIANCE WITH THE INTERNATIONAL COVENANT ON ECONOMIC, SOCIAL AND CULTURAL RIGHTS

Marcio Alexandre M. GUALBERTO (Brazil)

Introduction

The process of preparing Brazil's civil society report on compliance with the International Covenant on Economic, Social and Cultural Rights began in May 1999, when the National Conference on Human Rights[1] decided to assign high priority to this issue, urging the Brazilian government to present its report to the UN Committee on Economic, Social and Cultural Rights and preparing the parallel or shadow report by civil society, in counterpart to the report presented by the government. However, as the government did not present its report, what was intended to be a parallel or shadow report became an alternative report that is the only one presented so far to this Committee.

Based on the presentation of this Report, two possible scenarios appear:
1. Brazil presents its official report in good time;
2. Brazil does not present its official report, and the alternative report provides the input needed for the Committee to analyze the status of economic, social and cultural rights in Brazil.

Should the first scenario come to pass, Brazilian civil society will have to build up networks rapidly in order to present fresh elements for consideration by the Committee, based on the matters covered in the official report. Under the second scenario, constant contacts must be maintained with the members of the Committee in order to reply to their questions, extending the alternative report through case studies portraying violations of economic, social and cultural rights in Brazil.

---

1 Held annually in Brasília, the National Conference on Human Rights is organised by the Lower House Committee on Human Rights, the Brazilian Law Society (OAB – Ordem dos Advogados do Brasil), the National Human Rights Movement (MNDH – Movimento Nacional de Direitos Humanos) and the Federal Attorney-General's Office for Citizen Rights, in addition to a large group of non-governmental organisations working to defend and promote human rights in Brazil.

Methodology

The preparation of the civil society report on Brazilian compliance with the international Covenant on Economic, Social and Cultural Rights involved some 2,000 organisations in 18 of the 26 States of Brazil.

This was possible only because the organisations coordinating this process – the Lower House Human Rights Committee, the National Human Rights Movement and the Federal Attorney-General's Office for Citizen Rights – decided to encourage the State Legislative Assemblies to hold public hearings on the implementation of economic, social and cultural rights, while analysing case studies of violations of these rights. For methodological reasons, these case studies were not included in the alternative report, as not all sectoral systemization coordinators presented emblematic case studies of such violations.

The public hearings initially generated a total of 5,000 pages that were divided up by topic among several organisations for an initial round of sectoral systemization. The initial round of sectoral systemization trimmed these 5,000 pages down to 800, which were then edited down to the 130 pages presented in the Report after the final round of systemization.

Report Structure

The civil society report on Brazilian compliance with the international Covenant on Economic, Social and Cultural Rights is structured in order to:

- Assess the legal framework of Brazil, presenting specific aspects related to this Covenant, and linking them to Brazilian law;
- Identify topics in order to score each of them for the rights listed in the Covenant, and outline problems in the application of these rights;
- Assess State actions in terms of complying with the Covenant, because it was felt that merely presenting situations portraying violations of these economic, social and cultural rights was not sufficient, as an effort should also be made to showcase the progress achieved by the State in implementing these rights;
- Qualify and quantify the problems – using social and economic indicators from official sources for this purpose, or produced by highly respected non-governmental institutions, which were used to illustrate the problems presented.

Presentation of the Report to Brazilian Society and the UN Committee on Economic, Social and Cultural Rights

A delegation was appointed to present this report in Geneva, consisting of federal congressman Nilmário Miranda (at that time chairing the Lower House Human Rights Committee); Luciano Mariz Maia (attorney, Federal Attorney-General's Office for Citizen Rights); Romeo Olmar Klich (national coordinator, National Human Rights Movement); and Marcio Alexandre Martins Gualberto (assistant at FASE, the final organizer of the report). They presented this Report to the UN Committee on Economic, Social and Cultural Rights, together with a set of international organisations.

There were two elements that had a marked impact in Geneva: the first was the methodology used to prepare the report. Never before had so many organisations gathered together to prepare what was to have been an alternative report. The fact that 2,000 organisations from almost all over Brazil were involved in the preparation of a report of this size had a marked impression on the members of the Committee.

The second factor was the scope of this report. Of the sixteen rights listed in the Covenant, only one – the right to science and technology – was not systematised, due to last-minute difficulties. In Geneva, the Brazilian delegation gathered that it is quite usual for societies or organisations in other countries to present counterpart reports on specific issues such as education, minority problems, gender-related issues. But the methodology used in Brazil ensured that all relevant topics were listed and discussed, with their problems analysed and presented.

Furthermore, the report clearly demonstrated the massive levels of inequality in Brazil, particularly in terms of racial issues, as the gap between blacks and whites remains patent for almost all rights presented.

Concomitantly with the presentation of the report in Geneva, partner organisations in Brazil released it to the press, while also disseminating it to civil society organisations and government sectors through the electronic media and speaking in public. By year-end 2000, the Process of Articulation and Dialogue (PAD) between protestant agencies in Europe and their counterpart entities in Brazil (working closely with this organisation and providing the necessary support) ordered this report to be published as a book, with the Lower House Human Rights Committee following suit in January 2001.

Objectives Achieved

The objectives listed at the start of the Process were successfully achieved:

- A broad-ranging report was produced on violations and the non-application of economic, social and cultural rights in Brazil;
- Under the aegis of civil society, economic, social and cultural rights were endowed with greater visibility;
- The range of institutional alliances was expanded, building up a significant dialogue with sectors of the Judiciary and the Legislative; and
- Work began on reviving and restructuring the Brazilian Chapter of the Inter-American Platform for Human Rights, Democracy and Development, which had been dormant for some years.

Results of the Report

The resuscitation of the Brazilian Chapter of the Inter-American Platform for Human Rights, Democracy and Development not only boosts discussions on the topic of economic, social and cultural rights in Brazil, but also streamlines the process of monitoring the discussions in Geneva, focused on the alternative report. The Brazilian Chapter of this Inter-American Platform is being structured to build up a cluster of networks in Brazil – but without the slightest intention of taking over any other functions – covering a wide variety of standpoints on issues related to economic, social and cultural rights. Within this context, the Brazilian Women's Network (*Rede de Mulheres Brasileiras*) and the Negro Entities National Coordination Unit (*Coordenação Nacional das Entidades Negras*), as well as networks working on issues related to housing, urban sanitation, agrarian reform, etc., are being – and will be – invited to join the Brazilian Chapter, in order to extend their agendas through adding tools promoting and defending the human rights recognised by the Covenant.

Using the Report as a Tool for Promoting and Defending Human Rights

The many dissemination strategies engendered by the group of organisations involved in the preparation of this report were basically designed to spotlight issues related to economic, social and cultural rights in Brazil. However, from now on this report must become a broad-ranging tool for Brazilian society as a whole, leading the institutions that promote and defend these rights towards an understanding that human rights are far broader than might have been thought.

It is necessary to alter the view that has developed recently in Brazil, which seems to believe that the defence of human rights necessarily means protecting those who are outside the law. The fact that Brazil emerged from a military dictatorship only sixteen years ago has prompted widespread acceptance of the concept of defending civil and political rights. Concomitantly, the discourse of the Brazilian left – where most of the organisations working with human rights are located – has always been to rate the issue of violence as a structural problem that would tend to disappear as social, economic and educational progress is achieved. However, even with the consolidation of the democratic process, an upsurge of violence is assailing major urban centres, worsened by the apparent inability of the leftist parties that have taken over State and local governments to draw up firm and fast-acting proposals for pruning urban violence.

Consequently, much work is needed to extend the scope of the concept of human rights. Just as the return of democracy nudged the struggle for human rights upward on political agendas, with civil rights being implemented as a basic requirement of democracy (even if violations are still matters of much concern for their defenders), the neo-liberal economic model preferred by subsequent federal administrations is causing widespread economic and social hardship among the Brazilian people. Ranking economic, social and cultural rights high on modern agendas means that this struggle for all human rights will result in the appearance of fresh concepts of these rights.

Consequently, it is vital to use the international Covenant on economic, social and cultural rights as an innovative tool, with the civil society being one of its key instruments. People promoting and defending human rights must be empowered to an increasing extent, helping them expand the field of dialogue and draw closer to others whose rights are constantly violated. It is important to ensure that the masses not only understand but also assimilate and deploy the tools offered by this Covenant, because then will we be in a position to reshape the idea of human rights held by the common citizen, while pressuring government and society and demanding that economic, social and cultural rights should be dealt with at their rightful level: as the inalienable rights of each human being.

SECTION IV
SUBJECTS AND PROCESSES

SOCIAL SUBJECTS, HUMAN RIGHTS AND THEIR POLITICAL RELEVANCE

Pedro Cláudio CUNCA BOCAYUVA (Brazil)

"Through the promulgation of a written text containing a Declaration of Human and Citizenship Rights, modern Constitutionalism is endowed with a core factor for development and achievement, enshrining the triumphs of the citizen over authority".
(*Dictionary of Politics,* Norberto Bobbio)[1]

Introduction: Constituent Authority

Enshrined in Brazil's 1988 Constitution, International Human Rights and more particularly Economic, Social and Cultural Rights are a yardstick for questioning the limits of government policies and examining the structural inequalities that characterize Brazilian society[2]. This paper analyzes the meaning of the dispute between the concept of rights as tools for emancipation and equality, compared to rights in terms of the ideology of domination and the logic of the global expansion of capital. On the following pages, we offer a brief overview of the political meaning of the topic of rights, as part of the thorny political issue of implementing substantive democratisation within the Brazilian society in an open international context at the start of a new millennium.

The issues of the type of constitution and functioning of the political covenant, the distribution and balance of the division of powers among State institutions, and the relationships between direct and representative democracy will not be covered by this paper. We will rather start out from a viewpoint affirming the pluralistic and dynamic meaning of the forms of democracy as a political, social and material process. This is based on the inner differences found in civil society, as well as the dynamics of

---

1 Norberto Bobbio, Nicola Mateucci & Gianfranco Pasquino, *Dicionário de Política,* Brasilia (Editora University of Brasília), IIId edition, 1986.

2 Article 6 of the 1988 Brazilian Constitution affirms that "the social rights are education, healthcare, work, housing, recreation, safety, security, social welfare, protection for mothers and children, and aid for the homeless, as established in this Constitution", in: Geraldo Magela Alves and staff (eds.), *Constituição da República Federativa do Brasil,* IIId edition, Rio de Janeiro (Editora Forense), 2000.

political pluralism, elective processes and the division of power – in brief: the rules of the game under a democratic system. The crux of our reflections focuses far more on the social and material aspects of the links between freedom and equality. Our concern addresses aspects of economic, social, cultural and environmental human rights that are not always acknowledged, although directly linked to the process of expanding civil and political rights.

Since the late XVII century with the Glorious Revolution in the UK, and the French and American Revolutions during the XVIII century, the power of political processes and contemporary revolution has built up a set of rights grounded on peoples' struggles. This has been the cornerstone for developing the political process of forming democracy and citizenship through broadening and extending civil, political, economic, social and cultural rights throughout the XX century. Struggles for rights, political upheavals, social and political reforms, and constitutional covenants rooted in historically significant crises and conflicts all demonstrate the vitality and weight of the links between the culture of rights and pressures from grassroots movements throughout the course of contemporary histor. They are all calling for the establishment of democratic processes, governments, regimes and institutions.

The XX century continued the battle over the thorny issue of rights through combating totalitarian regimes, dictatorships and imperialism. Liberal democratic revolutions, socialist movements, revolutions, civil and political reform processes and struggles for independence from colonial rule all provided platforms mobilising the call for rights, forming the foundations of new political pacts ushering in changes in material structures and even the State itself. This broad-based view of rights as correlative to the institutive and constitutive powers of the peoples is related to discussions on the source of the ethical and regulatory powers that underpin the democratic covenant. This power of united individuals, the power of the masses as the creative source of rights and its relationship with democracy were identified by Spinoza within the widespread crises that characterised the XVII century.

The supporters of the Social Contract and the Enlightenment were both grounded on a more general delegative and representative view, as the basis of the theory of Sovereignty, the State, the Government or the Prince. But as affirmed by Antonio Negri, it is the immanent power of the subject, the masses, the union of the people that developed the potential power of social construction and active politics[3]. In contrast to the concept of Rousseau – who rated the general will and the constituted power as the source of the sovereign power of the people, reflected in the social contract that defines a generic abstract field for the production of equality – the political treatise of Spinoza indicates the constitutive authority as the basis for democracy: "if two individuals unite and join forces, they will increase their power and consequently their rights. And with more individuals joining the alliance, all of them together will have more rights". The right of constraint that is grounded on the basis of common law features an active collective characteristic that is not alienated in the function of sovereignty. To a certain extent this anticipates the concept of modern mass democracy: "this right, which is defined by the power of the masses, is usually called the *STATE*, and anyone who through common consent strives for public matters is in full possession of this right, meaning the establishment, interpretation and repealing of laws, strengthening cities, deciding on war and peace, etc. If all of this is handled by an assembly drawn from the masses, the State is called a *DEMOCRACY*. If it consists of a few privileged men, this is an *ARISTOCRACY*. And if it consists only of one person, this is a *MONARCHY*"[4].

Universal Declaration of Human Rights

The international aspects of the process in historical breaks and gaps draw close to the discussion of rights. They relate to the sovereign power of the State, with the aspects of freedom and equality, fuelling social conflicts that update the conceptualisation of the collective players through dialectics that extend beyond the framework of the conflict at the national level. The historical milestone of the Universal Declaration of Human Rights (1948) expresses the historic tension of the triumph of citizens over authority, linked to the problem of unequal relationships among the States in different political systems, and in view of the globalised nature of capitalism. This Declaration is distinguished by the unification of different historical generations of rights, unifying the indivisible policy of these rights by ranking economic, social and cultural rights (including the rights to work, education, housing, etc.), alongside civil and political rights. In the view of Flávia Piovesan, "by linking the value of freedom to the value of equality, this Declaration outlines the contemporary concepts of human

3 Antonio Negri, *Le pouvoir constituant. Essai sur les alternatives de la modernité*, Paris (Presses Universitaires de France), 1997.

4 Spinoza, *Tratado Político*, Rio de Janeiro (Edições de Ouro), undated.

rights, through which human rights are conceived as being inter-related and indivisible, endowed with an interdependent unity."[5]

The problem of extending these rights through social and national struggles speeded up during the 1960s. It took on fresh meanings in different contexts, including the return of democracy to Latin America and Brazil, as well as the collapse of socialism and the upheavals and conflicts linked to the process of globalisation launched by the crisis of Capitalism over the past thirty years. In the XXI century, awareness, practices and struggles to defend or even establish rights still offer ample headroom for building platforms and conflicts over freedom and equality, with human rights serving a tool for their materialisation and enforceability, particularly through the courts. Through the acknowledgement of citizenship, human rights form the formal, subjective foundations of both national constitutions and international law, highlighting the active, creative power of citizenship as a condition for political democracy.

As World War II drew to a close, the world faced the challenge of a new type of relationship among the Nation States, where different types of sovereignty and political blocs had to organize a complex system of mediatory relationships through setting up the United Nations Organisation. This was designed to deal with the after-effects of nazism, fascism and Japanese ultra-militarism, through establishing rules for mediating and settling disputes between the capitalist and socialist blocs; tackling the problems of rebuilding the global economy that had been undermined by the decline of the European system; dealing with the process of achieving independence from colonial rule for the peoples of Africa and Asia; and coping with the set of geo-political and economic dynamics that characterised the post-war context.

The thirty years that followed the establishment of this system reflect the combined effects of small-scale wars and crises linked to the cold war process, discussions over the development and non-alignment of outlying countries, and the steady expansion of regulated or organised industrial capitalism. Based on the effects of crimes against humankind and the hegemony of the USA, the regulation of the international system – grounded on the leading role assigned to State players – was always characterised more by geo-political and economic dynamics than the standpoint of rights. But after the Declaration of Human Rights paved the way for the appearance of international human rights, covenants and

[5] Flavia Piovesan, *Temas de Direitos Humanos*, São Paulo (Editora Max Limonad), 1998.

conventions ensuring their implementation opened up a significant ideological and political arena for dealing with the challenges of building up a hegemonically stabilised international order.

The End of the Cold War and Globalisation

Ushered in by the end of the cold war and the collapse of the bloc headed by the former USSR, crises in mass-production and accumulation systems, the speed-up of globalisation, the spread of the information and communications revolutions, and difficulties assailing classic national regulations, authorities and international rights, all shaped the international political arena for disputes over the establishment and legitimation of the new conditions needed for hegemonic stability. Meanwhile, gaps and loopholes in the field of human rights, in parallel to squabbles over their indivisibility exacerbated tensions and struggles calling for their enforceability – particularly through the courts – as the way to protect individuals, peoples and nations. The eternal dilemma running through the notion of the rights re-emerged as an international issue, promoted by clashes between capital flows and power with the simpler life-styles of communities scarred by the many different types of exploitation, domination and inequality that characterised a wide variety of military, political, economic, cultural, religious, ethnic, class and gender conflicts, replicated in many social and environmental settings.

As the century drew to a close, a huge range of social conflicts loomed: urban issues; the power and participation of women; social and environmental conflicts; demographic problems and the strategies of bio-power; social and production networks; flows of goods, services and capital; new non-material production processes and the culture industry; the process of turning social life into a spectacle; widely-disseminated violence and criminalisation processes; the increasingly precarious nature of labour relations; fiscal crises undermining the State; adjustment and restructuring processes; economic integration and the formation of regional blocs; neo-liberal political processes; streams of migrants; ethnic and racial conflicts; location-specific skirmishes, etc. As affirmed by José Maria Gómez, at the universal level it is hard for the democratic principle and the guarantee of rights to speak with a single voice within this context, characterised by the asymmetries and inequalities caused by globalisation. When subject to the universalisation of capitalist mercantile relationships structured as international links, the democratic principle clashes with the real expansion and use of democratic and social institutions that extend beyond their subjection to the rules of formal procedure. The links between democracy and the globalised market through transnationalised capital flows and networks whose spatial distribution is hierarchised in fact reflects a basic contradiction with the hypothesis of the active take-over of democracy by the various social and political forces of peace.[6]

According to Luis Carlos Fridman, the counterpart to globalisation – with its volatile capital flows and their social, productive and technological transformations reshaping the post-modern culture through the logic of newly-arrived capitalism – is the build-up of an entire set of excludatory frontiers. Alongside the cosmopolitan struggle of peoples, movements and individuals for a polyphony of new lifestyles, we still see the predomination of a "new social stratification", shaped by "capacities for movement in time and space", defining a context of extraterritorial and global mobility for the elite, and territorialised exclusion or forced displacement for the "others"[7]. Processes that extend beyond national borders require an approach from civil societies and grassroots movements that blend a redemption of the culture of creating rights and guarantees, in parallel to an approach grounded on a paradigm that takes into account the widespread dilemma of these "frontiers". New hordes of the excluded and vulnerable place a global agenda high on the order of the day, founded on the alternative use of international covenants and instruments. This experience is being urged in Brazil and the Americas by the Inter-American Platform for Human Rights, Democracy and Development.

The Dilemma of Human Rights: Banalisation × Emancipation

If the West and the capitalist world claim that much of its world-domination logic and the legitimacy of its "civilising" interventions were undertaken on behalf of human rights, under a conflictive logic and also on behalf of their rights, peoples have risen in revolt and built up strategies for political emancipation. This clash between asymmetrical powers, authorities and forces in the international order follows the driving forces in the dilemma of the history of peoples, moving towards covenants and national political constitutions. In the dialectics prompted by the polarisation between the "part of the Prince" and the "part of the People", a permanent tension has been built up in the relationships between the institutions of power and juridical systems as strategic devices structuring social relationships. Those at the bottom of the social scale are awarded a set of negative freedoms

---

6 José Maria Gomez, *Política e democracia em tempos de globalização*, Petrópolis (Editora Vozes), 2000.

7 Luis Carlos Fridman, *Vertigens pós-modernas. Configurações institucionais contemporâneas*, Rio de Janeiro (Editora Relume Dumará), 2000.

whose significance lies in the fact that the State cannot deploy the power of the legitimate use of force beyond a certain limit. On the other hand, we have the positive freedoms in terms of guarantees and rights which are the starting-point for central integration in the political pact "between equals": the democratic covenant.

The risk of juridical and institutional fetishism or the banalisation of rights characterised the post-war period, due to the sterilisation of the regulatory social welfare state, as well as government policies, social security and wage relationships. But when the organised forms of capitalism slipped into crisis, this did not prevent rights from being relocated in terms of social conflicts and fresh prospects for redeeming their historical dimension. This means recovering the mobilising capacity of human rights on the basis of new and active subjectivities through grassroots movements and individual actions that endow them with material solidity.[8]

The attempt to find a standpoint to analyze the rights in all their complexity is driven by the vast diversity of the aspects of social life characterised by the relationship between the State, rules and laws. The weight of the issue of rights in daily life for a wide variety of types of institutions and symbols that affect social life, the weight of international conflicts and the types of regulations, as well as disputes between countries and the struggles of their peoples almost always lead back to the factors required for the socialisation and institutionalisation of political covenants and systems as devices and practices of a juridical and political nature. In order to cover this process from the standpoint of the rights, we could select some paradigms to explain how legal and regulatory frameworks are built up, as well as political pacts, legal systems, and the frameworks of justice and security that constitute the legal order of what is known as the State of Law. Explanations based on the naturalisation of rights and their confirmation or implementation indicate problems linked to the issues of sovereignty, representation and the immanent power of the active construction of the subjects, while discussions continue on the different sources for establishing the rights. The dialectics over conserving forms of domination based on the alienation of power in the hands of the sovereign and problems of the active, emancipatory ethics of social subjects lie at the heart of the difficulties encountered in interpreting the meaning of the rights as tools for constructing democracies.

---

8 Boaventura de Sousa Santos, *A crítica da razão indolente. Contra o desperdício da experiência,* São Paulo (Editora Cortez), 2000.

In an attempt to identify the real nature of the State of Law, François Châtelet and Évelyne Psier-Kouchner warn that "as the ideal type, the State of Law has no legitimate function other than militant: a reminder of a demand. Furthermore, it functions only as ideology"[9]. This active principle is linked to the concept of the Democratic State expressed by Claude Lefort through the notion of the overwhelming experience of expanding the frameworks of the State of Law. He feels that "rights that have not yet been included set the stage for a state of peace whose purpose is not limited to conserving a tacitly established pact but is rather formed through approaches that the authorities cannot fully dominate. From the legitimation of the right to strike or set up trade unions through to the right to work or the right to social security, the foundations of the Rights of Man have built up a lengthy track-record that extends beyond the borders that the State attempts to define, in a history that remains open"[10]. But in contrast, the loss of the capacity to affirm new rights may result in backsliding and loss of ground even for existing rights that have already been formally established. The ups and downs of the democratic struggle in today's Brazil offer good examples: the upside features progress by the Landless Peasants Movement in forcing the early introduction of elements of agrarian reform; the demarcation of indigenous lands; women's rights; affirmative action for negroes; and assistance for the descendants of runaway slaves who once found shelter in clandestine rural communities known as *quilombos*; the downside includes: removal of the mobile wage scale; elimination of the wage policy; a sluggish income redistribution policy; the introduction of temporary work contracts; and slashed budget allocations for social policies, all in the name of adjustment and stabilisation.

The Core Issue of Democracy

The core issue of democracy is a crucial problem in terms of the challenges thrown up by the relationship between freedom and equality, characterising the thorny issue of human rights as the focus of reflection on the statute of rights in the political covenant and the form of organisation and distribution of power within society, for the dynamic definition of institutions and practices that ensure the dynamics of justice. In social and political terms, justice consists of the set of practices distributing and applying the rights, ensuring equality and their universal application to individuals, brought into operation through conflicts, crimes and claims.

---

9 François Châtelet, & Évelyne Pisier-Kouchner, *As concepções políticas do século XX. História do Pensamento Político*, Rio de Janeiro (Zahar Editores), 1983.

10 Claude Lefort, *A invenção democrática. Os limites do totalitarismo*, São Paulo (Editora Brasiliense), 1983.

In today's modern society, justice is characterised by dynamics that are related to other ways of building up laws and rules, reflected in the devices and processes that reflect links among coercion, sanction and force through the standards of legality and legitimacy in so-called rational modern political orders. The other side of Sovereignty, Authority and the State is the Constitution, the Law and the Right, as categories defining the complex field of power relationships and structures of domination, in addition to the symbolic and material authority of the arrangement of the juridical and political devices.

The issue of the Democratic State of Law and Human Rights is rated as a purpose that is just as relevant as the national order, if not more so, characterised by modernisation processes and the complexity of the social class system, types of urban development and mass cultural standards. The issue of International Human Rights and relationships among interstate and international agencies and institutions lies at the heart of disputes over hegemony and "world government" within the new international order, which is hegemonised by globalised capital. Rule and Coercion, Law and the Use of Force as the bases of a national political and juridical order are deeply rooted in the structure of international power, where the right appears as an established ideological form, an area for regulating the exercise of disputes by those under the yoke of domination, burdened by the structural inequality of material and military forces. But through an effect similar to that of the field of internal disputes and conflicts assailing nation states, this right is also rooted in conflicts and emancipatory projects urged by social forces and the lower classes, oppressed nations, minorities, the vulnerable and the excluded.

International Human Rights

The local, national, regional and international levels are permeated by the tension between coercion and consensus which characterizes new displacements and functions shaping relationships between States within the international system. The Empire of Capital must administer the crisis and guard its borders against fragmentative tensions, in order to stabilize its standards dominating the fields and flows of transnationalised material and immaterial networks. The power of banks and corporations is related to new systems and links in global networks, as well as fresh crises and local conflicts, redefining the functions of power and regulation of the Nation States. As a universal category within the juridical arrangements, international rights have an aspect and loophole open to emancipatory logic and the claims of peoples and the victims of violation by the processes, seeking active deployment at all levels of human rights on the whole, as this expresses the minimum conditions for the quality of life and equality among peoples. "Human rights are a way of holding the States responsible for the situation of vulnerable individuals and groups, as well as future generations. Human rights are reaffirmed and coded through International Law. The tools and mechanisms found in International Law and related to human rights may be deployed and strengthened by the NGOs"[11], as well as by grassroots movements, provided that they are firmed up in the objective field of their practices and correlated to political and juridical actions implemented through national and local processes.

The contradictory legacy of the democratic and social struggles of the people is reflected in the quest for the concrete expression and enforceability of human rights – particularly through the courts – as expressed in the Universal Declaration of Human Rights. However, this implementation depends on the effective application of international covenants[12] and conventions. As a subjective factor and tool in this struggle of oppressed men and women, human rights are an integral part of a universal historical process redefining these rights, whose political clout for ushering in freedom and equality depends on their deployment as a driving force behind the active demands of selected subjects at the local, national and international level. The link between democracy and rights runs through the field of a universal, selective *praxis* for social subjects, as explained by Marilena Chauí: "the democratic society establishes rights through opening up the social field to the creation of real rights, extending existing rights while also introducing *new* rights"[13].

The International Covenant on Economic, Social and Cultural Rights

Striving to ensure the active deployment of human rights to strengthen a strategic backbone for the substantive democratisation of Brazilian society, the National Human Rights Movement (*Movimento Nacional de Direitos*

---

11 International Secretariat – FIAN, *Direitos Humanos Econômicos e Sociais: seu tempo chegou*, Goiás (CPT, FIAN, MNDH), 1995.

12 The main covenants guiding specific conventions, such as the Convention against Torture, and the optional Protocols for their implementation are: the International Covenant on Economic, Social And Cultural Rights adopted through Resolution 2,200-A (XXI) by the UN Assembly General on December 16, 1966 (in effect since January 3, 1976, pursuant to Article 27) and ratified by Brazil on January 24, 1992; and the International Covenant on Civil and Political Rights, adopted and open for signature, ratification and adherence through Resolution 2,200-A (XXI) by the UN Assembly General on December 16, 1966 (in effect since March 23, 1976, pursuant to Article 49) and ratified by Brazil on January 24, 1992.

13 Marilena Chaui, *Convite à Filosofia*, São Paulo (Editora Ática), 1997.

Humanos) has been working with other institutions, pressuring the Brazilian State to meet the demands for compliance with the International Covenant on Economic, Social and Cultural Rights (PIDESC – *Pacto Internacional dos Direitos Econômicos, Sociais e Culturais*). These efforts have produced an Alternative Report on Brazilian society that will serve as the grounds for a set of actions designed to ensure compliance with these rights, which are enshrined in the Brazilian Constitution. Prompting a fresh approach to the strategies for handling lawsuits and underpinning the introduction of a new subjectivity, this will allow grassroots movements to be perceived as institutive players with the powers to lobby for alterations in restrictive, minimalist and excludatory government policies[14]. The view of grassroots movements and individual actions as shaping the subjects of these rights forms part of a fresh reading of the strategic horizon of the battle for democracy, redeeming the achievements of earlier historical social struggles and urging redistributive justice through the radicalisation of democracy. The dual nature of the inclusion of economic, social and cultural rights as an Article in the Brazilian Constitution and through an International Covenant underpins and fosters a new form of unification for democratic struggles and platforms, permeated by the political set of rights as a tool making room for the life of the citizen and redeeming democratic and socialist traditions of an emancipatory nature.

The strategy of the struggle for rights within the juridical and legislative frameworks, as well as the autonomous social actions of the movements involved, all spotlight the possibility of considering the expansion of Democracy as broadening social changes, from the standpoint of progress within the democratic order and along the lines indicated by the view of the constituent authority indicated by Florestan Fernandes. The somewhat fuzzy nature of Brazilian Democracy and the limits and constraints in the nation's 1988 Constitution – although lightened to some extent by neo-liberal reforms – do not prevent the use of this sensitive organised core as a modern instrument in the struggle for democratisation. The use of economic, social, cultural and environmental[15] human rights as tools for

14 There are two editions of *O Brasil e o Pacto Internacional de Direitos Econômicos, Sociais e Culturais. Relatório da Sociedade Civil sobre o Cumprimento pelo Brasil,* do PIDESC, one published by the National Human Rights Movement (Movimento Nacional de Direitos Humanos) and other entities coordinating the process of preparing the report, and the other published by the Lower House Human Rights Committee, National Congress.

15 Although the approach of the International Covenant on Economic, Social and Cultural Rights includes the topics of quality of life and the right to development, the weight of the environmental issue and the topic of social and environmental sustainability frequently prompted us to use a broader-based concept that includes environmental rights, instead of just economic, social and cultural rights, when referring to these rights as a whole. Due to

establishing the platforms of social struggles for citizenship by the workers and the people are related closely to the view believing that: "the emancipation of the oppressed and the working classes should start within the existing State and civil society through a worldwide struggle whose purpose is to trigger a political revolution within the order"[16].

Public Sphere and the Active Experimentalism of Social Subjects

The prospect of guidelines unifying struggles based on the universal nature of human rights, in parallel to affirmative action that distributes benefits to the excluded who are victimised by various types of oppression and discrimination, extends the scope of the view of the problems of Democracy in Brazil, including elements from the international social experience and challenging the limits imposed by authoritarian power and the oligarchies and monopolies that dominate local life. As noted by Carlos Nelson Coutinho: "the 'restricted' political sphere introduced by the elitist States – both authoritarian and liberal – is progressively making way for an 'extended' public sphere characterised by the political protagonism of broad-ranging and expanding mass organisations".[17] The programme for Brazilian democracy and the platform of the struggle for economic, social, cultural and environmental rights is nurtured by the creative power of new grassroots movements being the collective subjects of the struggle for rights through organised networks and the disorganised masses. These are now appearing on the public stage, demanding social and political justice as a gateway to the reorganisation and redefinition of the purposes of national development, in terms of alliances and the dilemmas faced by human society within the context of globalisation and consequently with regard to international human rights. This means that local and national actions have shifted to the level of international institutions, altering the meaning of the definitions shaping the current structural framework of the United Nations.

In the terms proposed here, human rights need to be reinvented, slanted more towards materialising social development processes as the construction of Democracy is extended by the constituent power of individual and collective subjects. The prospects for organising civil society are viewed from the standpoint of rearranging their collective actions, working towards

---

the relevance of the environmental issue and its relatively recent arrival within the juridical framework, the interpretation of this set of rights should be expanded.

16 Florestan Fernandes, *O processo constituinte*, Brasilia (National Constituent Assembly), 1988.

17 Carlos Nelson Coutinho, *A dualidade de poderes. Introdução à teoria marxista do estado e revolução*, São Paulo (Editora Brasiliense), 1985.

guarantee and protection systems that are the outcome of political socialisation and new public spheres of participation, pledging political enforceability with rights ensured through the courts, under State powers and the international system. As affirmed by Mangabeira Unguer: "progressives should reinterpret rather than reject the idea of fundamental rights". As there is "a dialectic link between protecting individuals through sheltering vital interests, and the capacity of individuals to prosper in the midst of accelerated experimentalism", the collective subjects emerge as the subjects of rights, established as a condition for the implementation of Democracy.[18]

[18] Roberto Mangabeira Unguer, *A democracia realizada. A alternativa progressista*, São Paulo, Boitempo Editorial, 1999.

HUMAN RIGHTS AND THE AFRO-BRAZILIAN POPULACE

Marcio Alexandre GUALBERTO (Brazil)

Introduction

As we draw near to the III World Conference against Racism organised by the United Nations Organisation, we feel it is important to analyze racial relationships in Brazil, seeking to cross-reference them to the issue of human rights. Examining gaps between blacks and whites from the standpoint of violations of human rights means moving into a sector where violence, lack of respect for the dignity of others, the total withdrawal of the State etc., indicates to what extent Brazil still clings to the concept of black slavery, social genocide (Negroes and indigenous communities), prejudice and racism.

Initially, it should be stressed that when speaking of human rights, we mean the broad-based concept of this term, indicating the indivisible and universal nature of the links between civil and political rights, and economic, social and cultural rights. According to Antônio Augusto Cançado Trindade, Chief Justice of the Inter-American Court of Human Rights:

> "What is the right to life worth, unless minimum conditions are provided for a decent existence, if not survival (food, housing, and clothing)? What is the right to freedom of movement worth without the right to adequate housing? What is the right to freedom of expression worth without access to basic education? What are political rights worth without the right to work? What is the right to work worth without a fair wage that covers basic human requirements? What is the right to freedom of association worth without the right to health? What is the right to equality under the law worth without guarantees of due legal process? (...) This stresses the importance of the holistic or integral view of human rights, taking them all together. We all experience the indivisible nature of human rights in our daily lives. All human rights for all, this is the only sure path for acting lucidly in the field of protecting human rights. Focusing equally on economic, social and cultural rights, in view of the wide diversity of the sources of violations of human rights, is what recommends the concept of universal accep-

tance today, of the inter relationship or indivisibility of all human rights"[1].

Consequently, analysing the situation of the Negro populace from the standpoint of human rights means understanding these rights to their fullest scope. We have consequently selected three areas that we would like to examine here: the right to education; the right to culture; and the use of legal mechanisms for obtaining these rights.

Although Brazil's return to democracy in 1995 ushered in a more open regime, with the return of its exiles and the release of political prisoners, little progress was made in terms of seeking to resolve structural problems that have more direct effects on the Negro population. There is a widespread idea that there is no racial prejudice in Brazil, but rather social prejudice. Consequently, heavier investments in education, healthcare and housing should logically ease larger numbers of Negroes in better social and economic situations, phasing out racism. However, racial prejudice is being reinforced to an increasing extent as common sense notes the apparent inability of Negroes to rise in society, particularly as the Negro population is found at the base of the social pyramid. This concept is incorrect, precisely because it fails to take into consideration the fact that the legacy of slavery remains present in the life of the Negro population, although latent. When slavery was abolished, the Negro population was left without work and with no source of income, forced to struggle for survival in a wide variety of ways. So there is a gap in equality that is still clear today, and which is growing even wider.

Right to Education and Social Mobility

Speaking of violations of human rights is extremely difficult without taking into account a series of other factors that are interconnected into a broad-raging network. However, it is impossible not to perceive the extent to which violations of the right to education have expanded the gap between blacks and whites. According to data drawn from the National Household Sampling Survey (PNAD – *Pesquisa Nacional por Amostragem Domiciliar*) presented in Brazil's Report on Human Development[2], 35.2% of Negroes and 33.6% of mulattos over the age of 25 years were illiterate, compared

---

1 Antônio Augusto Cançado Trindade, 'O Brasil e o Pacto Internacional de Direitos Econômicos, Sociais e Culturais', in: *Report, IV National Conference on Human Rights*, Lower House (Publications Coordination Unit), 2000, p. 24-25.

2 Wânia Sant'Anna & Marcelo Paixão, *Desenvolvimento Humano e População Afro-Descendente no Brasil: uma questão de raça*, Proposal n° 73, 1997, p. 29.

to 15% of whites[3], in a universe where 18% of the Brazilian populace is rated as illiterate. As the funnel narrows, the difficulties encountered by Afro-Brazilians in achieving access to education become even more severe. Only 18% of Negroes and 23% of mulattos are able to get into university, compared to 43% of the whites. These distortions are reflected even more clearly on the labour market. The best jobs and careers go to the whites, while Afro-Brazilians are forced to accept positions requiring fewer skills with lower pay, or are edged into under-employment generating a vicious cycle from which these sectors of the populace are unable to break away. According to a study by a researcher from the Institute of Applied Economic Research (IPEA – *Instituto de Pesquisa Econômica Aplicada*), Sergei Suarez Dillon Soares[4], the difference in income between whites and blacks (men and women) show that education and training, placement and wage definition are determining factors in wage levels. In the view of Soares: "If society is restricting the access of Negroes to good education or to good jobs, then the government should guarantee this access, particularly in educational terms".

This violation of the right to education is crucial for understanding the level of impoverishment of Afro-Brazilians. Logically, education itself cannot solve all the problems of a specific group in the population. However, denying education to Afro-Brazilians has helped perpetuate the view that the Negro is inferior and incapable, right from the earliest days of Brazilian history.

Even taking into account factors other than access to education as significant elements for better development of the Afro-Brazilian population, we cannot fail to note that the effects of limited access to education reverberate throughout society, with everyone affected by this to some extent. We have not yet examined in detail studies of the economic impact caused by racism. Yet, if we take into account all State outlays on combating violence, loss of tax revenues caused by underemployment, healthcare budgets etc., it becomes quite clear that discrimination and racism impose heavy economic effects on the country as a whole. As an example, we

---

3 It is worthwhile noting that the Brazilian Institute of Geography and Statistics (IBGE – *Instituto Brasileiro de Geografia e Estatística*) classified the Brazilian population into white, black, brown, yellow and indigenous. By these ratings, blacks account for 5.5%, of the population, with browns at 37.2%, yellows at 0.6% and whites at 56.4%, according to the 1987 National Household Sampling Survey (PNAD). We prefer to use the term Afro-Brazilians, which covers both brown and black people, and offers a more faithful reading of the level of inequality among these groups and the white population.

4 Sergei Suarez Dillon Soares, *O Perfil da discriminação no mercado de trabalho – homens negros, mulheres brancas e mulheres negras*, Discussion Paper n° 769, Brasília (IPEA), 2000.

mention the increasingly fragile relationships on the labour market that have direct effects on Afro-Brazilians (see map below).[5] This shows that the Afro-Brazilian sector of the population is not outnumbered by whites anywhere in Brazil in terms of underemployment. This leads to the conclusion that the impact of underemployment on the Social Security System, for instance, causes severe economic problems for society as a whole. Ironically, the government prefers to introduce surtax policies that burden registered workers, rather than combating the causes of underemployment. An interesting aspect is the way that the government deliberately overlooks the causes and effects of racial discrimination, as well as its economic impacts.

Similar to Brazilian society, the State attempts to endow racism with an ethereal nature. Like the Spanish saying: "*Creer en las brujas yo no creo, pero que las hay, las hay*", the State acknowledges the existence of racism in many situations, indicates that actions could be taken to combat it, but places itself in a position where it is society that should act in order to change this situation. In turn, society agrees that racism exists, but does not see itself as the practical agent of this racism[6], and consequently does not admit that it can act either separately through individuals or altogether as a whole, in ways that would alter this scenario. Above all, it is vital that the government and society should acknowledge that the problem of racism does not involve only Negroes, as this affects everyone.

Right from the start, the Fernando Henrique Cardoso administration acknowledged the existence of the race problem in Brazil – which is not surprising, as Brazil's Sociologist President has published several well-known academic works on this topic, and was also a member of the School of Thought headed by Florestan Fernandes which began to indicate flaws in the idea that Brazil was a racial democracy. In the Inaugural Speech for his first term of office, President Cardoso was already mentioning the need to combat racial inequality in Brazil. In 1995 he signed a Presidential Decree, in response to demands from the Negro Movement[7], setting up the Interministerial Working Group for Enhancing the Value of the Negro

[5] Marcelo Paixão, *Maps of Inequality*, available on the web page of the *Rede Nova Abolicionista*, 2000.

[6] Survey carried out by *DataFolha*, the polling arm of the Folha de São Paulo newspaper in 1995, indicating that 89% of the Brazilian population acknowledges that racism exists in Brazil, while only 10% admitted that they had practiced some racist act at some time.

[7] In 1995, when the 300th anniversary of the death of Negro Independence hero Zumbi dos Palmares was commemorated, the Negro Movement organised a large-scale march to Brasília in order to present a series of proposals to the President of Brazil, designed to upgrade the living standards of the Negro population.

Population. Consisting of representatives from several different Ministries, militant sectors of the Negro Movement, and the black intelligentsia, this Interministerial Working Group was established to present proposals to the government for firm actions that would upgrade the living conditions of Afro-Brazilians.

Once again, in his speech commemorating the signature of this Presidential Decree, President Cardoso affirmed that:

> "Those who are here today are well aware that it is not due to a lack of laws that things do not function better in Brazil, but rather due to a lack of practice. The laws are there, the Constitution is there, and the laws stipulate equality. The problem comes from Brazil's burdensome heritage as a slavocracy, a culture that dissimulated discrimination through apparent cordiality, which does no more than repeat and reproduce forms of discrimination.
> All of us are well aware that the way to effectively extend the course of democracy lies through equal opportunities. And they are closely linked to schooling. This is why we are insisting so much on an active education programme in Brazil at the basic, primary school level. With our support, the Ministry of Education forwarded a set of measures to Congress, including some constitutional steps that would usher in a fresh definition of how the government deploys its resources for education"[8].

However, it is interesting to note that the proposals put forward by the Interministerial Working Group (GTI) became an item on the agenda of the Negro Movement, which the Brazilian government has not yet implemented – although some were included in Brazil's National Human Rights Programme, launched in 1996.

The initial version[9] of Brazil's National Human Rights Programme was launched by the Federal Government, with some specific proposals that affect the Negro sectors of the population:

---

8 *Construindo a Democracia Racial – Atos e palavras do Presidente Fernando Henrique Cardoso.* Signature of the Decree setting up the Interministerial Working Group for Enhancing the Value of the Negro Population, Planalto Presidential Palace, November 20, 1995. Federal Government website: http://www.plantalto.gov.br.

9 Brazil's 1996 National Human Rights Programme committed a conceptual error when separating these rights into three generations: civil and political; economic, social and cultural; and collective, as today there is a certain convergence, appearing through the logic of the indivisible and universal nature of human rights. The 2000 update of Brazil's National Human Rights Programme consulted several institutions in civil society on the intentions of the Federal Government to fix this mistake, which required absorbing a series of proposals related to economic, social and cultural rights.

"Short term:
Support the Interministerial Working Group established by Presidential Decree on November 20, 1995, in order to suggest actions and policies enhancing the value of the Negro population;
Inclusion of the issue of "colour" in all and any information systems and records covering the population and public data-bases;
Support the Working Group for the Elimination of Discrimination at Work and occupations (GTDEO – *Grupo de Trabalho para Eliminação da Discriminação no Emprego e na Ocupação*) established under the aegis of the Labour Ministry through a Decree on March 20, 1996. This tripartite Working Group should draw up an Action Programme and propose strategies for combating discrimination at work and in occupations, pursuant to the principles of Convention 111 issued by the International Labour Organisation (ILO);
Encourage and support the establishment and installation at the State and Municipal levels of Negro Community Councils;
Encourage the presence of ethnic groups constituting the Brazilian population in institutional advertising contracted by direct and indirect civil service entities, as well as by State-run entities under the Federal Government;
Support the definition of actions enhancing the value of the Negro population, as well as government policies;
Support actions by private enterprise underpinning affirmative action;
Encourage State Public Security Bureaus to run recycling courses and seminars on racial discrimination;

Medium term:
Revoke discriminatory standards still found in infra-constitutional legislation;
Fine-tune standards and rules combating discrimination against the Negro population;
Set up a data-base on the status of the civil, political, social, economic and cultural rights of the Negro population in Brazilian society, in order to guide affirmative policies designed to promote this community;
Encourage the charting, mapping and preservation of heritage sites, as well as documents and places containing historical remains, while also protecting Afro-Brazilian cultural manifestations;
Submit a Draft Bill in order to regulate Articles 215, 216 and 242 of the Brazilian Constitution;
Undertake affirmative actions ensuring access for Negroes to vocational training courses, universities and state-of-the-art technology areas;

Order the Brazilian Institute of Geography and Statistics (IBGE – *Instituto Brasileiro de Geografia e Estatística*) to adopt the criteria of rating mulattos, persons of mixed race and blacks as members of the Negro population;
Adopt the principle of criminalising the practice of racism in the Criminal Codes and Criminal Procedural Processes;
Encourage textbooks to stress the history of the struggles of the Negro people in building up our country, eliminating stereotypes and discrimination;
Publicise International Conventions and the provisions in the Brazilian Constitution, as well as infra-constitutional legislation dealing with racism;
Support the production and publication of documents that help disseminate anti-discriminatory legislation;
Encourage discussions and networking among entities in the Negro community and various government sectors, for the development of Action Plans and Strategies that enhance the value of the Negro community;

Long term:
Encourage actions that help preserve the heritage and foster the cultural output of the Negro community in Brazil;
Formulate compensatory policies that foster the Negro community in economic and social terms"[10].

Particularly noteworthy is the significant progress achieved through the existence of a National Human Rights Programme, particularly as Brazil is acknowledged as a stubborn violator of human rights. Consequently, the existence of this Programme to some extent reflects the commitment of this Government to respecting human rights and the implementation of others. Nevertheless, there are some extremely complex aspects of this Programme. The first is the fact that the pace of the government is not necessarily the pace of society. Consequently, measures that we see as urgent may be assigned to short, medium or long terms by the government, although without stipulating the time and space constituting these deadlines.

A concrete example of this is the item indicating the intention of the Government to order the Brazilian Institute of Geography and Statistics (IBGE – *Instituto Brasileiro de Geografia e Estatística*) to include mulattos,

---

10 Department of Justice, *National Human Rights Programme*, Brasília 1996, p. 29, 30 and 31.

people of mixed race and blacks as members of the Negro sector of the population. Although this was presented in the National Human Rights Programme in 1996, and the Brazilian population census took place in 2000, with its successor scheduled only for 2010, which means that for all effects and purposes, what should have been implemented over the medium term in this Programme, in fact becomes long term, and subject to implementation by subsequent administrations.

It is also interesting to note that this order forwarded to the Brazilian Institute of Geography and Statistics (IBGE – *Instituto Brasileiro de Geografia e Estatística*) has been called for over many years by the intelligentsia and sectors of the Negro Movement, always meeting strong resistance from this Institute. In fact, it is worthwhile stressing – with all the emphasis warranted by this topic – that race relations in Brazil become more visible only when the Negro intelligentsia began to work with the concept that browns and blacks should be viewed as members of the same group. The fact that the official statistics have always skimmed over these data leads us to the conclusion that there is a strong wish to keep things the way they are, grounded on a set of factors that are intended to reflect the "non-existence" of racism, with prejudice being a cause rather than an effect"[11].

Another important point highlighted in the words of President Fernando Henrique Cardoso, as well as in Brazil's National Human Rights Programme, is the existence and consequently the need to implement laws that have already been approved, in order to ensure equality among all men and women. Articles 215, 216 and 242 of the Brazilian Constitution cover access to culture, cultural heritage and teaching the history of Brazil, taking into account the contributions from the many different cultures and ethnic groups that form the Brazilian people.[12] However, these constitutional provisions lack regulations and consequently are laws that cannot yet be fully applied.

In parallel to the fact that we can perceive that juridical elements do in fact exist, there is also some acknowledgement of the problems, with some solution strategies defined; however, the political will to implement them is still lacking. And here we ought to acknowledge that there is also a lack of strategy in the sectors of civil society interested in this topic, particularly the Negro Movement, which is not alone. Civil society itself must learn to work with the logic of pressure, through lobbying Parliament, in order to

[11] Wânia Sant'Anna, & Marcelo Paixão, *o.c.*, p. 25.

[12] *Brazilian Constitution 1988.*

ensure that matters that are of vital interest are not left pending, halted and dependent on the goodwill of the government. This is why it is vital that this same civil society, as well as the rest of Brazilian society, should accept the fact that racism and racial prejudice are problems that extend throughout society. It is not sufficient for major organisations to work on topics related to violence, the lack of access to basic sanitation, the precarious nature of the educational and healthcare systems without initially acknowledging that there is a race issue implicit here. This means that the Negro Movement is mistaken when it takes up the position that it is the sole agent endowed with legitimacy on racial issues, while civil society organisations are also wrong in maintaining a passive stance on this matter.

The lack of political will and the strategic mistakes of civil society are added to the atavistic fear of Brazilian society in seeing Negro men and women in positions of power in our country. The prejudice found in all Brazilians, which appears through jokes and teasing – but never admitting *de facto* prejudice – becomes flagrant when better positions open up on the labour market, or through the struggle for political office.

Brazilian society has been structured right from the start through an inflexible logic keeping each sector in its place. A survey carried out by the Networking Centre for Marginalised Populations (CEAP – *Centro de Articulação das Populações Marginalizadas*) in 41 towns in Rio de Janeiro State shows that 50% of the people interviewed replied that they would feel somewhat uncomfortable having a Negro boss, compared to 47% who replied that they would not, and 3% who preferred not to answer. The interesting fact here – and this is very close to the survey carried out earlier by the *Folha de São Paulo* newspaper – is that 93% of the people interviewed replied that racism does in fact exist in Brazil. However, 87% of them said that they had never practiced racism.[13] As noted by Ivanir do Santos, the Chairman of CEAP, "no one admits to being a racist. Prejudice is always found among other people, never within oneself. This unconscious nature is a specific characteristic of Brazilian racism. Initially, people do not see racism. Then they see it, but always in other people"[14]. Once again, this is the old strategy of ignoring the problem, as though racism were something in the air, affecting some people, but for which no one is to blame.

---

13 *Folha de São Paulo,* newspaper, May 12 2000.

14 *Ibid.*

Affirmative Action – Why Not Now?

A study on the Human Development Indicators run under the Brazil 2000 Programme: New Targets for Race Relations shows the high level of inequality among blacks and whites in Brazil. Supported by the Ford Foundation and Terre des Hommes, this project was run by the Federation of Social Welfare and Educational Entities (FASE – *Federação de Órgãos para Assistência Social e Educacional*), co-ordinated by Professor Marcelo Paixão[15] from the Institute of Economics, Rio de Janeiro Federal University.

The Human Development Indicators were drawn up by the United Nations Development Programme (UNDP) rating the 174 countries in the world. This ranking consists of a summarised indicator reflecting three basic variables: *per capita* income, life expectancy, and literacy rates, together with schooling levels. By this Index, Brazil rates 74th in the UNDP ranking, classified as a country with a medium human development index.

This task consisted of applying this same UNDP methodology to measure the disparities between Afro-Brazilians and groups with white ethnic roots, taking Afro-Brazilians as being brown and black people living in Brazil. The basic data were taken from the National Household Sampling Survey (PNAD) carried out in 1998.
According to this study, the following items are particularly noteworthy:

1. In 1998, Brazil placed 70th. When applied to the white and Afro-Brazilian communities, it rated 49th and 108th respectively;
2. The life expectancy of white people in 1950 was 47.5 years, while the figure for the non-white community was 40 years. In our study, from 1990 through 1995, the life expectancy of the Afro-Brazilian populations is 6 years less than that of the white population. Whites live an average of 70 years, while the figure for Afro-Brazilians is only 64. Maintaining this average rate, this disparity would vanish in 160 years;
3. The educational inequalities between Afro-Brazilians and whites are so vast that the educational ratings for 1997 for whites were just below those of Chile, while those of Afro-Brazilians were close to those of Swaziland;
4. Based on the average *per capita* family income for 1997, the indicators reach 0.74% for the white population and 0.60% for the Afro-Brazilian population;

---

[15] Marcelo Paixão, *Desenvolvimento Humanos e as Desigualdades Étnicas no Brasil: um retrato de final de século.* Proposal n° 86, September/November 2000.

5. A ratings table was drawn up for the human development index ratings by ethnic origin, covering the States of Brazil. This list was headed by white people in Brasília, with the lowest level assigned to Afro-Brazilians in Alagoas;
6. The human development index ratings for Afro-Brazilians were no higher than the figures for the white population in any part of Brazil. This means that racial inequalities continue in all Brazilian States, regardless of their development levels.

A Gender-Based Human Development Index (IDG) was also drawn up by ethnic origin for Brazil. In this case, including the ratings for women, the IDG value fell compared to the IDH, reflecting a similar gender gap.

Based on these data, one question is asked constantly by all those dealing with the issue of race relations in Brazil: why is there so much resistance to introducing affirmative action policies? Replying satisfactorily to this question is a difficult – if not impossible – task. Consequently, over the short and medium term, we do not see any more efficient measure for shrinking the gap between blacks and whites in Brazil. According to the eminent Jurist Hédio Silva Júnior: "affirmative action is the acknowledgement of the principle of equality of all before the law being insufficient to guarantee this among the citizens"[16]. Consequently, other principles should be sought with the necessary urgency. As already stressed by several jurists and the President of Brazil himself, the nation has some of the world's most advanced laws, although they are almost never applied, facing the nation with increasingly severe problems that build up to become monstrous, when they should have already been resolved long before.

When sociologist Herbert de Souza launched his programme to combat hunger, many people accused him of being paternalistic. He replied by saying that he agreed that hunger would only be resolved as the structural problems causing it were eliminated, but as long as this did not take place, people would be dying of hunger, and he could not allow this to happen without doing anything.

Discussions over affirmative action today are at exactly this level, divided between those who urge it not as a permanent measure but rather as an emergency step to deal with a situation that which is becoming increasingly serious and those who view it as paternalism, pure and simple. Between these two extremes there is a middle path, followed by those who are in

[16] *Raça* magazine, 'Por que políticas afirmativas'.

favour, in principle, but are concerned about how whites and non-whites would be classified as "deserving" affirmative action policies. This is in fact a spurious issue, as Brazilian society is well aware of how to distinguish whites from non-whites. If this were not so, Brazilian television and advertising would not be so Anglo-Saxon, and would rather feature more people of mixed race. We feel that all those affected by poverty and the lack of opportunity (most of them almost always black) should be targeted by affirmative action.

However, discussions over affirmative action cannot be based solely and exclusively on whether or not a quota system should be introduced for advertising media, government universities and the labour market. Further thought should be given to how a broad-based set of strategies could concomitantly extend through a wide variety of sectors. Based on the logic of sociologist Herbert de Souza (Betinho), we could say that just as it is vital to introduce a quota system at government universities, it is also crucial to invest heavily in basic education, so that the struggle for places will become fairer over the coming decades and the quotas policy can be phased out. Similarly, the mind-sets of those who produce the image of the nation should alter, showcasing the ethnic diversity of the Brazilian people. As long as this is not achieved, we should impose quotas in the advertising media, the field of education, and the labour market. After all, we should always be thinking about immediate strategies for shrinking inequalities, with long-term strategies that will allow us to achieve greater parity between blacks and whites.

Black Culture – from Appropriation to Invisibility

As already mentioned previously, Articles 215, 216 and 242 of the Brazilian Constitution cover access to culture, cultural heritage and including the contributions of different cultures and ethnic communities to forming the country, taught as part of the history of Brazil.

However, it is interesting to note that, over time, those sectors of the population producing culture with marked influences on the cultural formation of Brazil fail enjoy the benefits offered by this culture, particularly economic advantages. One of the most appalling examples of this is the fact that Brazil is presented in the communications media as a country where Negroes do not exist. Advertising and television soap operas, among other media, form and deform Brazilian society, leaving Afro-Brazilians virtually invisible. Programmes targeting the children's public are invariably presented by young blond women; there are no cartoons featuring Negro characters; variety shows with live audiences are hosted by whites, with the odd exception. This has marked effects on the self-esteem of Brazilian Negroes, making the ideals of whiteness a constant in their lives. Unfortunately, we often note Negro children, adolescents and young people denying their ethnic roots, as they are unable to see the racial diversity of Brazil reflected in the main communications media.

Furthermore, there is a perverse strategy in "whitening" Negro characters that can only be explained as part of a drive to bequeath the lowest portions of our society to the Negro, starting with the destruction of personal pride. A good example of this is the greatest Portuguese writer after Camões, Machado de Assis, who is constantly shown as a white man. Over the past two years, blatant cases have occurred of Afro-Brazilian characters being portrayed as white on the stage and screen, including painter Arthur Bispo do Rosário and singer Chiquinha Gonzaga. The popular soap opera entitled *Porto dos Milagres* that is currently being aired by Brazil's leading television chain, repeats these stereotypes that have already been enshrined by the Brazilian communications media through: 1) whitening the work of Jorge Amado by assigning white actors as the protagonists of the soap opera based on his work, shot in Bahia; 2) assigning Negro actresses Camila Pitanga and Thaís Araújo the roles of an emotionally unbalanced girl who is constantly pursuing the hero, who scorns her, and a prostitute respectively; 3) the role of a simple fisherman is assigned to a black man, who begs for the love of the girl who is in love with the hero, and in order not to be flagrantly scandalous, attempts to even out these scales by giving the role of a priestess (*Mão de Santo*) to black actress Zezé Motta.

In fact, Brazilian television has out-performed itself here. More than any other media, it strengthens the idea of everyone in their rightful place, by always ensuring that Negroes – when not playing slaves or outback gunmen – fall within the traditional stereotypes of criminals, prostitutes, voodoo priests etc. There are very few cases where a Negro character is portrayed as someone "normal", like a bank manager or something really worthwhile.

There have been many attempts to heighten the awareness of the communications media to the disservice rendered to the Negro population and the need to alter this approach. However, it is quite often heard in advertising circles that Negroes do not sell. But this claim was rebutted powerfully when the *Raça* magazine was launched in 1995, targeting Negroes and rated by many people as the most striking success in the Brazilian publishing world over the past few years. The fact that the early editions of this magazine were sold out as they reached the news-stands caused surprise initially, through the discovery that there was a large potential Negro market in Brazil. Over time, we have noted that some advertising items are starting to include – although still timidly – Negro men, women and families, particularly those targeting mass publics such as advertising for banks, cleaning materials, clothes etc. However, advertising items addressing specific sectors of the public still lack sufficient Negro participation. This includes automobile advertising, real estate, travel agencies etc., demonstrating that the advertising world still retains the narrow view that the buying power of the Negro sector of the population is not up to purchasing these products.

Looking at traditional events in Brazilian culture such as Carnival, for instance, the Afro-Brazilian population is loosing ground steadily, in terms of power relationships as well as its participation in the organisation and participation in the parades. This take-over of Afro-Brazilian culture is also appearing in fields such as *capoeira*, music and others. Two years ago, the Zumbi dos Palmares National Bureau set up a complaints desk during Carnival in Bahia to receive claims of racism occurring mainly in the Carnival groups of Salvador, where the participation of Afro-Brazilians is shrinking. A similar phenomenon is taking place with the *funk* dances in Rio de Janeiro that can draw 1.5 million young people on weekends, but when the power of these youngsters becomes apparent, it is deployed to elect a Rio de Janeiro City Councillor: a woman nicknamed *Blond Mother*.

In counterpart to all this, some flowers are blooming in the desert, through the resistance of organisations such as the Negro Performers Information and Documentation Centre (CIDAN – *Centro de Documentação e Informação do Artista Negro*) which registers and encourages contacts between black actors and stage, cinema and television producers, while keeping alive Afro-Brazilian traditions such as the *jongo*, *maracatu*, and *samba-de-côco* dances, as well as many other aspects of Negro culture.

It is a matter of much concern to see how a country such as Brazil that is endowed with such a rich culture has implemented so few policies designed to preserve and enhance its value. Once again, we return to the problem of education, because we feel that it is only on this basis that it is possible to ensure that the Afro-Brazilian cultural elements in particularly and the cultural heritage of the entire population in general are respected. As long as there is only limited awareness that access to culture is an inalienable right, we will continue to see the Afro-Brazilian population becoming increasingly invisible in terms of one its greatest assets: cultural output.

This is why heavy investments are required in producing educational materials, providing refresher courses for teachers and changing the mind-sets of editors, publishers, advertising people, producers, directors and leading communications entrepreneurs in Brazil, in order to ensure that the Negro population begins to appear more frequently in the media. However, this is closely linked to the political will to ensure that the Afro-Brazilian population obtains increasingly more headroom in Brazilian society. The questions remains: other than the Afro-Brazilians themselves, does the rest of society want this?

Juridical Tools as Allies – Is This Possible?

The possibility of interlinking racial issues with discussions on human rights can only benefit both sides. We can affirm that much progress has taken place in Brazil so far: the issue of race relations is no longer limited to the sphere of action of the Negro Movement, and today runs through many different sectors of society, although not yet at the necessary depth. Discussing whether or not racism exists in Brazil today has become secondary and unnecessary, with progress made in finding solutions for solving this problem. The use of social and economic indicators by some sectors of the Negro Movement, as well as the Negro intelligentsia and non-governmental organisations (NGOs) have today brought us to a satisfactory level of consensus on the racial inequalities found in Brazil.

Similarly, extending the notion of human rights to include economic, social and cultural rights will force all of us to become more flexible in our analyses, impelling us to acknowledge a wide variety of factors in our reflections on the problems of Brazil. Consequently, based on this new and extended concept of human rights, the idea gains force that inequalities based on race and gender lie at the root of all the problems found in Brazil. We will only progress towards being a decent country, when we tackle these inequalities successfully.

To do, the use of juridical instruments and the International Covenants signed by Brazil and backed by its Constitution, should be the cornerstones of these actions from now on. It will be important for both the Negro Movement as well as other sectors of civil society to deploy tools such as the International Covenant on Economic, Social and Cultural Rights, as well as conventions such as the International Convention on the Elimination of All Forms of Racial Discrimination, so that they can – together with current legislation – generate lawsuits that force the nation to ensure greater equality among its ethnic groups.

Another useful element is the Alternative Report of Civil Society on Brazilian Compliance with the International Covenant on Economic, Social and Cultural Rights (*Relatório Alternativo da Sociedade Civil sobre o Cumprimento pelo Brasil do Pacto Internacional de Direitos Econômicos, Sociais e Culturais*) produced by 2,000 Brazilian organisations and presented to the UN Committee for Economic, Social and Cultural Rights in Geneva. Due to its high level of legitimacy, it could well serve as a crucial tool for civil society.

As indicated by Joaquim Barbosa Gomes[17], the acknowledgement by Brazil's 1988 Constitution of the tools for protecting "collective" and "diffuse" rights such as the Public Civil Action, allow the Department of Justice and social organisations established for over one year to file suit before the Courts, defending segments whose rights are being violated. Consequently, it is vital not only to become familiar with these tools, but also to acknowledge that sectors of the Judiciary such as the Department of Justice and the Federal Attorney-General's Office for Citizen's Rights are entities that can and should be brought into action in order to ensure the validity of Brazilian laws, which – if not complied with – would result in apartheid affecting Afro-Brazilians.

There is not the slightest doubt that much progress is still required in becoming familiar with the juridical labyrinths that must be followed in order to ensure the validity of the rights of the Negro population. However, under a democratic regime – even though this democracy may be criticised for not ensuring full rights for all its citizens – this is the path opening up to us for effective actions designed to upgrade the living standards of our population.

---

17 Joaquim Barbosa Gomes, 'Discriminação Racial: um grande desafio para o direito brasileiro', in: *Ceap Pesquisa*, www.alternex.com.br/~ceap/pesquisa.html.

THE ESSENCE OF THE EARTH CHARTER

Aziz AB'SABER (Brazil)

Introduction

For reasons of personal sensitivity and based on any knowledge that I may have acquired of the nooks and crannies of Rio Grande do Sul State, I would like to stress that there could be no better place to hold the World Social Forum than the City of Porto Alegre. A land of people with a lengthy history and a long-standing tradition of struggle, but accepting renewal and rethinking the world from the standpoint of social improvements while enhancing democracy.

The guardians of the nation's borders in the past and fraternal citizens today, friendly neighbours and neighbourhoods have much to teach Brazil about the importance of building up permanent bridges between power and knowledge. Above all, thinking about social aspects and a correct approach to the modern world, before supporting (neo)liberalism and all the strategies of stubborn speculators, or supporting untrammelled capitalism that is culturally insensitive.

My task focused on commenting and justifying the main topics of the recently-prepared Earth Charter. This request was very timely, as my highly esteemed colleague, Patricia Morales, has analysed and reviewed all the messages and topics in this significant document. In the limited amount of time available for my presentation, I intend to highlight some facts that I was able to select from the context of this Charter. I will not run through the full structure of the Document, but rather wish to underscore some crucial aspects that need more specific, detailed treatment.

The Context of the Reaction to the Earth Charter

The preparation of the Earth Charter extends and to a certain extent completes – half a century later – the masterly messages in the Declaration of Human Rights. Consequently, it must be said right at the start that there are no clashes or substitutions between today's expanded document and yesterday's notable and eternal statement. The Universal Declaration of Human Rights was drafted after World War II, interring forever the execrable ideals of Nazism. Today's Charter is a document fostering interaction among people, inhabitants and the different domains of nature that are occupied, modified or affected by cumulative anthropic actions. With all its ecological and anthropological physical variations, the Earth is the Living Planet *par excellence*. A set of predominantly sub-sky areas where plant, animal and micro-organic life has developed. A vast world underlined by biopic and social inequalities that needs enlightened protection to survive through various time-frames. A core issue: the Earth Charter was drawn up to issue a warning about all this.

During the closing decades of the XX century – above all from 1970 onwards – environmental awareness expanded worldwide. Grounded on many different themes and approaches, non-governmental organisations were established, each with its own preferred themes and struggle strategies. Some are smarter and better prepared, others more restrictive and repetitive. However, they all share a single set of ideals, working together to expand their environmental and ecological awareness.
Although so well trained to carry out surveys in their respective fields of specialisation, academics have remained largely silent on basic national problems. And they are even more aloof from the problems prompted by massive social inequalities that assail the excluded, constituting the swollen base of the social pyramid in the under-developed countries. Almost all of them are more eager to obtain funding for their own research projects than seek out ideas and projects for the suffering poor population of their own countries. There are celebrities who have more funds available for their work and travel than time for the research projects in question, or even for their own lives. This is due to a mistaken approach in the behaviour and sensitivity of both the members of some non-governmental organisations as well as at public and private universities.
In Brazil, it is becoming very difficult to find academics and intellectuals working at the tip and base of such a complex society. Nevertheless, collaboration is required in order to (re)balance this disastrous situation. It is no longer possible to accept that all projects – no matter how odd they may be – are imposed on the nation through the sole choice and will of the powerful, hand in glove with subservient bureaucrats subject to this type of pressure from the powerful.

The responsibility of sensitive and enlightened men – living at a certain time – is far higher than is generally assumed. The human species consists of the only living beings able to trace their history back through time and space on the planet Earth. In fact, man is the only participant in the Earth's biodiversity with sufficient cerebral elasticity to care for and upgrade multiple cultural values. However, the permanent collection of these achievements is so vast and has extended to such an extent that democratising knowledge has become an extremely difficult task. It is hard to prepare and provide the necessary backup for a new generation of educators, in both social and economic terms. The art+science of selectively retrieving accumulated knowledge – by many different age groups – is blocked and curtailed at all turns by government leaders, bureaucrats and insensitive entrepreneurs. It is urgent to re-train teachers and qualify new educators, making better use of certain available technologies to produce a "balance" in the information and knowledge processes. Consequently, the facilities offered by radio, television, videos and computers should be widely used in order to usher in a true revolution in the field of education, involving the acquisition of knowledge and cultural values, sublimation, beauty and ethics.

It has never been so necessary or urgent to work in the field of ideas in order to assist those who remain excluded from the society that calls itself modern. Among the elite, insensitive to need and poverty, there is no interest in considering the fate and problems of the suffering bases of the social pyramid. They have not yet learned – at the end of the second millennium – that profound, Christian human lesson that states: "no-one can choose the place, womb or social and economic condition guaranteeing their place in society". Irreversible biological reality leads children and adolescents along a wide variety of paths in life. Some of them are the privileged offspring of the powerful of all types, the scions of quasi-feudal families. Others are born and grow up in rural and urban communities, running wild, marginalised and isolated from social life, subsisting in environments that are more than oppressive in any corner of Mother Earth.

Faced with this dramatic situation, traditional demagogues and governors always claim limited funds and a shortage of partners. However, the problem does not lie only here, because it is also related to the lack of knowledge, ideas and political will. References are made to poverty within a setting of weak-willed commitment and sporadic attention. Commonplace truisms are repeated. Poverty is mapped. And finally, it is shoved into the dead-end street of powerlessness and forgotten. There is no doubt that this is the leading problem in a nation with such a huge population, scattered all over a continent-size country. Yet another reason for authorities and scientists to get to work, alongside supportive and enlightened people, thinking seriously about hundreds or even thousands of strategies for modifying this cluster of inequalities. These should be based on well-analysed proposals, no matter how simple they may be, provided that they are both feasible and useful, and above all trigger expansion with multiplicatory effects. Reading thousands of intelligent proposals, while imposing justified pressures on bureaucracy, corruption and abuse, could well launch a significant social (re)vitalisation process.

I have always been very interested and moved by the fate and needs of those whose lives are isolated by distance, forming islets of humankind. Contrasting sharply with the mass economy and the fallacious mass democracy is a human geography that is more than martyred in many places all over the vastness of Brazilian Amazonia and the harsh drylands of the Northeast. My contacts with these dwellers in solitude – whether single families or small groups subsisting on staples – date back to surveys carried out since the middle of the century now drawing to an end. One day, on the banks of the Gaamá River – having crossed a long tract of *várzea* floodland forest blanketed with tall trees – I and my research colleagues arrived at the banks of a pool where a family of simple mixed-race *caboclos* lived in an adobe shack, taking care of an undeveloped estate for a merciless absentee landlord. Amazed by the poverty and the solitary life of this riverbank family, we asked some questions about the daily life of this couple and their four small children. They were starving, while living between the rich forest and the river, allowed to use only a tiny cassava plantation carved out of the side of a hill.

The isolation of poverty-stricken families or small groups has been a sad reality throughout many centuries of social life in Brazil. Solitude is found almost everywhere all over this vast land. This is far worse than the conditions facing the indigenous peoples living in their huts and bound to a culture of survival. Or even their later successors, living in clandestine settlements seeking refuge from an oppressive society.

As urban networks grow denser, with highways running between them, new relationships are being built up between town and countryside that will help ease this inhumane isolation. However, the great forests cut through by rivers, streams and inlets still shelter a dramatic set of cases consisting of islets and mini-islets of humankind. This situation is repeated for different reasons in the more rustic parts of the *sertão* drylands of Northeast Brazil.

Based on our meditations and experience of the dramas of isolation and the suffering human geography of traditional communities in the heartlands of Brazil, we can better appreciate the situation of some extractivist reserves that are being upgraded through a series of improvements, ushering in hope and respect. They include extractivist reserves in Acre and the RECA Project on the border between Rondônia and Acre States, the Brazilnut Cooperatives on the banks of the Jari River in Amapá State, and the rational use by smallholders of the rich soils of the vast alluvial floodplains of the Amazon and Solimões Rivers, together with well-planned multicrop plantations along the banks of the Acre River and its tributaries that supply the towns of Rio Branco and Boca do Acre. These are the embryos of an ecologically self-sustainable economy that can multiply and become more profitable. To do so, the presence of enlightened, democratic leaders is required.

These experiences are directly contrasted to the devastating and almost useless activities of the huge agribusinesses set up in Amazonia with subsidies from the Amazon Development Superintendency (SUDAM) – which is an institution guilty of the worst corruption in the history of these Regional Superintendencies that were set up to even out inequalities in regional development throughout Brazil. Inadequately staffed and incompetent to assess projects, these institutions were happy to work with speculators and powerful fund-raisers through impractical or even fake projects, most of which resulted in the savage criminal devastation of biodiversity in Amazonia, showing no interest in the necessary resources.

Interdisciplinary Approach

Once again, young people endowed with permanent intellectual curiosity are requesting their teachers for a quick and valid definition of science. The questions continue. Science is always innocent. It is always ethical. And then the simplistic argument arises: so what about Hiroshima and Nagasaki? How can bio-weapons be justified? Based on these lines of thought and stimulated by a steady fire of questions, an atmosphere of disbelief is engendered, with anticipated disapproval. This is why the challenge must be dealt with patiently.

Initially, it should always be recalled that the basic attributes of the human condition include three values and principles: man is the only living being on the face of the planet able to (re)trace the history of our species through widely-varying time and space, including our own (pre)history. This is followed by his capacity to produce cultural values in a wide variety of sectors: logic, sociology, technology, the arts, music and even play, with principles and values that depend on producing and polishing knowledge in a wide variety of domains of science: the Universe, the Earth, Life, Materials, Water, the Atmosphere, Biodiversity, Humankind, Society, Economics, Genetics, Health and the Biosciences.
It is important to bear in mind the inter-disciplinary links among these various fields of human knowledge. There are sciences (perhaps most of them) that involve mandatory interdisciplinary structures. Outstanding

among them is Ecology, which extends into Biogeography and Geoecology. Similarly, Geomorphology involves the Earth Sciences (Geology and Pedology), Material Sciences, Climatology, Limnology, Hydrology, Ecology and Geoecology. Internalised transdisciplinary structures are also attributes of Biochemistry or Physics and Chemistry.

At the crossroads between the ecological sciences and the geographical and space sciences are high-level concepts of interdisciplinarity, such as the ecological concept of total space, studies of the urban metabolism and above all studies forecasting the physical, ecological, social and psychosocial impacts. All this does not even take into account the art+science of forecasting impacts, based on a wide variety of time-frames extending through an uncertain and variable future. Despite the immense and almost impossible challenges of forecasting forthcoming events, particularly in view of the vast time-scales involved, these are tasks that can and should be undertaken, moving ahead in this direction and tackling them whenever possible.

MORAL AND GLOBAL CHALLENGES OF THE III MILLENNIUM: HOW TO IMPLEMENT THE EARTH CHARTER

Patricia MORALES (Argentina/The Netherlands)

Introduction

This paper is dedicated to analysing how the implementation of the Earth Charter could be encouraged, in keeping with the inherent characteristics of this document, with the Universal Declaration of Human Rights as a vital precedent and taking as the next objective its adoption by the United Nations in 2002 as soft law. To do so, the following topics are listed: initially, the Earth Charter is interpreted as a shared global system of ethics, respecting and caring for humankind and the Earth. Then the Universal Declaration of Human Rights is analysed as the source of inspiration for the Earth Charter examining the effects of its implementation. The third section examines the principal elements in the implementation of the Universal Declaration of Human Rights, explored in the light of the elements of the Earth Charter. Then a brief comparison is drawn between the Earth Charter and other global ethics documents in terms of implementation; finally, the presentation to the UN in 2002. In parallel to the UN Conference on Sustainable Development, this is a vital element for guaranteeing the implementation of the Earth Charter, and to do so, it is suggested that its similarity with the Universal Declaration of Human Rights should be stressed, in addition with cooperation with other global documents and a positive interrelationship be built up between the provisions of national constitutions and the contents of the Earth Charter.

The Earth Charter (2000) is a document that lays down guideline principles for global ethics tackling the challenges of contemporary interdependence. This document is the outcome of a collective process of worldwide consultations in order to achieve sustainable development. Representatives of the sciences, international law and philosophical and religious traditions from all over the world were invited to participate in drafting it. Its theoretical sources included the declarations and proceedings of the Seven UN Conferences, Declarations and Codes of Ethics, Government Declarations and Treaties of the Peoples, with real-life examples of sustainability taken as a practical source.

In 1992, the UN Conference on Sustainable Development and the Environment was held in Rio de Janeiro, and drew Agenda 21 on a consensual basis, as the guidelines for sustainable development. A Declaration of Global Ethics to underpin this sustainability-based project, which had already been requested by the UN World Commission on the Environment and Development in 1987, remained outstanding yet again. Through joint efforts launched in 1994, the Earth Council (Maurice Strong), the Green Cross (Mikhael Gorbachev) and the Netherlands Government (Ruud Lubbers) as well as thousands of individuals and experts from many institutions, the Earth Charter was completed in March 2000, and officially launched at the Palais de la Paix at The Hague, the Netherlands, on June 29, 2000.

Once launched, the formulation and consultation stage made way for its implementation, in all its complexity. Its submission to the UN Assembly-General was scheduled for 2002, the same as the UN Conference on Sustainable Development (Rio+10).

The Earth Charter consists of a Preamble, four parts, and an Epilogue:

The *preamble* shows us how the interdependence and fragility of the Earth to which we belong as part of "one human family and one Earth community", requires us to take a moral decision in order to "bring forth a sustainable global society founded on respect for nature, universal human rights, economic justice, and a culture of peace". The positive and negative elements of global interdependence and particularly the worldwide environment crisis and the potential of science and technology offer an unprecedented framework for human decisions, with unquestionable moral demands.
An affinity can be noted in the introduction to the Earth Charter and the Universal Declaration of Human Rights, as expressed in the Preamble to the Earth Charter: "Whereas lack of awareness and neglect of human rights has resulted in acts of barbarism that outrage the conscience of human kind, and as the highest aspiration of Man has been proclaimed as being the advent of a world in which human beings, freed from fear and poverty, enjoy freedom of speech and freedom of belief; whereas it is essential that human rights should be protected by a system of Law ..." (Universal Declaration of Human Rights, Preamble). Both documents arise in response to historic demands to reshape human actions, due to the vast size of the dangers that surplus or harmful human activities have prompted. Human kind found itself in an unprecedented situation, due to the widespread atrocities committed during World War II. With the Universal

Declaration of Human Rights, it aspires to a world where human rights reign supreme, together with the fundamental freedoms, and through this, a moral decision is symbolised, promoting peace and security all over the world.

The Earth Charter reflects aspirations leading to a sustainable world as a pre-condition for human rights and fundamental freedoms, for both current and future generations, with respect for the Earth as a whole: "The choice is ours: form a global partnership to care for Earth and one another or risk the destruction of ourselves and the diversity of life. Fundamental changes are needed in our values, institutions, and ways of living" (Earth Charter, Preamble).

In its four Parts, the Earth Charter outlines the principles and grounds for rights over the Earth. *Part I* of the Earth Charter lists the four general principles that essentially stipulate "care and respect for the community of life". A core element in this postulate is respect for human dignity, translated into human rights. Entitled Ecological Integrity, *Part II* contains the specific principles for protecting and conserving eco-systems, and summarizes proposals for curtailing human actions, particularly with regard to production, consumption and reproduction standards, as well as scientific and technological activities. *Part III* supplements the required responsible actions, focused on the human community. The target of "social and economic justice" is urged through the eradication of poverty, rectification of economic actions and gender equality, while condemning discrimination. *Part IV,* entitled Democracy, Non-Violence and Peace, lays down the essential foundations for human kind to regulate its own living conditions, with adequate governance, education, tolerance, ethics of non-violence and a culture of peace.

The *Epilogue* is a broad-ranging and comprehensive invitation to implement the principles of the Earth Charter, stating that: "To fulfil this promise, we must commit ourselves to adopt and promote the values and objectives of the Charter. This requires a change of mind and heart. It requires a new sense of global interdependence and universal responsibility. We must imaginatively develop and apply the vision of a sustainable way of life locally, nationally, regionally, and globally."

The Earth Charter as a Shared System of Ethics

The Earth Charter is a project that is open for sharing by the entire human family. Its principles are possible only when global "sharing" can be consolidated through these three paths: shared values, agreement on theory; shared responsibilities, action guidelines; and the shared earnings resulting from these activities.

The Earth Charter strives to consolidate a system of ethics based on shared values for a global society, based on universality through multiculturality. Through multicultural processes of dialogue and understanding, it can finally be made clear that there are values shares by the majority of the world's cultures. The concepts outlined in the Earth Charter correspond to this phase of global dialogue, where universality is managing to firm up its position through multiculturality. Both acquire legitimacy through the respectful meeting of cultures.

This involves sharing values in order to consolidate global ethics for an interdependent world: "We urgently need a shared vision of *basic values to provide an ethical foundation for the emerging world community*. Therefore, together in hope we affirm the following interdependent principles for a sustainable way of life as a common standard by which the conduct of all individuals, organizations, businesses, governments, and transnational institutions is to be guided and assessed" (Earth Charter, Preamble).

All social players are invited to participate in this act of multicultural sharing, as proven by the Epilogue: "Our cultural diversity is a precious heritage and different cultures will find their own distinctive ways to realize the vision. We must deepen and expand the global dialogue that generated the Earth Charter, for we have much to learn from the ongoing collaborative search for truth and wisdom" (Earth Charter, Preamble).

In contrast – and due to the historic conditions of its formulation – the Universal Declaration of Human Rights is not the outcome of a full multicultural and multifaith dialogue and consensus. The acknowledgement of cultures came later, peaking at the UN Conference of Human Rights held in Vienna in 1993, which reaffirmed the universal nature of human rights and validated them on a transcultural basis. In its Preamble, the Universal Declaration of Human Rights lists universal values from the viewpoint of the peoples of the United Nations, achieving a common concept: "Whereas the peoples of the United Nations have reaffirmed in the Charter their faith in the fundamental rights of man, dignity and the value of the human person, as well as equal rights for men and women... whereas a common concept of these rights and freedoms is of the utmost importance for full compliance with this commitment,... the Assembly-

General proclaims this Universal Declaration of Human Rights as a common idea ...." (Universal Declaration of Human Rights, Preamble).

On the other hand, the Earth Charter issues an invitation to accept and ethically share the responsibility for all, in taking decisions and implementing actions. This involves active participation in transparent democratic processes taking decisions, striving to ensure fair representation of the many different sectors of society: gender, age, culture, races and traditions, to the extent that "we are at once citizens of different nations and of one world in which the local and global are linked. *Everyone shares responsibility for the present and future well-being of the human family and the larger living world.* The spirit of human solidarity and kinship with all life is strengthened when we live with reverence for the mystery of being, gratitude for the gift of life, and humility regarding the human place in nature" (Earth Charter, Preamble).

This responsibility is exercised through a process of human solidarity that is not curtailed by the limits of the current human family, but rather extends through to future generations and the community of life, as expressed by the Earth Charter: "Towards this end, it is imperative that we, the peoples of Earth, *declare our responsibility to one another*, to the greater community of life, and to future generations" (Earth Charter, Preamble). This states that: "Every individual, family, organization, and community has a vital role to play. The arts, sciences, religions, educational institutions, media, businesses, nongovernmental organizations, and governments are all called to offer creative leadership" (Earth Charter, Epilogue).

Considering that the cooperation between civil society, governments and the private sector should stress correct governance, the Earth Charter makes explicit mention of the word "implementation" in its principles, when referring to the responsibility of the governments to build up a sustainable global community, affirming: "...the nations of the world must renew their commitment to the United Nations, fulfil their obligations under existing international agreements, and support the implementation of Earth Charter principles with an international legally binding instrument on environment and development (Earth Charter, Epilogue). This rates the "implementation" of the principles as "Hard Law" through a tool to be ratified and complied with, like a convention. Here the dual model would be followed, between the Universal Declaration of Human Rights (Soft Law) and the International Convention on Civil and Political Rights (1969) together with the International Convention of Economic, Civil and Political Rights (1969) (Hard Law).

The Universal Declaration of Human Rights appeared as a proclamation of governments acknowledging universally valid human rights for each individual on the Planet, "as the Member States have agreed to ensure, in cooperation with the United Nations Organisation, effective universal respect for the fundamental rights and freedoms of man, the common ideal for which all the peoples and nations should strive, in order to ensure that both individuals and institutions should be constantly inspired, and promoting through teaching and education respect for these rights and freedoms, and assuring their acknowledgement through progressive national and international measures, together with their universal, effective application among the peoples of the Member States, as well as among those of the territories placed under their jurisdiction" (Universal Declaration of Human Rights, Preamble).

The Earth Charter requires that social and economic justice, or sustainable development should be ushered in, achieved on the one hand at the *intra*generational level and on the other at the *inter*generational level. This is only possible when human actions respect the natural limits on production and consumption. "Sustainable development" was defined by the UN World Commission for the Environment and Development in 1987 as "development that meets the need of the current generation without adversely affecting the capacity of future generations to meet their own needs".

With this "sharing" which also includes future generations and criticizes the uneven contemporary distribution of goods, this extends well beyond the sphere of the Universal Declaration of Human Rights: "*The benefits of development are not shared equitably and the gap between rich and poor is widening.* Injustice, poverty, ignorance, and violent conflict are widespread and the cause of great suffering" (Earth Charter, Preamble).

The Soft Law Model of the Universal Declaration of Human Rights for the Earth Charter

Over fifty years after it was first drawn up and translated into over 300 languages, the Universal Declaration of Human Rights is the most significant predecessor of the Earth Charter. This Declaration is the core moral commitment for the peoples of the world to ensure universal human rights, which are being implemented in many different ways.

– This document is the cornerstone of UN Hard Law, and its contents translate the Hard Law in the international conventions on rights, as well as other international covenants, declarations and agreements.

– Most national constitutions have been reworded in the wake of political systems that wielded power unlawfully, and characteristically include some excerpts from the Universal Declaration of Human Rights, which in some cases is even ranked higher than National Law. When the provisions in a National Constitution establish the rights and duties of its citizens, this inclusion is very significant in terms of implementation.
The declaration is a key factor in many educational curricula, and is also included in formal and non-formal education programmes; it is also used when drawing up codes of ethics. As a guideline for shaping and assessing scientific, economic, political and social actions, the Universal Declaration of Human Rights has played an unparalleled role.

– Many non-government organisations also encourage its application. The most famous case is that of Amnesty International, which adopted this Declaration as the key document for demanding human rights worldwide, demanding the abolition of the death penalty, the elimination of torture and the release of political prisoners.

Initial Phase of Implementing the Earth Charter

The Earth Charter heightens awareness of contemporary global problems, and suggests that we assume a moral commitment for tackling the risk of destroying the world's eco-systems, inviting us to firm up its principles through sustainable implementation at all levels, and by all social sectors. In the Universal Declaration of Human Rights, the Earth Charter finds its most powerful inspiration, guiding its way from the enunciation to the implementation of ethical principles, in addition to a broader-ranging view that is inclusive, multicultural and participative. Compared to the Universal Declaration of Human Rights, the scope of the field of implementation of the Earth Charter is far more complex and broad-ranging. As a project for a sustainable future, it requires the participation of all social sectors, from local through to global; it extends from immediate impact in contact with the Earth on which we stand, through to its consequences in outer space; and it also includes many widely-varying individual and group actions (not only political, educational and social, but also technical such as production and consumption).

The Draft International Convention on the Environment

As formulated by the International Union for Nature Conservation, development requires an exhaustive list of the principles to be complied with by the Nation States in order to usher in sustainable development and environmental protection, and has been formally submitted to the United Nations. Should a convention be accepted as such by the United Nations, the next step is ratification by the minimum number of countries required for it to be implemented as UN Hard Law.

One way of fostering the adoption of the Earth Charter is to compare it with National Constitutions and other legislations. This could prove very convincing for the implementation process, based on the compatibility and mutual support found among many recent constitutions in terms of human rights, the environment, sustainable development, peace, and the Earth Charter. A review of some National Constitutions shows that most of the principles of the Earth Charter are illustrated by several National Constitutions; the principles that are definitively represented cover wild life and other living beings; the younger the constitutions, the more clearly the principles of the Earth Charter are formulated and represented. It can be noted that the Earth Charter has similar possibilities to the Universal Declaration of Human Rights for use as core document for drawing up or reviewing National Constitutions, and the Earth Charter can also function as a meeting point for national legislations, with regard to human rights, the environment and sustainable development.

A campaign is being run to endorse the Earth Charter, which is gathering support from both individuals and institutions. Once endorsed, the Earth Charter will take on the status of a treaty of the peoples, and a guideline for civil society. The Earth Charter is being endorsed at meetings and conferences, and is also being promoted through the communications media and education, with the support of universities and non-governmental institutions being particularly outstanding, such as the International Council for Local Environment Initiatives (ICLEI), indigenous organisations on various continents, the Amazon Parliament, and many towns and cities.

A suggestion that was also approved in 2000 is to set up the Ombudsman Centre for Sustainable Development, as a common effort undertaken by the Earth Council, the International Union for Nature Conservation and the Peace University. This international function provides assistance in settling conflicts over sustainable development among countries. It has already adopted the Earth Charter as one of its guidelines for assessing situations and proposing solutions. It has already begun to function in certain cases, such as Bolivia and Korea.

The Earth Charter and Cooperation with Other Global Documents for Implementation

In response to the risks and possibilities of global interdependence, the appearance of documents outlying global ethics has been very significant over the past few years. Cooperation with other global documents is also growing into a useful element for the development of the Earth Charter.

– The Earth Summit held in Rio de Janeiro in 1992 symbolised global awareness that environmental protection, management of natural resources, and the implementation of human rights in all aspects were closely linked; an international process of dialogue and consensus began here, working towards the establishment of common standards for achieving sustainable development, which resulted in *Agenda 21*. The Earth Charter offers value guidelines and moral principles for Agenda 21. In turn, it is supplemented by National Councils for Sustainable Development that are set up to develop national sustainability plans, and could provide a vital springboard for the implementation of the Earth Charter. These Councils are dedicated to assessing and implementing Agenda 21, and translating it to the national level, and the Earth Charter offers them a global overview of values that enrich this process for Agenda 21. These National Councils have a significant role to play in the organisation of the UN Conference on Sustainable Development in Johannesburg in 2002.

– The *Millennium Declaration* (issued in September 2000) and the *Declaration and Action Programme for the Millennium Forum* (issued in May 2000) are very important documents that formulate the demands of the contemporary global situation. The former is the document drawn up by government representatives and the latter represents civil society, both containing significant proposals for sustainable development as a system of global ethics. It should also be stressed that the Millennium Forum (2000) called upon the governments to endorse the Earth Charter through the UN General Assembly, and urged civil society to adopt this document in order to promote values and actions underpinning sustainable development.

An element benefiting the Earth Charter is that as a Treaty of the Peoples and a document to be submitted to the UN General Assembly, it is located in a no-man's land between these two documents, aspiring to play a mediatory function as a document of civil society and as a UN Soft Law.

Global Policy: Global Proposals Guided by Ethics

The following elements are te be taken in consideration during the presentation of the Earth Charter to the UN Assembly-General in 2002:

– *Millennium Declaration:* commitment to firm measures by the Heads of State to provide solutions to global problems such as poverty, pollution and violation of human rights.

– *Millennium Forum:* innovative proposals for implementing rights designed to reserve the adverse effects of globalisation, putting forward proposals from control and prevention institutions.

– *Earth Charter:* general principles to be supplemented through implementation measures, together with other projects such as the Sustainable Development Ombudsman.

– *Manifesto 2000:* with the support of UNESCO and an endorsement campaign, this initiative has achieved unprecedented support. The clarity and concision with which its principles have been drawn up streamline this process. This Manifesto urges a culture of peace, and one of its six principles is dedicated to respect for Nature. The contents of both documents are fully compatible, although with different objectives and languages. The Earth Charter consequently finds a supportive companion in the Manifesto 2000, moving steadily ahead along the same path.
Global interdependence has demonstrated quite clearly that the economy cannot function without a clear, well-defined context of ethics and legality. The Universal Declaration of Human Rights and other international documents are used to provide solutions to problems not covered by the law, and damages that assail human dignity.

– In response to the inadequacy of the legal tools guiding economic actions, the UN Secretary-General proposed the *Global Contract* (1999) inviting the private sector to participate with NGOs in order to build bridges between economics and respect for human rights for the current and future generations, and the Earth itself.
The Global Contract responds to a pressing need to moralize the economy, but has encountered adverse reactions in a variety of sectors. In turn, the Earth Charter offers a broader-ranging and integrative overview, endowing economic activities with a social, environmental, civil, political and cultural framework. The Earth Charter devotes one of its sections to social justice and economics, allowing economic activities to be viewed in perspective,

driven by global demands and contemporary models. An element favouring the Earth Charter is that it is a proposal addressed to all players in society, of which the economic sector is a part.

– The *Universal Declaration of Global Ethics* has been playing a significant role in finding common ground for many different religious beliefs, as an innovative agreement for ushering in universal principles seeking common foundations and fostering the culture of peace among the people. This drive attempts to produce firm results from implementation by counterbalancing unfamiliarity or rivalry among many different beliefs through an enriching dialogue urging peace. Conceptual agreements are being reached through multiculturality and inter-faith dialogue. The Universal Declaration of Human Rights is a cosmo-anthropocentric system of global ethics introduced through an agreement among the world's secular and religious sectors, in parallel to the Earth Charter. This system of global ethics is the outcome of the most broad-ranging consultation process ever undertaken for a global document.

– Drawn up to celebrate the 50th anniversary of the Universal Declaration of Human Rights, the *Declaration of Human Duties and Responsibilities*, has been widely welcomed for its efforts to supplement this Declaration through listing the duties and responsibilities that ensure the implementation of human rights at the global level. Its quality, clarity and clear enunciation of these duties and responsibilities was greatly appreciated by UN Representatives, NGOs, representatives of the arts and sciences, and leading politicians. For the moment, its implementation is being urged through conferences, university education courses, and communications media.
This Declaration and the Earth Charter find common ground in the emphasis laid on universal human responsibility as a condition for implementing universal human rights. Cooperation for its implementation at the level of shared responsibility could well constitute a second area of common ground.

Presentation to the UN Assembly-General in 2002, as a Key Element

The adoption of the Earth Charter by the UN Assembly-General in 2002 will basically depend on the formal support that it receives from the representatives of the Nation States. The fact that this document could well be adopted as UN Soft Law would make it easier to implement its provisions.

As a final comment on this article, we note the elements that should be taken under consideration during the UN presentation process in 2002:

- The common elements between the Earth Charter and the Universal Declaration of Human Rights, and the continuation of the fresh ground broken by this Declaration in order to ensure the full implementation of human rights, with a view to intra and inter-generational equity;
- Its compatibility with other contemporary global ethics documents;
- The affinity between the wording of National Constitutions and the Earth Charter in many cases, which will be strengthened through the formal adoption of the Earth Charter;
- The similarities found among many national Constitutions containing recent provisions on environmental rights, development and peace, with the shared adoption of the Earth Charter strengthening cooperation on these topics, transcending national borders;
- The complementary aspects through which certain principles in the Earth Charter are included in a group of constitutions, with other principles included in another cluster of constitutions. This could be viewed positively as an invitation to rethink the standards and values system from a broader-based standpoint, understanding the Earth Charter as a broad-ranging and comprehensive document;
- The assistance offered by the Earth Charter to National Constitutions that have not yet been updated or renewed: it could be argued that its adoption would serve as a catalyst for reviewing the issues in these Constitutions. In either case, a country whose constitution has not yet been updated would not be exempt from legal responses to such vital issues, due to this omission.

Documents Mentioned

Agenda 21, issued by the UN Conference on the Environment and Development (1992)
Earth Charter (2000)
Declaration of Human Duties and Responsibilities (Valencia 1998), presented to UNESC
UN Millennium Declaration (September, 2000)
Declaration of Vienna, UN Conference on Human Rights (1993)
Universal Declaration of Global Ethics, issued by the Council for the Parliament of the World's Religions (1993)
Universal Declaration of Human Rights, adopted by the UN General Assembly (1948)
Declaration and Action Programme of the Millennium Forum – We the People: Strengthening United Nations for the XXI century (May 2000)

The Global Contract, proposed by the UN Secretary-General to the World Economic Forum (Davos 1999)
Manifesto 2000 for a Culture of Peace and Non-Violence, (UNESCO 2000)

AGRARIAN SECURITY AND LAND PROBLEMS IN PUNO

Ricardo VEGA POSADA (Peru)

Land Problems in Puno

Over the past fifteen years, 1,010,992 hectares in Puno have been transferred from associative enterprises set up through Agrarian Reform to 641 communities established through the Restructuring Process. Having also launched the breakdown and self-liquidation procedures for the 729,319 hectares shared out among 42 associative enterprises, the process of awarding land titles and straightening out the situation of rural properties should take place in both sectors, in what are now 1,274 peasant communities, and the remaining SAIS, CAPS and ERPS, as well as the rest of the farmland units. Titles should now be issued for all farmland and other areas in Puno that should be reorganised in legal terms.

Obviously, no-one will invest, develop and protect land without secure title, far less launch an Andes Land Protection and National Water Use Process on this legal basis. Initially, this role should be taken up by the peasant communities and their organisations, including long-established renewed or restructured entities, as well as their more recent counterparts that have arisen in the countryside over the past fourteen years. Local (municipal), governments and concerted inter-institutional efforts also play key roles in this Local Rural Sustainable Development Process; this means tackling land-based problems, in parallel to running soil and water protection programs, while striving to ensure a well-balanced environment.

Although the State and other levels of government are assigned greater responsibility in this process of straightening out the legal aspects of land titles and ownership, as they must implement agrarian development policies for the Sierra mountain region, the roots of our Andean culture should be empowered to undertake the political exercise of democracy, claiming and fighting for the civil rights assigned to us by society.

Looking at modernity, Andean culture, democracy, politics and civil rights for all: "we have plenty of cement but little has been built". Demands for decentralisation and new regional governments are appearing on the agenda. Respecting Community Autonomy, Community Reorganisation Processes in both the "old" communities (established before 1985) and "new" communities (established after 1985) should work towards strengthening the rural institutional structure, supported by peasant communities, rural district governments and peasant organisations, exercising civil and political rights in the countryside.

Agrarian Reform in Puno

The implementation of Agrarian Reform appears in several different ways. Through Law No. 15037 (Belaunde – 1964) which covered 38 estates holding 141,155 hectares; Decree Law No. 17716 (Velasco – 1969) covering 1451 estates holding 2,094,479.45 hectares; areas not covered: 315,054 hectares.

The Table below gives an overview of land awards through Agrarian Reform (Decree Law No. 17716):

Awards	*Hectares*	*Properties*	*Beneficiaries*
– 23 SAIS	1,024,476,42	553	7,183
– 14 CAPs	498,416,94	120	2,328
– 2 PRE-CAPs	24,805	2	55
– 5 ERPS	217,417,78	172	958
– 39 Peasant Groups	82,567,48	66	1,104
– 36 GAST	27,419,96	39	501
– 76 Peasant Communities	58,551,37	121	14,714
– 243 INDIVIDUALS	43,464,86	243	243
– 15 Assignment for Use	16,778,59	15	–
+ CENECAMP	239,44	2	22
TOTAL	1'994,137,84	1,333	27,108

Pending in Court: 118 estates holding 100,341.61 hectares
Source: Ministry of Agriculture, Puno, March 1985

Although it is quite clear that Agrarian Reform has swept away the huge ranches known as *haciendas,* most of the medium-sized land-owners at the time of the awards ignored much of the peasant population, settled in the 486 acknowledged communities (June 1985) and over 500 shared facilities. Out of some 1,000 peasant bases, only 76 communities have benefited, although with 88.5% of the land. The awards benefited 10,546 families in

23 SAIS, 16 CAPS and 5 ERPS; peasant communities received 2.9% hectares for 14,714 families.

The implementation of Agrarian Reform in Puno was prompted by a crisis situation among the associative enterprises due to oversized and unwieldy farms that were unmanageable on a centralised basis. Internal conflicts began to break out between the participants and Civil Service bureaucrats handling administrative activities related to wages. Management was weak, with chaotic administration. Land conflicts sprang up with peasant communities, and the lack of agrarian policies for the Sierra mountain region became very apparent, particularly after 1980.

Taking over the Land and Democratic Restructuring

Faced by unfair and unjust Agrarian Reform and wearied by memoranda, claims and complaints, on December 13, 1985, ten communities in the Macarí and Santa Rosa districts, headed by FUCAM and the FDCP, took over more than 10,000 hectares from the ERPS at Kunurana, calling for the democratic restructuring of the associative enterprises in favour of the peasant communities.

This peasant struggle was supported by the people of Puno; its repercussions in the local and national press prompted the government of Alan García Pérez to take firm steps on these calls for land. Just 54 days after the historic land take-overs at Macarí and Santa Rosa, on February 5, 1986, the García Administration issued Supreme Decrees 005 and 006, restructuring the associative enterprises in Puno.

Through Supreme Decree 006, Alan García appointed a Restructuring Committee in Lima that spent all 1986 negotiating with the leaders of the associative enterprises. It implemented a disorderly restructuring process that became entangled in red tape, replacing the democratic participation of the peasants and their organisations by its populist "*rimanacuys*".

Faced with the bureaucratic and long-drawn-out preliminary restructuring process, the Puno Peasant Department Federation (FDCP – *Federación Departamental de Campesinos de Puno*) embarked on a massive struggle for land that continued from January through June 1987 throughout almost the entire Puno Department. The squatter protests and marches of May 19 resulted in 172 communities receiving over 360,000 hectares. On 24 June, President García Pérez completed the Restructuring Process and began to award titles for land assigned to the enterprises.

These peasant land struggles in Puno were put down by the Army and Police. Additionally, from March 1986 through 1992, the *Sendero Luminoso* rebels clashed with peasant leaders through unsuccessful attempts to take over the leadership of the struggle for land. In the course of this dirty war, leaders such as Pedro Laura, Porfirio Suni, Tomas Quispe, Dionisio Cantani and Zenobio Huarsaya were murdered, in addition to countless prisoners and injuries.
The practical outcome of these land struggles and movements is a Restructuring Process that has delivered 1,010,992.14 hectares to 641 communities and cooperatives that are being set up.

This Restructuring Process is encountering many different problems: restructured titles were handed over without defining the plots of land, borders and markers, with their respective records and plans not properly cleaned up. These 1,010,992.14 hectares that have not been properly straightened out are the main land problem today in Puno. This process was not carried out in an efficient manner (optimum enterprise sizes were not specified and farms were broken up); it was bureaucratic and discussed with the management of the associative enterprises; there was no participation by the communities or organisations. It did not prompt any rural development plan for the resulting community and associative enterprises, which resulted in widespread chaos in the production sector, with the breakdown of enterprises, other than some exceptions that will be analysed.

Current Land Ownership Problems in Puno, Peru

The Land Act (Law No. 26505) that came into effect in 1995 and its application through the Special Land Title Program (PETT – *Programa Especial de Titulación de Tierras*) assigned priority to only the original lands for the 1,274 communities, leaving aside the legal and physical re-organisation of the 1,000,000 hectares covered by the Restructuring Process. Some areas are still awaiting solutions for matters related to demarcation and borders, with lawsuits under way. In turn, these are the areas where the main land division trends have been appearing undertaken in a disorderly manner with no legal backing, excluding the poorest peasants and in many cases running counter to the institutional framework of the Peasant Community. However, this does not undermine the fair aspirations of cases where decisions have been taken in a non-exclusionary and democratic manner, awarding individual land titles through sub-division processes run by the peasant community or self-liquidation. The case of Puno is very specific, because the communities have almost tripled since 1985 through to the present date, with communities now known as "old" and "new". Puno became the administrative region (*Departamento*) with the largest number of peasant communities in Peru: 1,274 according the III Rural Census (1994).

On the other hand, individual land ownership processes launched for peasants and farmers have been causing problems through overlapping titles and registered plans. In many cases, legal loopholes feed the private appetites of a few petty bureaucrats, causing conflict and instability in rural areas.

Five Years after the Land Act came into Effect (Law No. 26505)

Trends in the "New" Communities

The trend in the 662 "new" communities is towards newly-launched land share-out processes that often fail to meet legal requirements and in many cases exclude the poorest sectors. Set up after the land take-overs at Macari and Santa Rosa and the 1985 – 1986 Restructuring Process, these originally landless "old" communities, with no lands assigned to them through Agrarian Reform, were established with lands under the Restructuring Process since 1986; in some cases these communities have opted for liquidation.

Trends in "Old" Communities

In turn, the 542 "old" communities established since the land take-overs at Macari and Santa Rosa in 1985 and the Restructuring Process, are maintaining their peasant communities in most cases, dividing out part or all of the areas set aside for restructuring and strengthening communal levels according to the type of land held – whether original land divisions, community-based or mixed, through agrarian reform, or purchase and sale. It is in this sector that the "old" communities have been implementing intensive community modernisation and reorganisation processes, with interesting experiences making good use of their resources.

A Community Reorganisation Process under Way

Consequently, a community reorganisation process is appearing in Puno, with trends divided between the "old" and "new" communities (before or after the land take-overs at Macari and Santa Rosa in 1985, and the Restructuring Process). As these processes are compulsory, violent and exclude the poorer peasants, they result in marked contradictions; at places where the community takes decisions, interesting experiences have been taking place through associations of land share title-holders through production lines or sectors, while on the other hand community-run pilot production centres are being set up, or community enterprises that are being resized and reduced.

There are loopholes in Law No. 26505, particularly for its implementation in the Sierra mountain region, and even more particularly in Puno, due to unresolved problems with the Restructuring Process, which is why a Legal Provision of Exception is required for Puno.
The problems encountered among the communities with individual land titles, added to the unresolved problems of demarcating borders and straightening out the Restructuring Process are worsened by loopholes, with a lack of land title regulations for application in the Sierra mountain region.

Based on the Land Act (Law No. 26505), since 1985, the Special Land Title Program (PETT) has assigned high priority to awarding title for their original lands to peasant communities, leaving aside the conflicts prompted by the Restructuring Process at places where the main land division and/or individual land title trends are occurring. Five years after the implementation of Law No. 26505, a Legal Provision of Exception is required for Puno.

At the Communities settled on the original land divisions, where land titles have been awarded under the Special Land Title Program (PETT), severe conflicts are breaking out over community land titles that on the one hand include ancestral titles owned by peasant community families, and on the other, several cases of medium and small land-owners that have been included in community lands, while failing to settle problems that are still pending over land bordering the restructuring areas. This causes disorderly community breakdown processes, undermining the rural institutional framework.

Problems Involved with Land Protection

To an increasing extent, soil is deteriorating due to depletion. Overgrazing and improper land use in terms of water are speeding up erosion and desertification, leaving the soil unprotected. The isolated efforts of the Pronomachs and other special projects are insufficient, without the active participation of peasants and their communities protecting the Earth, Water and the Environment.
Inter-institutional agreements are required among the sectors involved with this issue, as well as the peasants and farmers, in order to move ahead from uncoordinated, isolated efforts.

Our Land is being Depleted and our Natural Resources are Deteriorating due to Soil Erosion

Among other factors, the deterioration of farmlands is caused by overgrazing, mainly herds of sheep that selectively consume only the more succulent species, preventing their natural propagation and resulting in the consequent impoverishment of pastures.

- Saline Soils. A marked increase in the salt content of farmlands is being noted, due mainly to the use of improper irrigation techniques and fertilizers.
- Air Pollution. This is due to sulphurous waste gases emitted by the copper smelters and affecting the eco-system.
- Water Pollution. Rivers are being polluted by discharges of liquid wastes and gases from mining complexes containing reactive agents and slag that affect plants and wildlife, as well as hydro-biological species living in these zones.

Biological Components Are also Deteriorating

– Modification and Pollution of the Habitats of Hydro-Biological Resources
Pollution by liquid wastes from mining and metallurgy complexes (heavy metals) is poisoning snails and shellfish, affecting bays and hills along the coastline and resulting in permanent desertification.

– Reduction in Forest Wildlife
Due mainly to poaching, pollution, destruction and/or the physical modification of their habitat, these processes are threatening many species with extinction.
In the mountains: rheas, wildcats etc.
In the forests: bears, wolves, alligators, lizards etc.

At the same time, many unidentified and unprotected animal, plant and fish species are being threatened by extinction through illegal trade in biodiversity that is driven by biogenetics, while still lacking any type of scientific evaluation.

Alternative Secure Agrarian Techniques and Proposed Solutions

Quest for a Secure Agrarian System

This project stresses the need for legal and physical reorganisation carried out in a democratic and non-exclusionary manner, issuing land titles for all farms and smallholdings in Puno, particularly the 1,000,000 hectares covered by the Restructuring Process. This would ensure greater juridical stability for rural areas, in parallel to developing a pro-active land resource protection program that strives to halt or reverse soil and water depletion with environmental degradation, while endowing our proposals for rural local development with sustainability. Community reorganisation processes under way should be accepted, respecting community autonomy.

This means that our suggestions urging a secure agrarian system are closely connected to our aspirations and needs to live and work on lands whose borders are demarcated by law, with their natural resources properly protected from depletion and degradation. This would endow the agricultural sector in Puno with stability and sustainability.

Main Demands

- Require the central government to issue a new law (Supreme Decree of Exception to Puno) regulating the application of the Land Act (Law No. 26505) and undertaking the physical and legal reorganisation of the 1,000,000 hectares covered by the restructuring process initially. Finally, it should issue land titles for all farms and smallholdings in Puno, accepting community reorganisation processes under way and respecting community autonomy (Legal Instrument).

- Require the central government to prepare a new Rural Records Plan for Puno, using state-of-the-art technology: radar satellite photographs and Geographical Information System – GIS (Technical Instrument).

- Require the Inter-Institutional Approval of the CTAR, Agriculture, PRONAMACHS, Special Projects and Municipal Governments, with active participation from peasants and organised communities, drawing up a pro-active Environment and Land Resource Protection Program for Puno, with international and Federal Government cooperation providing the resources needed to deal with these severe problems (Political Instrument).

- Require a Geographical Atlas to be drawn up covering the districts and provinces, using state-of-the-art technology and displaying our natural resources (land, water, micro-basins); our production resources (agriculture, fishing, mining); and our social resources (populace) in order to draw up base-line zero plans based on districts and provinces that underpin Sustainable Local Development Processes. This task should be assigned to the INEI, together with the agricultural sector, in parallel to special and municipal projects (Technical Instrument).

ANNEX 1

Table I: Peasant Communities In Puno, Showing Communities Before and After Land Take-overs and Restructuring Process 1985 – 1986

Order No.	Provinces	Peasant Communities	Heads of Families	Estimated Population	Awarded Hectares	Peasant Communities	Heads of Families	Estimated Population	Awarded Hectares	TOTAL PEASANT COMMUNITIES IN PUNO
		COMMUNITIES UP TO 1985 (OLD)				COMMUNITIES AFTER 1986–1993 (NEW)				
1	Azangaro	89	8240	29970	66740.06	186	14735	69791	105032.10	275
2	Carabaya	31	3713	12640	11600.73	14	1240	4131	3644.36	45
3	Ilave–Collao	58	6805	25848	3390.20	55	5003	25228	–	113
4	Huancané	59	6050	22983	47839.06	52	3971	15514	51459.22	111
5	Puno	86	12285	48843	18525.30	122	9750	39689	53575.36	208
6	Lampa	18	1375	5156	25230.05	76	5642	23684	249652.84	94
7.	Melgar	40	3462	15003	41442.74	40	2588	11113	27053.93	80
8	Moho	10	1125	5863	20511.64	12	1117	5904	6653.00	22
9.	Putina	10	1154	3976	10366.91	27	2256	9269	48555.74	37
10.	Sandia	23	4137	13040	8900.50	1	250	700	–	24
11	San Roman	18	2714	15159	87424.91	17	1469	6062	2944.50	35
12.	Yunguyo	16	5256	23866	–	7	1411	5928	882.90	23
13	Chucuito	84	15501	56587	6172.95	53	5306	21440	18293.85	137
TOTAL		542	71817	278934	344145.05	662	54738	238446	566747.80	1204

- According to official information on the Puno Department, this includes a total of 1,274 peasant communities (Source: III Agrarian Census 1994); Table 1 shows a total for this Department of 1204 peasant communities, with 70 communities left out that had been acknowledged through to 1994, which was the date of the III Agricultural Census.
- At the level of the land awarded through the Restructuring Process, Table 1 shows a total of 910,892.85 hectares.
  The official total amount of land returned to the communities through the Restructuring Process throughout the Puno Department is 1,010,992.14 hectares; the difference of 100,099.3 hectares in the Table is related to the awards to what are known as the "Communities in Formation" and include land that is still under dispute before the courts.

SOURCE: *Peasant Communities Directorate – 1993 / RJCM*
Prepared by the CCCP Staff – 2000.

SECTION V
STRATEGIES

ECONOMIC GLOBALISATION, CIVIL SOCIETY AND RIGHTS

Gertrude ROEBELING (The Netherlands)

Introduction

My field of work, International Development Co-operation has shown some interesting changes in the last 20 years. The most striking is that since the fall of the Berlin Wall in 1989 a change is becoming evident in how the power relations in the world are analysed. Before 1989, for the West the "good" was seen to be in the West, while for the East the "good" was in the East. Thus dividing the world into ideologically based visions of what is "good". After 1989 the World was confronted with a lot of "good" and "bad" on both sides. The West was economically far more developed and had relatively good social standards expressed in the social Welfare State. The East showed more vulnerable economies where social equality was practised, but at a lower material level than in the West. Therefore the dominant vision on Development was the Western approach, re-qualifying the liberal ideology of the free market in a neo-liberal appearance.

Western theories distinguish three main actors who influence the quality of a society: the state, the market and civil society.[1] These different fields are active and interrelated, with shifting power dynamics between them. The neo-liberal model, after 10 years of practice, shows a shift in the role of the state, from the pre-1989 welfare state towards a more facilitating model: opening up to the global markets (economical globalisation of financial capital and some human resources), market liberalisation (deregulation); privatisation of public services, decentralisation.

International Co-operation in general, and co-financing agencies like ICCO in the Netherlands in particular, have one objective in common: "to combat poverty". This vision is based on the urgent need to contribute to improving the living conditions of all excluded people, the poor, the marginalised, and the discriminated, in order to bring about global sustainable development for all. Twenty years ago the West talked about 'development aid' in relation to so-called underdeveloped countries; the idea was that underdevelopment was caused by a lack of knowledge and funds, and therefore could be solved with some good projects. Ten years ago the general concept

---

[1] M. Edwards, June 1998.

was 'development co-operation' from the North to the South, in which the working together with the people on development projects would bring about changes for the poor. Still development in general was linked to economic and market development, whereas development of the poor was to be ensured by the State, and partially by civil society institutions. Today we speak about 'international co-operation' between North/West, South and East. Not only the State or some institutions like churches or NGOs are made responsible for development for all. There is more interlinking between all actors in society: State, market and civil society. This does not necessarily mean that the situation of the poor has improved. On the contrary, in spite of the enormous economic growth during the last decade, there have never been so many poor. Things are changing; the global context is changing.

Globalisation

Globalisation as such is in fact a dream for many people on earth. It is adventurous to get to know the whole world, to discover new regions, to meet other cultures. For socialists, globalisation is also the dream of international solidarity. So why is globalisation so alarming? Because globalisation is interpreted only as economical globalisation; social, political and cultural elements seem to be kept away. It brings exciting development for those who have a market position, for those who have access to money and political power. However, this is a privilege to the 'happy few'. Most of these transactions are increasingly across the boundaries of National States and beyond their political control. Social issues are looked upon as interfering with business and free market conditions. So what is alarming is not the fact that economy is globalising, but the package of measures that the neoliberal model brings along.

Crucial elements in the globalisation of economy are the globalisation of capital, of communication and of some human resources. Since boundaries still play a protective role by restricting market possibilities, economic globalisation has to rely on powerful instruments or to reduce the power of National States. This liberalisation of the market goes hand in hand with the State playing a more facilitating role towards the market, by promoting deregulation, decentralisation, privatisation of State property, reduction of the role of the State in social issues, and issues of common interest: *by choice or by lobbying pressure? And how do different actors respond?*

The State

The State is changing its face as well. The social Welfare State that existed from the sixties to the end of the eighties is now considered to be too expensive, and therefore the "social face" is being replaced by a "facilitating face" State. National State reform helps the process of liberalizing markets by focusing on opening national markets as much as necessary to international investors and capital. This means removing market protection instruments like import duties, reducing income and capital taxes, reducing legislation that protects labour and imposes minimum salaries, opening up boundaries between partner States in economical unions like the NAFTA, EU, Mercosul etc. The National State itself becomes an enterprise, selling out State public utilities for water, electricity, oil, fuel, mining etc, either by privatisation or by subcontracting to parastatal organisations. Income from the sale these State enterprises is usually used to pay foreign debts or to reduce the State budget. The State thus reduces the social costs of its country, but continues to borrow money at international banks like IMF and the World Bank, and follow their monetary instructions (inflation reduction), Social Adjustment Programmes (in name or in practice) or PRSPs. Social issues like health, education, small farmers, food security, social welfare, pensions etc. suffer lack of income and are under reform, even if this is against the Constitution.

A positive aspect of State reform is the decentralisation of State power to more local and regional levels, because this might give people more direct influence on their own living environment. The democratisation process that is linked with the neoliberal model, however, mainly gives influence to the people who already have access to power and money in the local context. By decentralising State power, it becomes more difficult for the National State to control the division of power and of public funds. Whether this model leads to a well-functioning democracy depends on how far democracy is able to develop at a local level. In most countries cultural characteristics like clientilism, nepotism, tribalism, corruption at a local level, etc. impede true success, and merely lead to a reestablishment of ancient cultural mechanisms of 'divide and rule'. In more developed democracies it leads to fragmentation of political articulation making these new democracies more vulnerable.

Market Actors

First of all market liberalisation means greater freedom of capital transitions across boundaries, reduced regulations on imports, lower income and capital taxes, and profit being allowed to leave the country without being taxed, thus attracting foreign investments and capital. Labour protection and salaries have to be as low as possible to make the investment climate even more popular and to be competitive in international markets. Financial markets follow their own rules, being almost completely de-linked from the production market. This enables people to either become rich or lose all their money overnight. Transactions take place all over the world on stock markets, which are linked with each other. The leading principle is to earn money and to increase the market share. Many huge international companies have appeared, buying up the competitors, and creating monopolies and oligarchs like Microsoft, Shell, Unilever, and international private banks. These companies are sometimes being confronted in their home countries with legal procedures because of their monopolising practices.

Privatised former-State companies supplying energy, water, postal services, telephone, public transport, or oil and mining companies, are also increasing competition on the markets. They first showed some extra profit, increasing their share values on the stock market. In the mid-term these profits were not invested, leading to neglected investment in infrastructure and increased consumer prices (against their former promises).

All these developments give an enormous feeling of freedom, possibilities and success. Competition, though, is the wild beast luring in the bushes all the time, pulling companies into a vicious circle. The need for continuity forces these companies to reduce their labour forces and to scale up in larger companies and joint ventures. To maximize profits de-levelling of lower salaries and increase of top managers' salaries are common practice. As from a macro-economical point of view there can be no development without economical growth; the gap between rich and poor is seen as just one of the pickups to maintain economical growth[2]. From that perspective it is necessary to rationalize labour forces through replacement by computers and by more highly educated personnel.

At the social level, the free market mechanisms lead to an increasing gap between rich and poor. Rationalisation puts great pressure on the poorer and the poorest, and on less educated people in society. Competition is increasing, accompanied by scaling up and slimming down of big companies, and by subcontracting out former departments or branches, thus keeping down wages down putting the responsibility on the subcontractors. This leads to the fewer and weaker traditional and local small enterprises. In non-Western countries more and more people are unable to cope in the formal sector and have to set up or continue their small enterprises in the informal sector, where they cannot contribute to taxes or receive any social protection. In the end the gap between rich and poor is widening,

---

2 Drs. R.H. Meys, Netherlands Foreign Ministry; future Dutch Ambassador in Brazil (2001).

leading towards unemployment, and economical and social exclusion of the largest part of society.

International control over market functioning is taking place in world conferences like WTO, IMF, World Bank, European Union, NAFTA, G7 / G8, in all of which the big economies have most power. These conferences only take account of capital and profits, and of a good investment climate like a stable political situation. In the Netherlands 'good governance' is an extra demand.[3] In this perspective Human Rights like the right to food, adequate housing, labour conditions, land and environment are non-issues. Food production for instance is seen as an economical liability; not as a right to food security.

Civil Society

A newly discussed phenomenon is the so-called civil society, often spoken of these days in International Co-operation circles. It is difficult to understand what exactly is meant by 'civil society'. As a western concept, in its broadest definition it includes all organised actors in society that do not belong to either the State bodies or market oriented activities or enterprises. But should political parties, parliamentarians, universities, scientific institutions not also be considered 'civil society'? Therefore civil society organisations can be anything where citizens are organised formally or informally in-groups varying from a sports club to a church body, or a street gang. When we talk about civil society we also mean all the non-profit organisations with a social goal. In this field many changes are taking place as well. An enormous increase of NGOs and charitable organisations can be observed. This also increases their mutual competition, thus fragmenting their previously coordinated actions. Different kinds of organisations can be distinguished: political and lobby organisations, organisations of charity, organisation to relieve the poor with immediate help, organisation that help people to get access to public funds and public policies, organisations specialised in thematic issues, decentralised ex-State bodies, credit organisation, training organisations, trade unions, student associations and local councils.

Western theories focus on the role of civil society in securing individual freedom and democracy in the face of incursions by States. They emphasise a narrow range of roles, especially the promotion of "good governance."

---

[3] Drs. E. Herfkens, Minister International Co-operation, Ministry of Foreign Affairs (2000).

Non-Western theories include a much wider range of roles including: promoting broader participation in economical and social life as well as politics; organising the co-production and management of goods, services and resources; caring and nurturing for those in need; and preserving culture. Civil society is not always seen in opposition to the State, since States may be needed to guarantee the rights of groups to organise themselves, and the rights of individuals who may be left out of civil society completely.

Each of these civil society theories leads into different directions in terms of policy and practice. Western interpretations focus on "building civil society" as a fixed concept, making all societies fit the three-circle model, and all civil societies look like those in the West. Non-Western theories prioritise support for particular organisations within civil society, and the conditions in which civil society can shape itself more or less successfully. Whereas Western theories see civil society as a solution, non-Western theories are more interested in the interlocking power structures among States, markets and civil societies that combine to exclude or oppress particular groups of people.

Civil society is now generally recognised as being increasingly important to global development[4]. "A strong civil society provides a means by which the interests of citizens are represented in relation to the State and the market". Different theories converge in emphasising certain values as desirable, either as a natural attribute of civil society or as something to be actively nurtured: trust, accountability, co-operation, and non-violence. It is possible to make a choice between competing theories on the grounds of intellectual conviction and personal belief alone. But if we want to make as big an impact as possible on world poverty it is better to start with what we want to achieve and then answer the question of how civil society will help or hinder in particular contexts.

Implementation of Economic, Social and Cultural Rights

The Universal Declaration on Human Rights and other conventions on Labour, Children's Rights, Women's Rights, Minorities and Indigenous People seem to be the only human values internationally recognised by the majority of countries. At an international level, when it comes to social globalisation, these Human Rights seem to be the only firm ground which people have to protect their human dignity and protect them against exploitation and submission to powers beyond their individual control.

---

4 World Social Forum, Porto Alegre 2001 and World Economic Forum, Davos 2001.

Still, some countries have not subscribed the UN Declaration (China). Other countries have subscribed, but in practice ignore and violate Human Rights on a large scale. An instrument for monitoring Human Rights exists, the "State compliance reports to the United Nations Commission on Human Rights", but hardly any country produces these. Here civil society steps in by producing their own independent reports, thus showing the importance of actions by civil society. The UN's funds for monitoring are extremely limited, and some countries have not paid their UN-contributions to this UN-sector for years (United States of America). If there is any interest in Human Rights it is mostly on the side of the violations of civil and political rights. These cases are brought to court with varying results. Under the international Universal Declaration of Human Rights, these rights are indivisible, enforceable, and justiciable. The practice of bringing economic, social and cultural rights cases to court is limited to labour cases and land issues. In many situations attempts to claim economic, social and cultural rights leads to violations of civil and political rights. Impunity of these cases is a large-scale problem, especially in Latin American countries.

Shifting Responsabilities?

The *National State* used to be the most powerful and important force during the last centuries. With the neo-liberal model ruling since the beginning of the nineties the National State has opened its boundaries to the international surroundings. The influence of the National State has diminished, due to national and international economical pressure and lobbying, and by political choice. But many Western National States still do not comply with the social paragraphs of the Copenhagen Summit in 1995 in their budgets on education and health, even under a social-democratic/neoliberal government (The Netherlands, 2001).

In how far market actors feel responsible for social issues seems to be extremely contradictory. 'Social responsibility" is a slogan often used by international enterprises, but has no generally accepted definition. The form used to express this responsibility varies considerably, ranging from public relations pep-talks, to a charity foundation, to serious labour standards, or to projects aiming at inclusion of marginalised producers, social and environmental standards and certification.

To which ends is civil society supposed to be a means? Although the transmission mechanisms between a "strong civil society" and development goals are not well-understood at the level of national development performance, experience shows that the synergy between a strong State and a strong civil society is one of the keys to sustained poverty-reducing growth. Yet, this need not mean a strong civil society of Western-style, but it does mean a dense network of intermediary associations that act as a counterweight to vested interests, promote institutional accountability among States and markets, channel information to decision-makers on what is happening at the "sharp end", and negotiate the "contracts" between government and citizens that development requires – "I'll scratch your back by delivering growth, investment and services; you scratch mine by delivering wage restraint or absorbing the costs of welfare".

The economical or productive role of civil society centres on securing livelihoods and providing services where States and markets are weak, and nurturing "social capital" for use in economic settings – the trust and co-operation that makes markets work. The quality of relationships between people has a major influence on economic performance, and those relationships are nurtured above all in civil society. In Brazil for example, the skills and attitudes developed in migrant associations were critical in promoting co-operation between shoe-producers later on. Civil society and market are not divorced from each-other, their economic and social impacts are inter-related, and NGOs contribute alongside other civil society groups. A well-digging programme, for example, will have some impact on village organisation through the committee that is formed to manage water resources; that committee will develop capacities that can be used in building a region-wide federation of water users; and that federation might make an important contribution to "good governance" by connecting the grassroots with policy-making at the top. It is difficult assume civil responsabilites if you are starving. As globalisation extends its reach into every corner of life, the links between economic, social and political processes become even stronger, opening up a huge agenda for civil societies at a micro-regional level to engage with macro levels and transnational corporations and codes of corporate conduct.

In their social role, civil societies can be a reservoir of co-operative values, caring, cultural life and intellectual innovation. In general, it is civic groups that teach people the skills of citizenship and provide a framework for the expression of what they hold in their hearts. Liberals refer to this as social capital, but "social energy" is probably a better term since it conveys the importance of trust and co-operation in terms other than pure economics[5]. These qualities are nurtured in any civic setting, but choral societies, sports clubs and the like play little part in efforts to reduce global poverty. It is NGOs and community organisations that are at the forefront. Civil societies also help people to feel more secure and valued within the associations they

---

[5] M. Edwards, June 1998.

belong to, to find common cause with like-minded individuals, and to help each-other in very practical ways – caring for each-other's children, or helping out in times of emergency. But exclusion cannot be tackled by civil society alone, because many civic groups are exclusive themselves – like trade unions which may fight for the rights of their members but ignore the interests of the unorganised poor. "Both States and markets are implicated in the process of social exclusion, and the associations of civil society work in interaction with these institutions to attenuate *or* exacerbate the problem." Therefore, a "strong civil society" does not guarantee social inclusion. As in the economic sphere, what matters is what each institution *does*, with whom, and how, not just what it is.

Conclusions

It is clear that we live in a new era. The power dynamics between the main actor fields described, the National State, market actors and civil society, are shifting, responsibilities are changing. But who is assuming these responsibilities; who is the bearer of rights – who is the bearer of duties – and under which circumstances? People at different moments of their lives or even during the day change their roles depending on the situation they act in: as citizens, as employees, as owners.

The role of the State needs to be redefined, maintaining the flexibility and creativity that the neoliberal model has brought about, but improving the situation of the many who lack rights, without returning to the welfare State. A State of well being? And how can democracy function in this respect? How can one improve the implementation of Human Rights as the anchor of social civilisation?
What exactly can be expected of market actors? How do they relate to the other actors in society? When and under which conditions will they respond to social responsibilities?
In relation to the role and responsibilities of civil society an important question to be answered is: *Does civil society really make a difference in this shift of responsibilities?*

In terms of development and changing power relations on behalf of citizens it is most promising to look more closely into the possibilities of implementing economical, social and cultural rights, as these rights protect people beforehand, instead of reacting after violation of civil and political rights. The implementation of human rights can be a strategic instrument, a tool, in changing power dynamics, in which every actor field has to comply with its specific responsibilities and duties.

STRATEGIES AND PRACTICES IN THE CONTEXT OF CASTEISM

M.C. RAJ (India)

Introduction

India is once again passing through a socio-economic-political and cultural struggle. The Hindutva forces are trying vehemently and have succeeded to some extent to establish a socio-political system that will establish the economic hegemony of the dominant castes in India. When the British colonizers were leaving India there was a major conflict within the Indian society initiated by the Hindutva forces. They wanted to establish a Hindu Nation, a nation based on the dominant cultural values as enshrined in the Vedas[1], Puranas[2], Smirits[3] and Tantras[4]. They did not succeed. Through vote bank politics they are on the brink of achieving their objective of constructing a cultural nationalism that will take over the Nation-State in India. Their success will announce the dawn of a new phase in the hegemonic history of Brahminism. The new phase will mark the transfer and consolidation of power in the hands of the conventional foes of the poor and the marginalized people, the Dalits, the Women and the tribal people of India in a liberalized Globalization context. This will be a major site of violation of rights of the people of India. India is not one country. It is a multiplicity of countries. India does not have one culture. It a multicultural society. India does not have one language. It has thousand of languages. It does not have one people with one identity. It has people belonging to different religions and castes.

The people of India who have been traditionally oppressed and marginalized in the name of caste have started asserting their rights and fighting back on many fronts. This has resulted in escalated violence by the supposedly non-violent dominant caste and in increased violations of the Human Rights of the people by the State. The Indian State is a conglomeration of the dominant caste-class forces. The resistance and resurgence of the hitherto marginalized people is another site of violations of rights. In

---

1 Vedas are philosophical and theological writings of Hinduism that promulgate the religious doctrines of Brahminism.

2 Puranas are the story forms of transferring Brahminic doctrines to the common people.

3 Smritis translate the Brahminic Doctrines into normative order and normative prescriptions.

4 In popular understanding Tantra means trickery. They are instruments of popular consumption and internalization of what is said in the Puranas.

this Paper I try to explain how Aryan Caste forces have established and perpetrated systemic and structural violence, exploitation and oppression of the indigenous people, depriving them of their dignity, self-respect, land, labor, education, livelihood and life itself. I also trace the history of the strategies and programs of the Dalit people for claiming and gradually establishing their legitimate rights in the context of the emerging Nation-State in India.

Origin of the Caste System

Ambedkar quotes from Katyayana about the origin of the four castes[5]: "There is no difference of castes; this world, having been at first created by Brahma entirely Brahmanic, became (afterwards) separated into castes in consequence of works. Those Brahmans (lit. twice born men), who were fond of sensual pleasure, fiery, irascible, prone to violence, had forsaken their duty, and were red-limbed, fell into the condition of Kshatriyas. Those Brahmans, who derived their livelihood from kine, who were yellow, who subsisted by agriculture, and who neglected to practice their duties, entered into the state of Vaisyas. Those Brahmans, who were addicted to mischief and falsehood, who were covetous, who lived by all kinds of works, who were black and had fallen from purity, sank into the condition of Sudras. Being separated from each other by these works, the Brahmanas became divided into different castes".[6]

Caste – Division of Laborers

Many Hindu scholars have tried to justify this system of graded inequality through philosophical discourses. However, the type of exclusivism that caste system has effected in the society cannot be wished away, nor can it be pushed under the carpet through pious and high sounding philosophical gongs. The general argument forwarded in the legitimization of the caste system is that it is a division of labor. It is the way that the Hindu society has been ordered and that it has worked well for millennia. First of all it must be said that it is not a division of labor. As Babasaheb clearly points out it is a division of laborers. It is a division of people.

Caste system has worked till now because of the total objugation of the Dalit people by the Brahminic forces all throughout history. They have ensured an all-round surrender of the Dalit people through the technologies of

---

[5] Dr. B.R. Ambedkar who is the Father of the Constitution of India and who is a Dalit is called Babasaheb with affection by the Dalits of India.

[6] Babasaheb Ambedkar, *Writings and Speeches*, Vol. 5, p. 193-194.

unrestricted oppression, manipulative co-option, perennial dependence, and the denial of education and livelihood opportunities. It is a shame to say that a system has worked well for a long time this way. If the Dalits are being kept in chains as bonded laborers even today and they agree to all the terms and conditions of the dominant caste fellows while being kept in chains can we call it a good system. Do the Brahminic forces understand the fundamentals of what is good and evil?

The Dalit People – The Outcast(e)s

When the Aryans came into India the indigenous people were not one homogenous group. There were many groups of them living with or without close interactions. The groups that lived were not identified as caste. There were at least ten groups of the indigenous people in India when the Aryans arrived. "The Kol-Bhil of Koibhajan (now called Bharat) having ten tribes (viz.Yadu, Turvasu, Druhyu, Anu, Puru, Kuru, Panchala, Bharta, Tritsu and Dasyus[7]) were living in this country without any discrimination before the coming of Aryans. The Aryans came here, applied the policy of 'divided and rule', propounded the theory of casteism and converted all our ten tribes into about 6000 castes and also sowed the seeds of discrimination among our people".[8] The Dalit community is a casteless community. Dalitism is castelessness. Since people in India have internalized caste very much they cannot think of natural groups except as caste. Even Christians and Muslims in this country are considered to be different castes in many regions. It is a mistake on the part of the British to have registered the different communities of the indigenous people as sub castes.

The Brahminic, hegemonic forces objugated the native people of this land with a specific purpose of extracting their land labor, and dignity free of cost. We generally make a mental construct of barbarism as something that is repulsive to the sight. The general image of a barbarous person is black, with skin cloth, shabby, with an ancient weapon in his hand, with two horns, protruding teeth and a frightening image. If Brahminism attaches so much importance to knowledge and mind barbarism of the mind should be a reality and that is what Brahminism is.

---

7 The word, though clearly applied to superhuman enemies in many passages of the RG Veda, is in several others applied to human foes, probably the aborigines, especially in those in which the Dasyu is opposed to the Arayan who defeats him with the aid of the gods. The great difference between the two is their religion. The Dasyu are styled "not sacrificing", "devoid of rites", "addicted to strange vows", "god hating" and so forth. Thomas R. Trautmann, *Aryans and British India*, p. 208.

8 Subhas Chandra Musafir, 'A Section of Educated Dalits have Become Mini-Brahmins', in: *Dalit Voice*, July 15-31 1999, p. 22.

Untouchability – Objugating[9] Stratagem

The untouchability that has come to stay as an ascribed identity to the Dalit people is a mental construct, part of an objugating stratagem. Untouchability is metaphysical. It belongs to the realm of the mind. In the realm of the mind we need to see what is the cause and what is the effect. Where does the cause of untouchability lie? Does it lie with the one who is ascribed untouchability or with the one who ascribes untouchability? There is only one pollution in the mental realm of the Dalit people according to the Brahminic paradigms. This pollution is the refusal to accept Brahminic gods, religious dogma, customs, rituals and other practices of Brahminism. If this is the actual cause of the mental pollution and uncleanness for which untouchability is ascribed then it must be ascribed to all those who refuse to accept Brahminism as a way of life. However, Hinduism does not ascribe untouchability to people of other religions. If the cause of untouchability is the pollution in the minds other than the rejection of Brahminism then it can be only acceptance of untouchability as a mental category. The Dalit mind is not a reception center of the dogma of untouchability. In fact, in the Dalit mindset there is no space for untouchability. It is a mindset that likes to touch and be touched. It welcomes all. It provides unlimited space to all people. The Dalit mindset is the victim of this discourse of pollution and its consequent untouchability. Untouchability is suffered both in mind and in body. The effect of the discourse of purity-impurity and pollution falls on the Dalit community as a whole.

Untouchability – Tool of Violations

In India, as in many other countries of South Asia, the violations of right to life and dignity assume barbaric dimensions in the caste system. The State in India is not only an active conniver with economic forces of exploitation but has an identity with that part of the civil society which assiduously seeks to maintain the hegemony it has established over the indigenous people and women. Untouchability is the demon that acts as the agent of caste system. While the violations of Human Rights in many other countries assume an individual dimension, in India, which is governed by a ruling caste, it is a whole people who are denied their rights. Though legal rights are enshrined in the Constitution of India, civil rights are constantly being violated through the collaboration of the State machinery.

---

[9] For an explanation on Objugation read, M.C. Raj, *From Periphery to Center.*

Roots of Untouchability

If the forces of Globalization have succeeded in disintegrating the local people socio-economically and culturally, Casteism did it long ago and is continuing to make the Dalit people the worst victims of its hegemony. If globalization with its ideological roots in capitalism has created a class of people who are subjugated and makes them to struggle for survival Casteism with its ideological roots in Brahminism did it much earlier and created untouchability in its worst inhuman forms. It objugated the indigenous people to such an extent that even after three millennia it takes pride and legitimizes, through multifarious discourses, the establishment and sustenance of such a social organization. Therefore, we may arrive at a position that the sources of violations of Human Rights in India are religion, caste and the economic system.

Untouchability Today

A common discourse that is produced and dispersed with an evangelical zeal is that caste discrimination is a thing of the past and that all stories of caste atrocities are concocted. It must be stated here that such a discourse is in fact fabricated as a self-defense. The reality of India as reflected even in the caste dominated media is that caste discrimination, and the 'terrorist' practices attached to it continue even today in as crude forms as it used to exist centuries ago.

- The latest in the series of caste killings is the one in Kurnool District of Andhra Pradesh. The Nation-State is an active collaborator in perpetuating such heinous crimes against the Dalit people in different parts of the country.
- An example of such a state of affairs is the cleansing of the chamber of B. Prasad, a Dalit, and Additional District Judge in the Allahahabad High Court with water from Ganga by Ashok Kumar Srivatsava who took over from the Dalit Judge.

Speaking of the Supreme Court of India, R.K. Garg writes: "The citizen is often shocked; why did the Supreme Court lean in favor of vested interest? The reason is simple. Laws are enacted to recognize or to create old and new rights. These rights become vested rights defended by vested interest. The Courts are there to enforce these rights. By habit, training, and equipment, judges get used to paying an awesome respect for vested rights, which are the bedrock of the legal framework given to them for administering justice".[10]

The Extent of Untouchability

Some forward the argument that the recent increase in the atrocities on Dalits is an indication of a higher level of awareness among the Dalit communities about themselves. It is only now that these atrocities are being reported. There is truth in this viewpoint. However, it must be stated firmly that the atrocities on Dalit people, as on women, have been there for centuries. With the rising Dalit awareness of their identity and rights, these atrocities have been increasing recently with a qualitative difference. *These are now carried out systemically and structurally.*

The decade of development during Indira Gandhi's regime registered more than 40,000 cases of atrocity against the Dalits. According to a recent report in the Deccan Herald of 29 July 1998, Mrs. Maneka Gandhi made gave the following details to the Parliament. *"Despite the Constitutional mandate, untouchability is prevalent in 12 States – Andhra Pradesh, Bihar, Karnataka, Gujarat, Kerala, Madhya Pradesh, Maharashtra, Orissa, Rajasthan, Tamilnadu, Uttar Pradesh and Pondichery".* The report further states that it is prevalent in a mild form in six States and Union Territories, Jammu and Kashmir, Punjab, Haryana, Himachal Pradesh, Goa and Delhi. The rest of the States where, according to the government untouchability is not practiced are the North Eastern States and West Bengal. Therefore, we may conclude that the Government has accepted the prevalence of untouchability in the whole of India.

Untouchability – Causal Factors Today

It is not only the number of atrocities but also the type and the reasons that count. We may identify three major causes for the increasing atrocity on Dalits.

1. Whenever the Dalit people assert their cultural rights and refuse to accept the hegemony of dominant castes. The Tsundur atrocity in Andhra Pradesh and the one in Badanavalu of Karnataka are just two examples from the South.
2. Whenever the Dalit people assert their economic rights by laying a claim to natural resources, especially to land. The Soolanayakanahalli atrocity

[10] Professor D.N. Sandanshiv, *Human Rights and the Primacy of the Constitution's Directive Principles, Untouchable!*, Ed. by Barbara R. Joshi, p. 130-131.

in Tumkur District and the recent one in Kurnool District of Andhra Pradesh are large-scale atrocities that remain fresh in our memory. The whole Dalit community in a village has to pay a heavy price for a land dispute between individuals.

3. Whenever the Dalit people assert their political rights by courageously taking recourse to the provisions in the Constitution and independently participate in the legal system of the country.

Untouchability – Forms of Practice and Penalties

The type of reign of terror that is perpetrated on the Dalit people gives generally the picture of the forces that boasts of a superior culture but is truly in need of civilization. For those who live in the cities blissfully unaware of what is happening to millions of their fellow beings around the country the following may be shocking. It is important to remember that we are speaking of things that are taking place in 1998 and we are only one year and a half away from the 21st century.

- The Dalit people are served coffee and tea in hotels in separate glasses, which they themselves have to wash. They have to stand outside the hotel and sip their coffee.
- They are not allowed entry into places of worship. In many places the Dalit masons construct the temple but as soon as it is dedicated the Dalit people become untouchable.
- In village festivals they will be served meals separately only after everyone else has finished and only the leftovers will be served to them.
- The Dalit people are not allowed to draw even drinking water from tube wells of the government in the dominant caste streets.
- The Dalit people are also forced to perform conventional caste 'jobs' free of cost. Such duties include announcing the death of dominant caste person to relatives of the person wherever they may live; digging graves; removing dead animals; beating drums during funeral processions and village festivals; free labor during village festival etc.
- Any dissension on the above said matters will immediately be met with a thorough beating up of the Dalit people in order to teach them a lesson. When that fails there follows a social boycott of the Dalits, which practically is an economic boycott. In the event of a boycott the Dalits will not be allowed to walk through the main streets of the village, will not be given any provision in the shops, will have no entry into the flour mill to grind their grain. Dalit women will not be allowed into the fields at dusk to ease themselves, will not be given any work in the fields till the Dalits agree to the terms and conditions of the dominant caste

people. If anyone gives the Dalit people job in his field he/she will have to pay a fine.

Sites of Violations

These sites of violations of rights are common to both the forces of Globalization and that of Brahminization:

- Male Domination – Objugation of Women
- Domination over Nature, Ecology
- Assertion of Religious Superiority, assertion of one caste as supreme – caste first; assertion of the individual as supreme – individual first
- Assertion of cultural superiority and paradigms of universalism
- Based on religion – for Normative order, normative standards and normative prescriptions
- Religion for you poor (heaven in the next world) – wealth, power and status for us (in this world)
- Purity-Impurity; Superior-Inferior; Heaven-Hell; This world-Next world; Earth-Heaven; Body-Spirit; Rationality-Emotion dichotomies
- Cultural Unity – Cultural Diversity (Diverse Groups are enemies)
- Criminalisation of objugated people
- Claim to absolute truth, ownership of Truth, their science is more truthful, Universal science Vs Perspectivism
- Civilization – Barbarism discourse
- One Nation, One people, One culture, One language, One religion discourse
- Privatization, Liberalization, Democracy – the economic agenda of both
- One is to judge-the other is to be judged, not worthy of ruling

Strategies and Programmes

1. Religion as a Strategy

During the 1880s as elsewhere among the depressed cases, the Chandals developed the Matua cult, and re-named themselves Nama Shudras.[11]

The Chamars of North India have their history of protest. Ghasi Das (1756-1836) founded a sect called Satnami and preached the unity of God and equality of all human beings. This was a direct challenge to Brahminic hegemony in the name of religion.[12]

[11] *Ibid.*, p. 64.
[12] *Ibid.*, p. 66.

"The Chamar brethren of the northwest Punjab province gave a clarion call to all the depressed classes, during the second decade of the present century, through a newly founded (1925) religion called Adi Dharm:

> We are the original people of this country and our religion is Adi Dharm. The Hindu qualm came from outside and enslaved us. When the original sound from the conch was sounded all the brothers came together – Chamar, Chuhra, Sainsi, Bhanjre, Bhil all the untouchables- to make their problems known. Brothers there are seventy millions of us listed as Hindus, separate us and make us free (M.Juergensmeyer 1982: 46)

Now there is a new cry in Indian Dalit Scenario for the evolution of a Dalit religion centered around the earth and the ancestors.

2. Conversion as a Strategy

Many of us have the habit of viewing conversions to other religions only from a religious point of view. Most of the conversions to Christianity and Islam were also protests from the Dalits against caste oppression and untouchability. The best example of such a protesting conversion came from none other than our great Babasaheb himself. He converted himself to Buddhism as a mark of protest. However, in the light of the possibility of new religious formations the call to all Dalits of the world is to convert themselves to Dalitism.

3. Social Protest as Strategy

The movement includes two cases of direct action aimed at the demolition of the Hindu Social Order by applying dynamite to its very foundations. One is the burning of the Manu Smriti and the second is the mass refusal by the Untouchable to lift the dead cattle belonging to the Hindus and to skin them. The burning of Manu Smriti took place at Mahad on the 20th of December 1927. Babasaheb himself describes the significance of the burning Manu Smriti thus.

> "The burning of the Manu Smriti by the Untouchables at Mahad in 1927 is an event which has the same significance and importance in the history of the emancipation of the Untouchables which the fall of Bastille had in the liberation of the masses in France and Europe".

4. Political Nationalism as Strategy

Starting from 1906 the Hindu extremists were aggressively in pursuit of a cultural nationalist agenda. The professed objective of Hindutva was to establish a Hindu Rashtra (Nation). Cultural nationalism in India would mean the firm establishment of Caste system as an instrument of societal organization. Not only that, it would also lead to the Brahminic Order being recognized as the normative order of the Indian society. The legal system then would be designed based on this Order. This was untenable in the Indian context for many reasons. India is not one nation as one can see in many other nations. India is a continent of nations. Each State of India has a different language, different culture. The indigenous people do not belong to the Hindu religion. The Tribal people, who are more than 80 million, have their own religion. The Dalits who are more than 180 million are not Hindus. There are 130 million Muslims. There are many other minority communities in large number.

Babasaheb B.R.Ambedkar, and Periyar saw this shenanigan of the cultural nationalists clearly and the consequences for the Dalits of this country. We may also mention the names of Mangoo Ram, Swami Atchutanand and Birsa Muda as other untouchable and tribal leaders who fought for political nationalism. Such nationalism would ensure equal political right for the different communities living in India respecting fully their freedom. A Constitution that would ensure the equal rights of all people was made. It was written by no other than Ambedkar himself.

"The third thing we must do is not to be content with mere political democracy. We must make our political democracy a social democracy as well. Political Democracy cannot last unless there lies at the base of it social democracy.... We must begin by acknowledging the fact there is complete absence of two things in Indian society. One of these is equality. On the social plane, we have in India a society of graded inequality, which means elevation of some and degradation of others. On the economic plane, we have a society in which there are some who have immense wealth as against many who live in abject poverty......On the 26th January, 1950 we are going to enter into a life of contradictions. In politics we will have equality and in social and economic life we will have inequality....We must remove this contradiction at the earliest possible moment or else those who suffer from inequality will blow up the structure of political democracy which this Assembly has so laboriously built up".

5. Participation as a Strategy

No State will be complete unless the security of its entire people is adequately assured. Assumptions of individual liberty are to be addressed within the boundaries of the securities of communities of people. The protagonists of an end-state appropriate to themselves the right to eliminate those who produce countervailing discourses about individual and community security vis-à-vis individual liberty. The State proves itself to be the tormentor, the aggressor and the violator of human rights in this sense. The state either subdues or eliminates, by the indiscriminate use of the State Machinery, those who genuinely endeavor to make the State a level playing field for all communities of people. It believes in the total elimination either of individuals or of ethnic groups if they are seen to be inimical to its legitimizing ideology and formulae.

In the Globalization context one may point out to such big talks of a 'New World Order', 'Decentralization of Power', 'Democracy', 'Participation' etc. as the legitimizing ideology and Decentralization of power as the legitimizing formula. Therefore, we may conclude that the 'Project of power decentralization is a pet agenda of the State that has bowed its head and sold its freedom to the dominant elite of the world order.

It is in the specific context of the Dalits and local governance that the concept of power as participation needs to be looked into. Against the bipolarity of power as dominance and power as resistance we need to now move into a tripolarity of power as participation. Power as participation takes people deep into Governance. Here we take Michael Th. Greven's definition of Governance as a process of the allocation of values in a given society. Allocation of values implies the allocation of material resources and normative standards. By implication this would mean that participation in Governance is the power to make decisions at the community/societal level and the power to determine the functioning of systems. The road to the power of determination and decision making should be paved with the power of influencing the decision-making.

Programmes and Practices

1. A separate religion – a New Religion for the Dalit people. Booshakthi-the symbol of Dalit power. Ancestor Worship as the alternative to dominant order of society. Chains of Dalit spirituality and learning centers all over South Asia and wherever possible in the rest of the world.

2. *Dalitology* – the alternative ideology for Capitalism and Brahminism. A unified and integrated vision of human personality and community. The essence of communicative competence. The Dalit Science never will it claim to be universal or the only science.

3. *Dalitism* – the worldview. The value premise by which people live. Inclusiveness, providing unlimited space to all communities and people, hospitality, resilience, introversion as internal strength.

4. *Cultural Identity* – the Dalits, the broken people. Historically and culturally derived identity. Not permanent. Be proud to proclaim as Dalits. No more a shame. Identity as Untouchables – Yes, do not touch us any more. Purity-impurity around beef eating. Yes, we are beefarian. Discourse based on black complexion. Yes, we are proud to be black. We are a separate people. There is a need to develop our discourses that will pave way for a Dalit Normative Standard, a Dalit Normative Order and Symbolic Order and Dalit Normative Prescriptions.

5. *Economic Identity* – Laborers. Declare Dalit labor as a national resource. No more free labor. Fix maximum wages for Dalit labor. Indigenous people that we are, land should come into our hands. Each Dalit family should have a minimum of five acres of land.

6. *Dalit Politics* – Conventionally a bipolarity of Power as Dominance and Power as Resistance. But now, a tripolairty of power as Participation. The power to govern and effectively influence governance. Work towards a Dalit form of Governance – distribution of values – both material and spiritual. No space for oppression and exploitation. A space for everybody. The Nation-State of the Western order is not an end in itself. It is only a transient order. What we aspire for is a governance system of our own. However, till it is achieved the Nation State offers one of the best hopes for the Dalit people in a context which is overwhelmingly saturated with Brahminic hegemony.

7. *Dalit Panchayat* – The strategy for internal organization of Dalit communities. A normative order based on the conventional wisdom of ancestors. Conflict resolution within the Dalit Community itself. Access the Nation-State mechanism against the oppressive forces of caste. Greater and more effective participation in democratic processes through Dalit panchayats.

8. *Dalit Intelligentsia* – The need of the hour. Development of organic intellectuals. Convergence of Academicians and Development practitioners. Keep the cycle of learning growing and expanding. Develop intellectuals

from childhood. Residential schools for Dalit children. Alternative education for Dalit youth. De-learning and re-learning processes for adults.

9. Leadership Development – Brahminic forces are always on the alert. Their technology is one of co-option. They never allow any value-based leadership to develop in the Dalit communities. The education system is in their hands. Long term educational and community living programs for Dalit young men and women, especially for women for internalization of the value system of Dalitism.

10. Human Rights Campaign – National and International. Significant efforts have been made to establish Dalit Rights as Human Rights through the National Campaign for Dalit Human Rights. In fact, this campaign has spread out to many parts of the world. In recent history many countries of the world have started Dalit Solidarity Forum. Globalization of the struggles for the establishment of rights is a dire need and this is being done with utmost seriousness. On this line mention must be made of the inauguration of CEDAR South Asia with its base in Bangalore.

11. A Yuga for Dalits. Ambedkar – the symbolic representation of the Dalit people. This Millennium is declared as the Ambedkar Yuga (Era). Visualize Dalitisation as a long-term perspective and process, which has to be initiated immediately. Yuga – already declared in Tumkur of Karnatka in India on 10 January 2000. But the Mission has to be carried on.

AN EXPERIENCE OF THE STRUGGLE AGAINST CORRUPTION IN ELECTIONS

Francisco WHITAKER FERREIRA (Brazil)

The Social Situation in Brazil

One of the basic characteristics of the current situation in my country, Brazil, is the marked inequality in the living standards of its population, contrasting with an abundance of natural wealth, a vast land mass, the beauty of its landscapes and the friendliness of its people.

On one side are the privileged or wealthy, at levels varying from very rich to medium rich, who place the nation's resources at their own service. Next come what could be called the middle classes, also aspiring to become wealthy. All this results in a lifestyle that is similar or even superior to that of the middle classes in the developed countries. They also travel widely throughout the rest of the world, and the very rich belong to the international jet-set. At the other end of the scale is a vast majority living in poverty and even the most utter poverty.

This characteristic of Brazil is nothing new. It is rooted in its colonial status that extended through to the first two decades of the XIX century, and a production system based on slavery, which continued through to almost the end of this same century. This has remained in place, due to the rural exodus that expanded rapidly over the past century.
Today, social inequalities continue to worsen, paradoxically in parallel to the modernisation of the nation through the production of goods and services slanted towards exports and meeting the needs of those with ample buying power. Another aspect that worsens the situation lies in the unprecedented possibilities of building up wealth through the economic globalisation process and international financial transactions. During all this time, the "excluded" – such as second-class citizens whose formal rights are not respected – constitute a vast and forgotten potential market, subsisting on crumbs falling from the tables of those eating the fill. This situation could well extend through to the year 2015, when worldwide poverty should be cut by half – according to the leaders of all our countries.

The Banalisation of Social Inequality

If the wealthy and the middle class represent one-third of the Brazilian population, this third forms a market of at least sixty million people, a demographic mass comparable to that of major European countries and sufficiently large enough to fuel the functioning of a dynamic economy. This economy sets up a type of smokescreen that conceals the poorer sectors of the population, at the same time as it forces them farther away from their places of work and commercial areas, building "capsules" of modernity in cities and large towns that could well be in the wealthy nations.

The poverty and utter poverty of the majority certainly manages to penetrate the protected enclaves, bringing with them the violence that springs from the difficulty in surviving through work, a lack of prospects, and drugs that are spreading everywhere.
While shocking visitors from less inegalitarian countries, Brazil's social inequalities are grounded on another problem: their banalisation. This fact is accepted by most Brazilians as quasi-natural characteristic of our social reality. It is part of the daily lives of our people, who fail to view it with a critical eye. Even the privileged themselves feel not the slightest embarrassment at displaying their wealth.
However, all human beings have an undeniable right to live in dignity and enjoy the respect of their peers. This banalisation of poverty and social injustice can no longer be tolerated. Brazilian society is in fact living in iniquity.

Social Inequality and Corruption

Corruption is one of the ingredients of this inequity. It is a serious type of theft: siphoning off government resources from social welfare purposes to private pockets, absorbing resources that could not only do much to reduce hunger, but would also underwrite investments generating jobs. This effect is extended by the fact that globalisation has opened up the possibilities of very high profits – particularly through international financial transactions and massive privatisation processes, yielding vast sums of money that are skimmed off, in an economy such as that of Brazil.

When this is undertaken with impunity by political leaders – who should rather be setting an example of how to exercise power to foster the common good – all society feels entitled to follow suit. Corruption rots the social fabric, benefiting the selfish, the devious and the crafty to the detriment of those trying to build up supportive relationships with their peers and society as a whole.

When this phenomenon takes place in the poor countries, or where government funding is limited, fraudulent misappropriation of public funding becomes a crime of high treason, and should be subject to reproof and condemned with the same rigor as torture.

These issues affect both the morale and the future of the people, in terms of ethics in politics and their struggle for social justice, striving to combat this iniquitous inequality that is a source of corruption – a recurrent problem in Brazil. Quite recently, during a speech as the new Supreme Justice of the Brazilian Supreme Court was taking office, the chairman of the Brazilian Bar Association (OAB) stressed "the need to undertake serious investigations into denunciations of corruption that sully the functions of many different civil service sectors, as well as leaders, government offices and politicians, together with the need to punish the culprits". Jointly with thirty other institutions, including the National Conference of Brazilian Bishops, trade unions and leading grassroots movements, the Brazilian Bar Association has just launched a "civic vigil against corruption", urging civil society to become more involved in investigations of cases of corruption, starting with the identification of sanctions that have not yet been imposed.

This seems like an endless and even desperate struggle. For instance, this was the case with the denunciation by the Brazilian Commission for Justice and Peace (CBJP), where I work, of an unacceptable practice: under the pretext of facilitating free international circulation of capital – the golden rule for globalisation under the thumb of finance – the Brazilian Central Bank (which is a federal government entity) was authorizing the inflow and outflow of vast amounts of funding with no control over its origin and not subject to any tax declarations. The money brought in by organised crime, the drug traffic and corruption are now blended with earnings that may well be honest, and this murky stream follows the paths of international finance to tax havens – legal until now – and is then channelled along different paths of unlimited accumulation.

This denunciation is the outcome of a study undertaken by the Brazilian Commission for Justice and Peace (CBJP) of another serious problem involving corruption in Brazil: the *promiscuity* of public and private agents managing the nation's financial system. This study revealed a real scandal through what were known as CC5 accounts, named after the administrative measure that "legalized" them. This denunciation was not followed by the

measures it deserved, as the mass communications media are controlled by political leaders and powerful people who draw personal profit from this lack of regulation.
This general introduction was needed to locate within its real context the Brazilian experience that is the subject of my presentation: an action undertaken by Brazilian society, urged by the National Conference of Brazilian Bishops, against what we have called electoral corruption.

Elections and Corruption

We are all well aware that democracy means more than just electing political leaders through a popular vote. However, elections are so important in a democracy that they are almost synonymous. Without going quite so far, it could well be said that they are surely the sinews of democracy.
As elections are so important, they should necessarily be free and honest, with all candidates competing under equal conditions. This is the only way in which elected leaders acquire legitimacy.

Some tricky problem have arisen in many countries, such as how to finance electoral campaigns, for instance, which is often the reason for turning to significantly corrupt practices.
Among other aspects linked to the threat of fraud, this problem also exists in Brazil. Just a few years ago, it was covered by in-depth discussions in our national parliament, urging that electoral legislation should be introduced that could prevent candidates from abusing their economic and political clout.

However, through to 1997, a distortion in our electoral processes remained untouchable: ballot-buying by candidates that is quite properly called "electoral corruption". The struggle against this scourge that was not sufficiently denounced does not appear in any of the political reform bills under discussion. And for good reason. Most of the elected politicians owe their mandate to bought ballots. This obviously benefits candidates – for both the legislative and the executive authorities – who can invest more heavily in their campaigns, as well as those linked to sources "interested" in financing these campaigns.

Perhaps like almost all Third World countries, ballot-buying in Brazil is current practice, made easier by low levels of political awareness among the majority of their second-class citizens or the "excluded", as mentioned in the start of my presentation. They form vast "electoral reserve armies" who are happy to sell their votes in exchange for a "plate of beans". Due to the vast number of voters who can be persuaded to cast their votes for more "generous" candidates, this practice lies at the root of severe distortions in election results.

This is a perverse and even cruel political system, as it draws its strength from maintaining voters in poverty and utter poverty. It also undermines democracy, whose functions are flawed at the root.
This practice also results in the mediocre quality of a significant number of elected representatives from the municipal through to the national level. In fact, elected representatives who cheat their voters are not eager to struggle to resolve the social problems of Brazil. Moreover, having had recourse to fraudulent methods in order to be re-elected, they tend to use these methods during their terms of office. This is how corruption can put down roots as a widespread practice in the field of politics.

Project Combating Electoral Corruption[1]

The action that I would like to tell you about began with a Lenten campaign focused on Fraternity and Politics, launched in 1996 by the National Conference of Brazilian Bishops (CNBB). Known as Fraternity Campaigns, they select a significant social issue as their theme each year, requiring reflection and action by Christians. The Conference of Brazilian Bishops published a reference text on various aspects of the selected theme, through which it attempted to visualize reality and analyze this situation based on the teachings of Jesus Christ, while indicating the paths for action for those feeling the call. All the communities in the Roman Catholic Church received this text, together with other attached documents intended to assist reflection on the reality within which these communities lived, being invited to concentrate on them during Lent.[2]

These annual campaigns are of the utmost importance in the pastoral actions of the Roman Catholic Church, which also seeks to include other religious confessions and society as a whole in reflecting on the actions to be taken. From this standpoint, the 2000 Lenten Campaign was addressed not only by Roman Catholic Bishops through the CNBB, but also by an ecumenical group of churches brought together through the National Council of Christian Churches (CONIC). The selected topic of human dignity and peace covered all the key issues in the reality of Brazil, which

---

1 See Francisco Whitaker Ferreira, 'L'aspiration à des élections vraiment régulières – Échec à la corruption au Brésil', in: *Le Monde Diplomatique*, September 2000.

2 For more information on these Fraternity Campaigns, log on to the internet website: www.cnbb.org.br.

I attempted to outline at the start of my presentation. The issues proposed for reflection by Christian communities during the 1996 Lenten Campaign included the topic of electoral corruption.

As this reflection prompted an awareness that this issue was of the utmost importance for Brazilian democracy, the Brazilian Commission for Justice and Peace – which is an entity under the CNBB – decided to run a specific project extending this Lenten campaign, entitled 'combating electoral corruption'. In 1997, a survey was carried out to measure the effects of ballot-buying on the results of the 1996 elections. A series of public hearings was held in several States, in order to complete this enquiry through witness statements[3].

Based on these facts, and assisted by a group of jurists, the Commission reached the conclusion that it was necessary to modify Brazil's electoral laws. In fact, ballot-buying was already ranked as a crime under law, but due to its severity, the judicial procedures stipulated for punishing the guilty parties were very lengthy, and the actions of the electoral courts remained ineffective: the few decisions handed down emerged only many years later, when those elected though buying ballots were already in their second term of office.

The proposed modifications to the law stipulated that giving or merely offering voters any material goods, advantages or money during electoral campaigns in order to obtain votes was not only a crime, but also an electoral violation. An electoral violation is subject to administrative sanctions that are far easier and faster to impose. This sanction was far more radical than the criminal procedure: the candidate was disqualified, obviously before the votes were counted, or at least before being inducted into office. Candidates found guilty of electoral corruption were consequently stripped of their right to participate in the election under way.

This draft bill included a second section, which was also innovative: the electoral courts could also disqualify any candidate who wielded the administrative structure to obtain votes, meaning the use of civil servants, government vehicles and other services for campaigning or handing out favours to voters. Also frequent, until then, this practice had been punished only by a cash fine that was negligible compared to the vast amounts disbursed by candidates. This sanction was so light that Congress often voted to issue a general amnesty a few years later, before the penalties were

---

[3] For more information on the projects combating electoral corruption, log on to the internet website: www.cbjp.org.br.

imposed. The proposed innovations should have weighed particularly heavily on the municipal elections that were to take place the following year, when for the first time mayors could run for a second term without resigning.

A Difficult but More Promising Path

There were two ways to submit this draft bill to the National Congress: turn to the government, at the initiative of the House of Representatives or the Senators, or use a tool involving direct citizen participation established by the 1988 Brazilian constitution: a popular initiative on legislative matters. This tool had been used only once, and the draft bill submitted was still under discussion by parliament. The popular initiative required the signatures of one million voters on a petition – around 1% of the total electorate – which is the minimum required by the Brazilian constitution.

This second option was selected. Although obviously harder to implement effectively, the selection of this strategy reflected another very specific intention: the Commission for Justice and Peace wished to benefit from this initiative in educational terms. The practice of ballot-buying is widely accepted, with voters casting their ballots in each round of voting in order to receive something from the candidate. The problem is consequently crucial, with the collection of signatures offering a chance to discuss the value of their votes.
Sixty other national organisations joined the Commission for Justice and Peace in this campaign, and a slogan was launched: *A Vote Has No Price, It Has Consequences.*

It was obviously not an easy task to gather a million signatures, each accompanied by its voter card number, which is an item that not everyone carries around with them. Collecting these signatures required fifteen months' hard work.
Once submitted to Congress on August 10, 1999 this draft bill passed rapidly though the various levels of decision, thanks to the political weight of its one million signatures. Having been discussed and approved by the Lower House and the Senate in 35 days, it was promulgated almost immediately by the president of Brazil – just one day before the deadline for this new law to cover the elections in the year 2000.

It is not certain whether all members of Parliament were fully aware of the consequences for themselves of this law on which they voted. In the course of the discussions, a senator forecast that it would have a "devastating effect". But it was difficult for these parliamentarians to oppose a draft ill whose clear and simple objective was to punish a crime more effectively. To resist would seem like an advance declaration of an intention to commit this same crime.

The adoption of law 9840/99, on September 29, 1999, was a great triumph for Brazilian society, crowning the successful completion of the very specific procedure of a draft bill submitted by popular initiative for the first time in the nation's history.[4]

Controlling the Application of this New Law

However, it was quite clear that the mere existence of a new law would not be sufficient: the electoral courts could only hand down decisions on complaints filed against candidates in violation. Without these complaints, everything would continue as before, and nobody would be punished.

Faced with this challenge, the organisations that had sent in a million signatures to Congress set up yet another network, through a broad-ranging movement designed to ensure the application of the new law during the municipal elections in October 2000. The three hundred Brazilian bishops were mobilised yet again during their general assembly in late April, as well as the leaders who brought in the signatures. Committees were set up in many towns, named after the number of the law 9840. Each organisation also agreed to issue publications during this initial stage; meanwhile leading newspapers, radio and television chains also began to cover this problem.

A brief but detailed handbook was prepared on the contents of the law and the procedures to be followed when setting up these committees and keeping them running, published by the Commission for Justice and Peace.[5] The Brazilian Bar Association (OAB) – which had also helped collect the signatures – forwarded this handbook to all its regional and local chapters and sub-chapters, recommending its members to provide legal support for these 9840 Committees. In several States, local leaders simplified this handbook for use by the public at large. Stickers began to appear on vehicles. Additionally, an intensive education campaign was run to break down foreseeable resistance among the voters themselves, who

4 See the transcript of the discussions in Congress in: *Combatendo a corrupção eleitoral,* Brasilia (Lower House, Documentation & Information Centre, Publications Coordination Unit), 1999.

5 Brazilian Commission for Justice and Peace, *Vamos acabar com a corrupção eleitoral,* São Paulo (Paulinas), 2000 (www.paulinas.org.br).

did not necessarily cast a favourable eye on banning practices that often benefited them.

This handbook was made available over an Internet website set up especially for this mobilisation drive.[6] This website also published newsflashes on these initiatives, together with educational materials and legal information of use to the 9840 Committees, as well as posters and publications available for reproduction. This website also provided information on denunciations and sanctions handed down by the electoral courts. Exemplary sanctions were assigned high priority, due to their marked dissuasive effect.

Towards the 2002 Elections

However, the application of this law has not yet produced all the expected results. We still do not know – although a survey is under way –exactly how many sanctions were imposed. However, there is no doubt that the mere existence of this new law prevented many candidates from buying ballots. These sanctions also lowered the number of potential offenders. There was a high turnover on many Town Councils, and some of them – notorious for corruption – did not see the worst of their members return. Even where these dishonest candidates were been punished for their crimes, the voters themselves blocked their re-election, as they became aware of these accusations.

However, much still remains to be done for this law to be applied in full. Although very effective in some places, the Electoral Courts still fell well below expectations in many parts of the country. The Commission for Justice and Peace and a few of the organisations associated with it in this project – such as the Association of Judges for Democracy, the Democratic District Attorneys Movement, and the Brazilian Association of Non-Governmental Organisations (ABONG) – are already gearing up to take action before the 2002 elections at both the national and state levels. Among other actions, a national seminar for electoral judges and district attorneys was organised in August 2001, in order to assess the actions of the electoral courts in the 2000 municipal elections and define the types of action needed to ensure that law 9840 is fully applied nationwide in 2002. This seminar was supported by the Superior Electoral Court (TSE), which is the highest electoral court in Brazil, endowing it with added importance.

---

6 www.lei9840.org.br.

We are still working hard, guided by the purpose of ensuring respect for the human dignity of all Brazilians. The struggle against electoral corruption is limited but strategic, in view of Brazil's political lack of responsibility: it is designed to prevent dishonest candidates from competing at the ballot box, preventing the election of those who have no programmes other than handing out cash or favours to voters in order to be elected to positions of political power that they will use for their own profit. We believe that our efforts could well help reverse a tendency to mistrust democracy that is far too strongly marked among the Brazilian people, and which is a dangerous trend in a country where inequalities are so deep-rooted and with social problems that are so severe.

WHERE IT COUNTS: THE STRUGGLE FOR A PEOPLE'S BUDGET IN SOUTH AFRICA

Dale McKinley (South Africa)

Introduction

The Legacy of Apartheid Budgets

The historical legacy of South Africa reflects a double dynamic. On the one hand, apartheid produced gross racial, class and gender inequalities that rendered the vast majority of the population economically, socially, culturally and physically oppressed. On the other hand, the mass struggles waged against such oppression have endowed this country with a degree of politicisation and social organisation that is both varied and dynamic. The real challenge for the majority of South Africans since overthrowing the apartheid system then, has been the degree to which the latter inheritance can overcome the former.

During the apartheid years, the budget was used to institutionalise economic inequality and social injustice and the budgetary process itself was completely without any kind of involvement from the vast majority of the people. From the early 1980s onwards, this took place within a broader context of declining economic growth, massive accumulation of apartheid debt, impoverishment for the black majority (and to a lesser extent other 'non-white' racial groupings). This was coupled to an immense accumulation of wealth by a small minority of capitalists (predominately white) and generalised social degradation for most South Africans.

People's Struggles

The mass struggles that eventually toppled the apartheid system sought to usher in a new, democratic dispensation that would set about rectifying the damage done. Even in the context of the serious compromises that marked the negotiated transition to a new political order, the vast majority of South Africans based their support for the new government on a socio-economic programme – the Reconstruction and Development Programme (RDP) – that would, over time, fundamentally address the social and economic inequalities that had made the country the most unequal society in the world. The RDP was, of necessity, a broad strategic framework within which more specific tools of fiscal, monetary and social policy would follow – the budget being one of these tools.

A budget is a universal tool for setting the overall policy priorities of a government, a way of deciding how the wealth and resources of the country are going to be utilised. In the South African context, the overwhelming endorsement of the RDP, as the foundation upon which post-1994 budgets would be built, set the scene for the new government to implement the social and economic priorities of the people. These priorities were quite simple – to guarantee the most basic human, economic and social rights of the people through a radical redistribution of economic and social wealth and opportunity.

What has Happened?

The first two (post-apartheid) budgetary cycles reflected the content of many of the compromises that had been agreed to during the negotiations. People were patient. Yet, there was little indication of preparations for a decisive break with the past, both in terms of the content and process of the budget itself. When the new government finally decided to 'show it's hand' (mid-1996), it introduced the Growth, Employment and Redistribution (GEAR) programme as the strategic macro-economic framework within which the priorities expressly endorsed, and struggled for, by the South African people, would be pursued.

GEAR's understanding of how macro-economic policy would be pursued, and thus, the ideological foundation of the budget itself, rested on two key and inter-related assumptions:

1. That there was no economic and political space (blamed on the 'balance of forces') for the construction of a uniquely redistributive South African political economy grounded in the creative political and economic will of the majority as broadly captured in the RDP;
2. That the political and economic will of capitalists, as represented by domestic and international corporate and finance capital, would be better suited to South Africa's stated desire (through the 1994 electoral victory and the RDP) for redistribution, job creation and growth.

Not surprisingly, the cumulative result of the dogged pursuit of GEAR budgets has been to further institutionalise (even if not on the basis of racial categories) the very economic inequalities and social injustices that the struggle against apartheid had sought to abolish. Over six years after the demise of apartheid, the content and process of the budget has failed to respond to the will of the South African people. As this study will show, the extent of the redistribution of income, wealth and general resources in favour of the impoverished majority has been scant. Instead, the budget has resulted in furthering the gap between rich and poor and has been used as a tool to pursue a deracialised, 'free market' capitalism that seeks to meet the interests of small minorities of elites, both domestically and internationally.

The Need for Change

It has become patently obvious that the present strategic, macro-economic framework that has informed post-apartheid budgeting has to be abandoned. There is no use in tinkering at the micro-level of the budget – the core is rotten. An entirely new foundation needs to be laid that reflects, both in content and process, the frequently expressed (but frequently ignored) will of the majority of South Africans. This requires a political will that has been completely lacking. Even more importantly though, this requires that the people of South Africa raise their voices and intensify their struggles for a society in which social and economic rights are not held hostage to the ideological whims of a few elites, regardless of class orientation and/or skin colour. Nothing less than mass mobilisation for a people's budget is going to force fundamental change.

It is important to note that any meaningful analysis of budgets must do so over time. This provides a means of discerning specific budgetary patterns, continuities, results and contradictions. It should further be noted that there always exists an umbilical relationship between a chosen macro-economic framework and the specific contents and process of any budget – one cannot be understood without the other. Finally, it should be clear that the main intent of this study is to assist the majority of South Africans who are daily struggling to overcome economic inequality and social injustice and to make a powerful case for the need for, and realisation of, an entirely new, people's budget that speaks directly to those struggles.

General Economic and Social Indicators

South Africa is a wealthy country, endowed with abundant natural and human resources, a highly developed manufacturing sector and substantial capital infrastructure. At the same time, this endowment is highly concentrated in particular geographical areas of the country and the distribution of resources flowing from it has historically benefited a small (predominately white) minority. One the one hand, parts of South Africa resemble the most developed areas of the (First World) North, and on the other hand there exist parts that are as under-developed as the worst areas in the (Third World) South.

Taking a look at the most commonly used economic indicators of economic development (as Table 1 below does over most of the 1990s), one could be excused for immediately thinking that the economic health of South Africa is fine, if a bit uneven in places. Indeed, this is often the approach taken by mainstream economists and developmental 'experts', who point to the apparent normality of the economic 'road signs'. Nonetheless, as even the mainstream indicators provided below show, there has been a general lack of performance in the South African economy since the mid-1990s, giving an early indication that all is not as well as it appears.

Table 1: Overall key economic indicators for South Africa (1991-1998)[1]

KEY INDICATORS	UNIT	1991	1992	1993	1994	1995	1996	1997	1998
POPULATION	MILLIONS	36.19	36.99	37.8	38.63	39.47	40.34	41,23	42,13
GROSS NATIONAL INCOME AT CURRENT PRICES	US$ MILLIONS	122 297	130 781	128 882	134 504	147 238	140 021	144 415	129 699
GDP AT CURRENT PRICES	US$ MILLIONS	120 245	130 533	130 488	135 822	151 118	143 128	147 637	133 380
GDP AT CONSTANT 1990 PRICES	US$ MILLIONS	200 846	196 553	198 978	205 413	211 813	220 608	226 131	227 635
GROWTH IN GDP AT CONSTANT PRICES	%	-100	-210	1.20	3.20	3.10	4.20	2.50	0.50
GDP PER CAPITA	US$ MILLION	3323	3529	3452	3516	3829	3548	3581	3166
GOVT. CONSUMPTION AS% OF GDP		19.80	20.20	20.10	20.00	18.30	19.40	19.80	20.20
PRIVATE CONSUMPTION AS% OF GDP		63.40	63.70	62.30	62.10	62.60	62.70	63.40	63.00
GOVT. SAVINGS AS% OF GDP		-310	-730	-670	-590	-420	-490	-490	-390
PRIVATE SAVINGS AS% OF GDP		6.50	9.00	9.40	9.40	7.60	7.80	6.70	5.20
GOVT. INVESTMENT AS% OF GDP		3.40	2.80	2.50	2.30	2,4	2.40	2.50	2.50
PRIVATE INVESTMENT AS% OF GDP		10.70	9,5	11.00	13.10	13.70	12.80	11.60	10.00
INFLATION	% CHANGE	15.30	13.90	9.70	9.00	8.70	7.40	8.60	6.90
MERCHANDISE EXPORTS AS% OF GDP		19.80	18.80	19.00	19.40	19.90	21.20	21.10	21.80
MERCHANDISE IMPORTS AS% OF GDP		14.30	14.00	14.20	16.10	18.10	19.30	19.60	20.40
CURRENT ACCOUNT AS% OF GDP		1.90	1.50	1.10	0.10	-150	-130	-150	-160
CAPITAL & FINANCIAL ACCOUNTS AS% OF GDP		-140	-70	-390	0.90	3.80	0.40	3.30	1.40
OVERALL BALANCE AS% OF GDP		1.30	0.20	-230	0.70	1.80	-90	1.80	-70
DOMESTIC CURRENCY PER US$ – END OF YEAR		2.74	3.05	3.40	3.54	3.64	4.68	4.86	5.86
TOTAL DEBT AS% OF EXPORTS OF GOODS & SERVICES		89.60	93.40	94.30	98.80	101.70	96.30	105.40	106,8
BUDGET DEFICIT/SURPLUS AS% OF GDP		-421	-818	-869	-502	-516	-489	-302	-256
TOTAL PUBLIC DEBT AS% OF GDP		36.82	40.45	43.45	49.12	49.55	49.25	48.28	50,47

1 Source: *Southern African Political & Economic Monthly,* Vol.13, No.12, Sept/Oct 2000. SARIPS/SAPES Databank.

Taking a closer look at more specific developmental indicators such as the rate of poverty, inequality of income and general health give a better picture of the developmental state of the country. Thus, the fact that 3% of all household income is received by the poorest 20% of the population, or that 22.9% of South African infants suffer from stunting, gives indication of the extent to which there exists extreme poverty and inequality in a country with more than adequate resources and capacity to ensure the well being of its population.[1]

If the focus is shifted to infrastructural indicators such as the prevalence, geographical spread and racial composition of access to the most basic services (water and electricity) a picture emerges of a country in which the majority of its citizens (African poor), and especially those in rural areas, have yet to emerge from their under-developed status.

Table 2: Percentages of Total & African households with access to basic infrastructure (1996-1999)[2]

	Total households with access to infrastructure				*African-headed households with access to infrastructure*			
	1996	*1997*	*1998*	*1999*	*1996*	*1997*	*1998*	*1999*
Type of infrastructure in urban and non-urban areas (i)	%* (ii)	%* (iii)	%* (iv)	%* (v)	%* (vi)	%* (vii)	%* (viii)	%* (ix)
(a) Both urban and non-urban: Running water in dwelling or on site	62,2	64,3	64,1	65,9	47,6	51,9	51,5	55,3
Electricity for main lighting source	62,1	65,1	66,7	69,7	47,6	53,5	55,4	60,8
(b) Urban: Running water in dwelling or on site	869	88,4	87,3	88.8	77,8	81,5	79,0	82,9
Electricity for main lighting source	82,5	84,2	85,2	84,5	70,3	74,8	75,9	76,5
(c) Non-urban: Running water in dwelling or on site	25,4	26,8	29,3	31,2	20,9	23,4	25,7	27,3
Electricity for main lighting source	31,6	35,4	38,8	47,2	27,6	32,9	36,3	44,8

1 See Statistics SA, *Household Survey*, October 1999.
2 Source: Statistics SA, *Household Survey*, October 1999.

Once a more comprehensive perspective of the economic and social character of South Africa and its population has been obtained, it is then easier to understand why South Africa (described as a 'middle-income' country relative to global developmental 'standards') ranks among the worst in terms of income equality. South Africa's income inequality is one of the highest in the world, whether as compared to developing countries or countries that fall within the 'middle-income' bracket.

A brief perusal of another key indicator of the developmental health of a society, employment, confirms the link between economic and social 'health' and the ability of a society to generate employment opportunities. The falling employment rate, prior to the introduction of a new, post-apartheid government, gives indication of an overall economic decline that had begun many years previously and was only slightly mitigated by occasional surges in employment within the public sector. The late apartheid era record of the private sector in generating employment also provides a strong indication of the general tendency of private capital to shed jobs in an environment of political and economic uncertainty.[3]

And yet, employment trends in the post-apartheid 1990s reveal a continued shedding of formal jobs.[4] Despite the overthrow of apartheid, the coming to power of a democratically elected and popular government and the introduction of a new macro-economic policy framework, the South African economy has failed miserably to generate positive employment figures. Indeed, the negative rate of employment that characterised the pre-1994 period, has only accelerated, despite economic and political stabilisation. While there continues to be raging arguments over the exact number of jobs lost since the introduction of GEAR (although it is generally accepted that it has been in the hundreds of thousands), one thing is clear – that successive post-apartheid budgets have failed to stimulate employment in the formal economy. As with all countries, high rates of unemployment go hand-in-hand with increased economic inequality and social poverty.

The data on employment trends is made all the more negative when one looks at parallel trends in labour costs. Again, the declining nominal and real unit labour costs in the first half of the 1990s (as the figure below clearly shows) have continued, even if not so precipitously, in the latter half of the decade. This gives lie to the well-worn argument that the South African labour force is over-priced. But, it also reveals that the macro-

[3] See SA Reserve Bank, *Quarterly Review 1996.*
[4] See *ibid.*

economic approach of the post-apartheid government has sustained these negative trends in the 'labour market' in the vain hope that this will lead to increased private sector investment (both foreign and domestic) and thus the creation of jobs, neither of which has happened with any sustained intensity.

Non-agricultural nominal and real unit labour costs

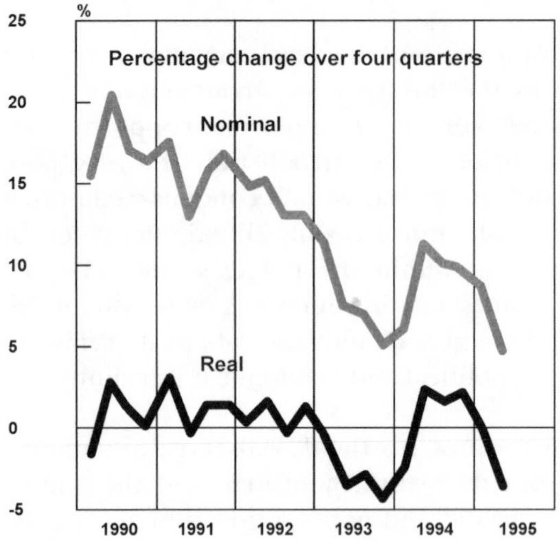

Source: SA Reserve Bank, Quarterly Review (1996)

The budgetary approach of the post-apartheid government has failed to fundamentally address the serious social and economic problems as briefly laid out above. Virtually none of the main economic indicator assumptions and result projections of GEAR for the five-year period from its implementation in 1997 have been achieved. The only projected assumption of GEAR that has been met (and even exceeded) is the budget deficit: GDP ratio. In all other respects, the budgets offered to the people of the new South Africa have, to put it mildly, been far below their legitimate expectations.[5]

The Income Side of the Budget

In a people's democracy (which South Africa makes claim to) there is always a 'societal contract'– i.e., a government is put into place to provide not merely a political representation of the will of the people but to meet

---

5 See John Newton, *Reforming the South African Public Finances,* (NIEP Occasional Paper Series No. 6 April 1997), Johannesburg (National Institute for Economic Policy), 1997, p. 21.

the basic needs of the population. In the context of a capitalist political economy in which there are social/economic classes that benefit at the expense of others (and in South Africa this is layered over with an apartheid past which makes things even worse for the poor), this means that the government is faced with the task of ensuring that the necessary capital is made available to address societal divisions (practically experienced by the lower classes through the unavailability of jobs, lack of basic services and general impoverishment).

Thus, the starting point for any income side of the budget must be to put the necessary mechanisms in place to access the maximum amount of capital that is available in order to fulfil the 'contract' with the people who placed it in power. In South Africa there is a tremendous amount of capital that is available for this purpose but it is mostly concentrated in the hands of a small and powerful minority (top quintile) that is most interested in ensuring that the capital it possesses remains where it is.

Given this scenario, the government of the day must have the political will (with which it has been popularly and democratically invested) to act in favour of those who otherwise will forever remain at the bottom of the economic and social societal scale. Income decisions are therefore not merely economic decisions about numbers and percentages but necessarily and predominately political ones because they go to the heart of addressing inequality, poverty and the possibilities for all South Africans to enjoy the most basic economic and social rights. In the present environment of seriously unequal global and domestic economic relations this is not an easy task but it must be tackled if there is to be any real societal progress towards realising the struggles that the South African people have waged, and continue to wage.

The Tax Regime

The most common means of accessing the capital available in a society is through various means of taxation. South Africa's tax regime has historically been regressive, not out of any general economic imperative, but solely as a means of benefiting the class (and in the past, racial) interests of a small minority. The impact of this regressive tax regime on the poor (and predominately black) majority has been all the more intense in a South Africa that has never had a sizeable middle class around which a more widely spread tax regime can be centred. The overall trend in South Africa has been a gradual increase in general tax revenue (outstripping expectation), giving further indication that despite low rates of growth there exists space for increased revenue generation.[6]

However, by looking at a more specific breakdown of where that revenue income has been derived (as the data below shows), it is clearly revealed that both the pre and post-apartheid trend point to a generally regressive tax regime. One of the most regressive single taxes (Value Added Tax – VAT) which is now set at a flat rate of 14%, has progressively taken up a larger share of tax revenue (multiplied when set against the household income of lower income earners), while at the same time company taxes have fallen as an overall percentage of revenue collection. Similarly, taxes that hit the poor the hardest, such as fuel taxes have risen over time (even more so in the last several budgets) as has the share of personal income tax, while taxes on gold mines has virtually disappeared.

In other words, the means of generating government revenue for the delivery of goods and services has increasingly been shifted to those who can least afford it. There is simply no way of getting around the fact that unless the decisions on taxation, within a budget, reflect the economic reality of South Africa (as addressed in the previous section), there is very little possibility that the rights and needs of the majority will ever be realised.

Table 3: Percentage Composition of Tax Revenue (1976-1995)[7]

Source	*1976*	*1980*	*1985*	*1990*	*1995*
Gold Mines	8.5	11.4	6.8	1.7	0.4
Other Companies	26.5	18.0	16.1	17.7	12.1
[Total Companies]	[35.0]	[29.4]	[22.9]	[19.4]	[12.5]
Individual	24.7	18.0	31.1	30.4	40.9
Sales Tax	0	12.2	25.0	27.0	26.4
Customs & Excise	21.1	12.7	8.1	14.4	17.9
Other	19.3	27.7	12.9	8.9	2.2
Total	100	100	100	100	100

6 See SA Reserve Bank, *Quarterly Review 2000.*

7 Source: Trudi Hartzenburg, Paper delivered at Women's Budget Initiative Workshop, March 1996, contained in: COSATU, *Submission of the 1996/97 Budget.*

Table 4: Composition of Tax Revenue – 1999/2000 – 2000/2001[8]

	1999/2000		*2000/2001 (*Estimates)*	
	R (Millions)	*% of Revenue*	*R (Millions)*	*% of Revenue*
Individual	85 953.70	42,5%	86 400.00	40%
Companies	21 263.30	10.6%	26 025.00	12%
Vat/gst	48 330.20	24.2%	54 000.00	25%
Fuel Levy	14 289.80	7,2%	14 900.00	6,9%
Excise Duties	9 740.40	4,8%	9 721.00	4,5%
Total Tax Revenue	200 958.70	89,3%	216 786.3	88,4%

The increased tax burden on the poor is a direct result of budgetary concessions to the rich. A host of corporate subsidies, tax holidays for foreign investors, a lack of specific luxury taxes, varying levels of tax deductibles for those fortunate enough to have investments, medical aid etc, and myriad other tax breaks for 'charitable' donations have all combined to make the South African tax regime a thoroughly regressive and anti-people fiscal instrument. Not only does this have a seriously negative effect on the daily lives of the poor majority but just as negatively, on the prospect of accessing adequate amounts of capital, through taxation, to carry out the people's mandate for meeting basic social and economic needs.

This situation is consistent with the economic orthodoxy that informs GEAR – i.e., a trickle down approach which stipulates that if a government 'removes' much of the tax burden from the private corporate capitalist class that they will, in turn, invest the windfall into the general economy and thus spur growth and employment. This kind of taxation policy is no less a political decision than any other and all international evidence points to the conclusion that following such orthodoxy in a country like South Africa has not, and will not, benefit the 'receptive' majority. Indeed, this approach can only serve to increase the tax burden on those who can least afford it while providing increasing relief to those who can most afford to pay.

The economic logic here is simply ludicrous – give those that already have more and trust that they will then use this to benefit those who do not (not

8 Source: Department of Finance, *2001 Budget Review*.

to mention society as a whole). A tax regime that is based upon such logic will only serve to further exacerbate economic inequality and social poverty. Confirmation of this is provided by the fact that the economic elite in South Africa have taken their tax windfalls and invested billions of SARands overseas rather than invest in the real domestic economy. The same applies to capitalists from outside the country who have given no indication, after several years, that they are at all interested in utilising tax benefits received for the greater good, but who prefer capital intensive, and short-term, 'quickie' investment.

Since GEAR (which has framed the specific tax decisions taken in successive budgets) premises the possibilities of economic growth and employment on such an approach, it then becomes clear that the present tax regime can, in no way, meet the economic and social needs of the majority it is supposedly designed to do.

Tariffs/Exchange Controls

Another means of accessing capital for purposes of meeting the needs of the people is through the application of tariffs, and the management of exchange controls. In the South African case, we have a scenario in which the government has followed a path of removing as many tariffs as possible, as fast as possible (in relation to other countries with similar levels of development and even in excess of that required by membership in the WTO/GATT). This approach has had devastating effects on employment in the most affected sectors (e.g., textiles), has seriously eroded the possibilities of catalysing domestic, productive investment and has led to a more general loss in relation to government revenue.

In a different, but no less important vein, serious questions need to be posed concerning the present federalist approach to 'control over' and thus ability to gain revenue from such things as water. While on one hand water has been proclaimed as a national asset that belongs to the 'people', the power over the control, use and 'taxation' of water has been given to the local government level – the level of government least able to do so effectively. Thus we have a situation of completely unequal access to, and use of, water services with little use of block tariffs and progressive structures of taxation (but rather increasing privatisation). Provision and revenue cannot be artificially separated, as is now the case with the national budget.

Likewise, the budgetary approach to exchange controls has dealt a double blow to the effective collection and use/employment of domestic capital (which is, after all, capital that has been 'produced' by the workers of this country). Not only has the relaxation and virtual disappearance of exchange controls resulted in massive capital outflows that have often outstripped any Foreign Direct Investment (FDI) coming into the country, but it has also deprived the domestic economy of taxable capital.

It is ironic, that while GEAR purports to be 'integrating' South Africa into the global capitalist economy to the benefit of all South Africans, such GEAR-informed policies are, in reality, depriving South Africa of the very capital foundation needed to be able to develop its economy as well as to be able to operate on much more equal terms in the global economy. The present trajectory is little more than the confirmation that the government is using budgetary means to fit in with the agendas of powerful international and domestic agents who do not want to see any 'barriers' to their manipulation and use of capital. Again, a situation has been allowed to develop where those that are privileged to have capital influence the 'rules' to their benefit, while the majority are supposed to hope that some sort of long-term indirect benefits will trickle down to them as a result. Nothing could be further from the reality.

Debt 'Income'

Although not technically a component of the income side of a budget, in the South African case it does apply. This is due to the fact that the accumulated apartheid debt (the very economic basis for the subjugation of the majority of the population for so long) continues to act as a serious break on the potential availability of capital in the budget to meet the necessary social expenditure needs for that same majority.

What we have had now for several years is the almost unbelievable scenario of a democratic government dutifully repaying (mostly in interest on the original principle), a debt incurred to prevent that same government from coming to power. The data provided in the expenditure section on debt gives a clear picture of the size of this debt relative to other areas of expenditure and shows how the government has religiously prioritised its repayment at the expense of other budgetary items. Given the fact that the vast majority of this debt is 'owed' to the Government Employees Pension Fund (GEPF), there is absolutely no economic sense in continuing to service an illegitimate debt that is maintained merely through the political decision to continue with a fully funded public pension scheme. Indeed, there is every reason to conclude that following such a path has much more to do with 'perceptions' of powerful economic actors rather than any economic logic.

Not only do the people of South Africa lose out on billions of capital that could be utilised for social expenditure, employment creation etc. (i.e., additional 'income'), but those that previously benefited under apartheid (both domestic and international) continue to benefit from the people's capital through receiving repayments on this illegitimate debt as well as benefiting from accruals gained through 'managing' debt capital held in reserve.

Privatisation 'Income'

Similar to debt 'income', the proceeds of the government's privatisation programme are not formally considered to constitute a part of the income side of the budget. Be that as it may, the reality is that the government has taken the decision to use privatisation of public assets as a means to gain additional income for budgetary expenditure.

In his presentation of the 2000 budget, Finance Minister Trevor Manuel explicitly stated that the government had received an amount of R6.9 billion in privatisation proceeds for the previous fiscal year (1999/2000) and that amounts of R5 billion for 2000/01 and R10 billion in 2002/03 were expected to roll in to the government's coffers. Minister Manuel even went so far as to say that the government considered these amounts to be below expectations but that the revenue gained from privatisation would go a long way to ensuring the better delivery of services[9]. Not surprisingly, Minister Manuel announced in his 2001 Budget speech that expected proceeds from privatisation over the next budget cycle would be raised to R18 billion and that it would be these funds that would cover the parallel expansion in infrastructural and service delivery.

Most all of this privatisation 'income' has been, and will continue to be, derived from selling off the most important public assets, whose continued public ownership and use are absolutely essential if the government is to address the needs of the majority. This privatisation process, which has become the rallying cry of the private sector across the globe and which the IMF and World Bank vigorously propagate, constitutes a double blow to the possibilities of social and economic equality and justice. Not only

9 2000 Budget Speech by Minister of Finance, Trevor Manuel, February 2000.

are the main public tools for service delivery being sold off, but they are being sold to the very corporate capital that has no interest in anything other than the amount of profit that can be derived from their use, profits that are then used for unproductive and speculative purposes of further accumulation. Already, the privatisation of water services has resulted (as it has internationally) in increased price structures and the contraction of delivery to poor communities who cannot afford to pay. The same has happened with housing and so too will it apply to the transportation and health sectors once the privatisation process speeds up.

As has been shown in the cases of the rail system in Britain, water services in many European countries or in a host of key social services in developing countries, privatisation is a failure, both in terms of income derived and the social and economic consequences the majority of people. Indeed, it is nothing more than an ideologically-driven means to further empower private capital and completely guts the potential for public enterprises to actually make capital for the public sector while at the same time fulfilling their role as economic catalysts and delivery agents. As long as the South African government continues to pursue the privatisation of public assets, in the false belief that this will benefit the majority and enhance the ability of government to deliver basic social services, references to a people's government ring extremely hollow.

The Expenditure Side of the Budget

The expenditure side of a budget represents the dominant tool of government, for provision of services, the redistribution of resources and is the main tool to stimulate and drive the economy. In the context of a capitalist political economy where the prevailing orthodoxy is, the less government the better, it is most often social and infrastructural expenditure by the public sector that is the first to suffer. While this orthodoxy is presented as the best means to 'free' the market to deliver services and grow the economy, the reality is much simpler.

Decisions relating to the character and amount of budgetary expenditure are, first and foremost, political decisions. There is absolutely no correlation between cut backs on the expenditure side of the budget and improved social and economic 'health'. Indeed, all international and historical evidence points to an inverse relationship between the two and private capital should be the first to acknowledge this. Capitalists themselves, have no problem with receiving as much government financial assistance as possible (after all, most tax regimes are essentially private welfare assistance) when it benefits their ability to make more profits and to receive certain services for free. Any successful private entrepreneur understands that without access to financing and credit lines, the chances of building and sustaining his/her enterprise are virtually non-existent. And yet, when it comes to government finances, it is the private sector that is the first to cry foul when the public sector desires to apply this basic principle.

The argument that has been used against increased government expenditure – i.e., the 'crowding out' of private sector expenditure – is not borne out either internationally or in the case of South Africa. On the contrary, increased government expenditure actually serves to 'crowd in' private sector expenditure by creating new avenues for economic growth and increasing the population's capacity for consumption, tied to the parallel expansion of employment. As has been the experience with all developed countries, economic and social opportunities for the majority of the population were premised on the accessibility to most all the basic services needed to maintain a decent standard of living (although this is becoming less so since the economic orthodoxy has been more aggressively implemented in the last two decades).

Data provided on the character and content of general expenditure patterns in South Africa over a number of years, gives the strongest indication of the proportional relationship between social/infrastructural expenditure and basic socio-economic indicators of well being. The record speaks for itself over the last several years. As real public sector expenditure has declined (whatever specific measurement is used), so too have the problems of unemployment, sustained access to basic services, quality of health and education and the general well-being of the majority of the population suffered.

And yet, it is not simply a matter of ever-increasing expenditure being the panacea to all of South Africa social and economic ills. In other words, increased expenditure is a necessary, but not sufficient, condition for redistribution of resources, economic growth, and meeting the rights and needs of the majority Unless it is properly directed and managed it can be wasted (as is shown specifically, in the realm of welfare). Arguing that, for example, the amount of monies spent on education in South Africa compares favourably with countries in the same developmental band misses the point. South Africa has an incredibly deep inequality that has to be overcome in the historical and more contemporary context within which it has been allowed to fester. Therefore, the requirements to ensure that such inequality is fundamentally addressed demands a distinct standard of reference than might apply elsewhere.

Nonetheless, there does exist a universal expenditure 'equation' to successfully tackle the kind of inequality and poverty that now threatens to engulf both South Africa and much of the world. It goes something like this – if the necessary expenditure is not taking place then this, in turn, impacts on the possibilities for economic growth which, in turn, impacts on the size of the budget to be made available for social priorities. Without this, talk of percentages and amounts mean very little in the context of what is required to address the problems confronting South Africa. This is even more the case in a scenario in which the rate of inflation and the increase in the size of the population outstrip any small increases in expenditure, as has been the case in South Africa for most of the last several years.

Besides direct government intervention to socialise/nationalise specific sectors of the economy (which was taken off the South African agenda prior to 1994), one of the only ways in which the government can adequately address the kinds of inequalities and maldistribution of resources is to intervene in the economy through expenditure priorities. This necessarily means doing so to benefit the majority poor. The relationship between social and infrastructural expenditure, economic growth and the raising of living standards is well established and this must be the priority of the government rather than something that is 'added on' to the budget after prioritising reduction of the budget deficit etc. The axiom that informed the RDP was 'growth through redistribution', not the other way round as is now the case with government budgets. Prioritising redistribution is fundamental to a complete shift in the way budgets are approached. The people must come first.

There has been a relatively stagnant level of expenditure throughout the 1990s and, rather than a rise in general and consumption expenditure (as a% of GDP) since 1994, there has been a slight overall decline.[10] This indicates that the post-1994 period has, at least, been true to one of its budgetary promises – namely, to reduce (real) overall and consumption expenditure.

Time-line studies that cover an extensive period leading up to the advent of a new government (1973-1996), give further evidence of several trends prior to the advent of a democratic government: declining public invest-

10 See Department of Finance, 1999/2000.

ment and more intense decline in investment by public authorities and corporations; relatively stagnant levels of capital expenditure (both in relation to GDP and to the budget); increasing amounts of debt servicing as a component of both overall expenditure and the budget; nominal rises in general expenditure but declines in real-term expenditure over time.[11]

The revenue: expenditure ratio has remained relatively constant over a number of years, with public sector deficits being experienced on a more intense level after 1990. Macro-economic policies followed over the period under review, spurred increasingly high interest rates – something that hits the poor the hardest and negatively affects the possibilities for economic growth. Since 1996, interest rates have risen even further and have maintained at the level of 18-21%, making life even more difficult for the majority of poor who often are forced to borrow money to finance the most basic purchase of goods and services.[12]

Table 5 clearly reveals the effects of a decline in public expenditure directed towards the poor – i.e., the knock-on effect. Poor households are unable to redirect their own expenditures patterns to purchase (for example) durable goods, as a direct result of the dominant portion of their incomes going to provide basic services. Thus, those in the lowest two quintiles (40% of the population) only account for a measly 3% of all expenditure on durable goods.

Table 5: Distribution of Expenditure between Quintiles by percentages (1995)[13]

Expenditure	*Quintile 1*	*Quintile 2*	*Quintile 3*	*Quintile 4*	*Quintile 5*	*Total*
Durable	0.1	0.2	0.5	0.13	0.79	1.00
Semi-Durable	0.3	0.7	0.12	0.22	0.56	1.00
Non-Durable	0.5	0.9	0.13	0.21	0.52	1.00
Service	0.1	0.2	0.5	0.14	0.79	1.00
Total	0.2	0.4	0.8	0.16	0.69	1.00

11 See John Newton, *Reforming the South African Public Finances,* (NIEP Occasional Paper Series No. 6 April 1997), Johannesburg (National Institute for Economic Policy), 1997, p. 17.

12 *Ibid.*, p. 35-36.

13 Source: Statistics SA, *October Household Survey and Income & Expenditure Survey 1995.*

Looking at specific budgetary item expenditure (Table 6 below) reveals that from 1997- 2001 real expenditure on water provision will register a negative growth of 7.5%, welfare will decline by 0.3%, education by 1.3% and expenditure on housing by a whopping 16.2%. Conversely, real expenditure on areas such as defence and prisons will register positive growth as will expenditure on general economic services and general government services.

Table 6: Real change in expenditure, 1997 to 2000[14]

R millions	*1997/8*	*2000/01*	*Real average annual change (%) 1997 to 2000*
Other social services (mostly arts/culture)	512	772	8.6%
Prisons	3,211	4,740	7.8%
Justice	2,211	2,981	4.6%
Other economic (mostly labour/tourism)	3,815	5,104	4.3%
General government	21,857	28,081	2.9%
Agriculture	2,963	3,785	2.7%
Defence	11,079	13,737	1.7%
Health	26,704	32,320	0.9%
Police	12,963	15,646	0.8%
Welfare	17,913	20,923	-0.3%
Education	44,794	50,712	-1.3%
Transport communication	8,420	8,815	-3.9%
Mining manufacturing construction	234	226	-6.4%
Water	2,487	2,321	-7.5%
Housing	5,880	4,075	-16.2%
Fuel/energy	695	351	-24.6%
subtotal	204,558	194,508	-6.9%
Interest payments	38,820	46,490	0.5%
Reserve	0	2,269	n.a.
Consolidated Expenditure	243,377	243,425	-5.3%
Growth excluding defence	242,866	242,653	-5.4%
Growth excluding defence and reserve	242,866	240,384	-5.7%

Note: Deflated using CPI for the middle income group, since CPIX not available for past years.

Debt

Successive budgets since 1994 have prioritised the servicing of the apartheid debt at the expense of social and infrastructural (real/positive) expendi-

14 Source: COSATU, *Submission on 1999 Medium Term Budget Policy.*

ture.[15] Like all budgetary decisions, this is a political decision and it is one that has tremendous impact on the availability of funds for other priority areas.

As even the World Bank has pointed out, South Africa could increase its debt: GDP ratio by several percentage points and still maintain fiscal responsibility. Indeed, international experience[16] confirms that running budget deficits in the region of 60-70% of GDP is a prerequisite (especially for a middle-income country like South Africa) for accessing sufficient capital in order to attain the kind of expenditure patterns that will spur growth, create employment and provide basic social services.

The case of the apartheid debt is a classic example of the present budget not reflecting the will of the people. The vast majority of South Africans have, time and again, indicated that they support the cancellation of the apartheid debt alongside feasible measures to reduce debt servicing (e.g., shifting the Government Employee Pension Fund payment scheme from a fully funded to a pay-as-you-go scheme) and yet the Ministry of Finance has steadfastly refused to even listen to the people, instead proceeding to tell the people of South Africa that they simply do not understand the financial complexities of the matter and should therefore trust the Ministry/government to do what is best for them.

This reflects one of the most basic problems with the present budgetary process – i.e., the unwillingness on the part of the government to actually listen to the people and to provide sufficient mechanisms and structures to facilitate their active involvement in democratic decision-making. It is simply incomprehensible how the South African government can arrogantly dismiss the possibility that people themselves are actually better equipped to debate and influence decisions that affect their economic and social well being, especially when such decisions involve removing an apartheid weight from around their necks.

As the progressive local and state governments in Porto Alegre (Brazil) have already found out, involving ordinary people in budgetary decision-making, while not without its problems, provides a sound popular mandate for government because it is actually taking participatory democracy seriously. If ever there was an example of a budgetary arena in which the government

---

15 See data on National Government Debt as a Percentage of GDP – SA Reserve Bank, *Quarterly Review*, 2000.

16 See Labour Caucus at NEDLAC, *Social Equity and Job Creation: The key to a stable future. Proposals by the South African labour movement*, Johannesburg (Labour Caucus at NEDLAC), 1996, p. 27.

might match its rhetoric with actual practice, it applies to the apartheid debt. The government must desist from a confined understanding and application of representative democracy, and begin to believe in the people themselves.

Education

The provision and maintenance of a good educational system, at all levels, is one of the most central components for the general welfare of any society. It is the starting point for all else. If educational provision in the South African context is not maintained and expanded to accommodate population increases as well as to address the massive inequalities that still maintain in the educational system, then there will be scant chance of South Africa improving its social and economic situation in the medium to long-term.

For example, in a country with immense wealth, alongside pockets of advanced development, there exists an illiteracy rate that is completely unacceptable. Not only does this impact negatively on the ability of younger people to become productive members of society but seriously hampers the capacity of the older workforce to maintain (not to mention, advance) their economic well being in an environment that severely punishes those without the requisite, basic educational skills such as literacy. Indications from the data show that expenditure on programmes such as Adult Basic Education & Training (ABET) are far from being sufficient to address this.

Ensuring the most basic educational rights of all citizens is not something that can be approached from a purely fiscal standpoint – it has to be a political decision taken to prioritise this as part of building the foundation for a prosperous citizenry. Here, it is instructive to look at the example of Cuba and its mass literacy campaigns, which were one of the first, post-independence priorities of the government. Its achievements speak for themselves.

Without the necessary funds made available it does no good to then call on people to become involved in educational provision and sustenance. This can only serve to discriminate against those who are least able to afford either the time or resources to involve themselves and thus contributes to furthering the divisions between rich and poor communities. Decisions taken in the 2000 budget, to reward, through tax concessions, charitable contributions to education only exacerbate division and inequality. This reflects a shift, by government, towards the effective privatisation of education, a situation that is already proving to be disastrous, both in South Africa and all over the globe.

Despite the amounts of expenditure dedicated to educational provision in the national budget, the inherited inequality in the provision and character of basic education has not been fundamentally altered since the democratic government came to power. The educational budget and its various components provide a good reason to sustain the argument that there is no necessary proportional relationship between amounts spent and positive character of effect.

Table 7: Education Spending Estimates and Enrolment numbers (1997-2001)[17]

Medium Term Expenditure Framework				
R Billion	*1997/98*	*1998/99*	*1999/2000*	*2000/01*
National Spending	6.098	6.498	7.268	8.005
Provincial Spending	38.680	38.870	40.746	42.238
Total National & Provincial Spending	44.778	45.368	48.014	50 243
*% Growth**	7%	4%	6%	5%
School Enrollment Estimates	12 466 100	12 859 000	13 277 800	13 728 200

(*These are nominal growth rates)

The challenge for South Africa's educational system is both universal and simple. Basic education, up to the level of matric must be provided free for all, and there must be a targeted prioritisation of public fiscal support for secondary educational expenses for the poor. Further, government must desist from targeted expenditure on private education and adult basic education and training (ABET) must be prioritised in community educational programmes that begin to involve the people themselves (e.g., mass literacy campaigns). This must be accompanied by the promotion, through budgetary subsidisation, of public technical education and prioritised subsidisation for higher education (linked to the specific social and economic needs of the country). It is far past the time for government to stop making excuses for the growing educational crisis in South Africa.

---

17 *Source:* Department of Finance, *Budget Review 1998.*

If the educational rights/needs of the majority are not met, then South Africa can forget about developmental progress across the board.

Health

It is in the field of health that the long-term effects of the apartheid system have been most intensely felt and experienced. The onset of the HIV/AIDs pandemic has only exacerbated the situation and, as always, has hit the poor the hardest. Provincial data reveals the extent to which the population in the least resourced areas of the country continue to experience serious health problems, access to health facilities and lack of adequate health infrastructure and personnel.[18] At the same time, the private health sector continues to possess a majority of medical specialists and highly trained personnel, not to mention more adequate facilities.[19] This maldistribution of human and infrastructural resources is made all the more intense by the fact that the vast majority of the private health care sector is to be found in the urban areas.

While the government has embarked on a Primary Health Care (PHC) programme that has, to some extent, assisted the most vulnerable and poor (e.g., maternal care, children under the age of six etc.), budgetary allocations continue to be wholly inadequate to maintain adequate health standards for the majority of poor South Africans. Even where there have been short-term improvements in health provision, the lack of sustained infrastructural investment in clinics, particularly in relation to the poorest and most rural provinces has seriously affected the longer-term provision of health care.

Such blockages to effective delivery most often result in the majority of people seeking medical care facing serious bureaucratic and service problems as well as lack of access to some of the most basic medicines. This is a direct result of diminishing budgetary allocations to non-personnel components of the health system. In addition, the serious lack of consistent training and skills development in the health sector only adds to the growing list of problems that have not been fundamentally addressed in budgetary terms.

While there must be recognition of the degree to which the sheer scale of the HIV/AIDs pandemic has placed extra burdens on the health care

---

18 See IDASA Budget Information Service, *Provincial Health Budgeting for 2000/01*; and Edwards-Miller et al., *Health Systems Trust's Health Review 1998.*

19 See William Pick et al., *Human Resources for Health: A Draft National Strategy,* 1999.

system, the budgetary response to the pandemic can only be described as pathetic. Increasing numbers of women, rural poor and the young are contracting the virus (more so in the least resourced areas of the country), with devastating consequences for the economic and social fabric of both families and communities. There has been a steadfast refusal on the part of the government to make the link between these facts and the need to prioritise allocation of resources to deal with the pandemic. Alongside this, there is the equally important necessity, on the part of government, to openly confront and demystify HIV/AIDs so that the educational and prevention programmes that are carried out can have maximum effect.

Table 8: HIV prevalence by age group: Antenatal clinic attendees 1997-1998[20]

Age group	*1997*	*1998*	*% Growth of Infection Rate*
< 20	12.7	21.0	65.4
20-24	19.7	26.1	32.5
25-29	18.2	26.9	47.8
30-32	14.5	19.1	31.7
35-39	9.5	13.4	41.1
40-44	7.5	10.5	40
45-49	8.8	10.2	16

Source: Health Systems Trust, South African Health Review, 1999

Similar to the educational needs of South Africa, there is a societal necessity to ensure that all basic health services must be free to the public. This is not merely a matter of increased expenditure (although it is clear that this is required), but also proper management, maintenance and upgrading of existing facilities and personnel. In turn, the well being of the health system itself is directly tied to a well functioning, relevant and dynamic educational programme that views health professionals and service personnel as being at the forefront of meeting the developmental needs of any society. Even though it might sound repetitive, the bottom line is one of prioritisation – to the poor and less advantaged who suffer most from an inadequate health system.

---

20 Source: IDASA, *The Department of Social Development's Response to the HIV/Aids Crisis,* (Budget Brief No. 55, 2000). HIV/AIDS in pregnant women is also a good indicator of HIV prevalence in the general population.

Without a healthy populace there can be no serious talk of societal progress. When children are going hungry and losing their parents to HIV/AIDs in the hundreds of thousands, and people are dying of easily preventable diseases amidst immense affluence, there can be little doubt of the need for fundamental change. One of the first starting points to catalyse such change is a budgetary process that is responsive to what the people themselves are experiencing, without even having to say so. Indeed, there is something seriously wrong in our society when health-care corporations can influence government to such a degree as to utilise precious budgetary resources for those who already have more than enough.

Welfare

If the state of South Africa's health system is not particularly good, then the state of welfare provision is in intensive care. Provision of welfare is (theoretically) designed specifically to target the most vulnerable amongst the population – i.e. children, the aged and the physically and mentally disabled. A society that does not place the provision of adequate services to these sections of the population at the top of its fiscal agenda unmasks its own claims to the protection and sustenance of basic human rights.

In the South African historical context, apartheid systematically denied these welfare rights to tens of million of South Africans who were left to fend for themselves in the midst of a sea of poverty and desperation (particularly as applied to rural women and children as a result of the migrant wage labour system and the creation of Bantustans). While successive post-apartheid budgets have recognised this reality by extremely minimal increases in expenditure and attempts to streamline the provision of welfare benefits, the picture after seven years does not bode well.

A real decline in provincial budgetary allocations has already begun and will worsen over the next three years.[21] Even where there has been budgetary support to the welfare function, hundreds of millions of Rand have yet to be spent despite increases in expenditure on human resource development.[22] Real expenditure on key welfare programmes such as poverty alleviation has virtually disappeared and budgetary support to welfare enterprises has seen a precipitous decline in the capacity of these enterprises to care for the most vulnerable.[23]

21 See IDASA Budget Information Service, *Provincial Health Budgeting for 2000/01.*

22 See *Auditor General Report 1999.*

23 *Ibid.*

The situation in South Africa's welfare system goes to the heart of one of the most basic budgetary problems that has yet to be fully recognised nor dealt with. It is not, once again, merely a matter of the amounts of monies allocated to specific social programmes, even though this is most often completely inadequate to deal with the problems confronted, but the absence of an integrated approach to the delivery of services whereby the lack of budgetary allocation in one sphere negatively impact on another. In the case of unspent welfare funds allocated to the provinces, this is clearly the case due to the fact that there is a lack of trained and management personnel and systems to carry out the basic functions of actually spending the monies. Cuts in personnel expenditure (as has been the case in provincial welfare departments) deriving from a contractionary budgetary approach, results in knock-on problems (blockages) when it comes to delivery. There is a need for an integrated budgetary package that does not set one component of the system against the other. If this continues then there should be little reason to express surprise when things fail to happen.

The example of the welfare budget over the past several years speaks directly to the need for an integrated approach to the budget. There has been the tendency when analysing budgetary cycles, to apportion blame in a manner that fails to recognise this. Thus, potential changes end up merely addressing the symptom and not the cause. The macro-economic framework (GEAR) that informs the budget purports to offer such an integrated approach. Yet, due to its unidimensional focus on fiscal 'fundamentals' as the means to 'deliver' both administrative efficiency and services, resultant budgets completely fail to 'see' that it is not the manipulation of capital that 'delivers' either, but investment in human and physical 'infrastructure. Blockages in delivery will never be addressed until such an approach begins to inform both the process and content of budgets.

Housing

One of the very first undertakings of the new government was to address the massive backlog in the provision of housing as well as to improve the character of the housing environment. Much like the approach to dealing with other areas of societal need though, the government made the fatal mistake of buying into the neo-liberal argument of big capital that the public sector had neither the capacity nor the financial means to do the 'job'. As a result, budgetary allocations to housing were seen as providing a facilitative environment for the private sector to act as the main 'delivery' agent. Despite the obvious fact that the private sector has absolutely no interests at heart other than the bottom line, government has doggedly pursued this approach and as a result, housing provision has remained completely inadequate.

It is clear from the table below that the expenditure by the National Department of Housing over the last several years has been relatively static. The programme with the greatest increase in expenditure is administration, while actual expenditure on housing programmes sees no real (taking inflation into account) increase in expenditure from 1997-2002.

Table 9: National Department of Housing – Expenditure by Programme (1996-2002)[24]

Expenditure (R –Millions)	*1996/97*	*1997/98*	*1998/99*	*1999/2000*	*2000/01*	*2001/02*	*2002/03*
Administration	19.1	21.1	21.8	28.3	36.2	47.0	58.5
Policy Dev.	51.1	46.8	56.8	62.0	43.8	32.8	27.1
Housing Performance	545.5	815.8	583.7	454.2	217.0	305.2	309.1
Sa Housing Fund	1 453.2	2 634.9	3 084.2	2 970.9	3 027.9	3 207.2	3 351.2
Communication	1.2	1.4	1.0	11.8	8.4	8.9	8.7
Total	2 070.1	4 520.0	3 747.5	3 527.1	3 333.4	3 601.3	3 754.6

Since 1994 the National Department of Housing has 'delivered' a total of 998 552 houses (built or under construction).[25] The RDP, which was adopted prior to the 1994 elections, conservatively estimated that there was a backlog of over 3 million housing units (this included the need to upgrade shacks and mud huts), although the Housing Department accepted a figure of 1.3 million (which considered shacks and mud huts as adequate housing). That was in 1994, and yet the government has failed miserably to deal with a backlog that has now mushroomed over the last seven years.

Clearly, the housing situation in South Africa requires a fundamentally new approach. Nowhere has the ideological foundation of the budget been more overtly applied than in the realm of housing provision, resulting in

24 Source: Department of Finance, *2000 National Expenditure Survey.*

25 See Department of Housing, *Annual Report 1999.*

a quantitative and qualitative failure. Not only does there remain a massive shortage of housing units in the most needy areas, but much of the character of what has been delivered is little different than that which graced the South African landscape during the apartheid years. Decent and affordable housing is another one of the core human rights guaranteed in the Constitution (as confirmed recently by a successful class-action suit – the Grootboom case – brought against the government in relation to government's duty to provide housing).

However, the present budgetary approach only responds with fiscal disdain. Like the example of welfare, there is a false separation between spheres of development, each being treated as though it can be addressed on its own. In the case of housing, there is simply no way that the need will be met unless dedicated housing expenditure is linked to dedicated expenditure on public works programmes and the capacitation/creation and use of those public agencies best able to respond to such needs. When government responds to the people's 'cry' for housing by telling them (through the budget) to make do with the thin slice of the fiscal pie allocated, it is not far removed from Marie Antoinette's infamous retort to the French people's desperate pleas for the provision of basic foodstuffs.

Land

In the context of a country whose black population was systematically removed from the land they occupied, and lived off, as the basis for the creation of racial supremacy and capitalist accumulation, it is incomprehensible that so little has been 're-delivered' since political freedom was attained. At the heart of any productive society lies the question of property, whether rural or urban. It is a productivity that is umbilically linked to the ownership and distribution of that property. It is unfortunate that within the capitalist land framework that exists in South Africa (and which was entrenched as part of the negotiated compromises) the only real basis for addressing the historic racial and class inequalities that have arisen from the concentrated ownership and maldistribution of land, is for the government to wield the weapon of the budget as a means to provide the maximum number of people with access to, and sustained use of, potentially productive land (as applied to both rural and urban land).

However, the budgetary approach to the land question has only allowed for the privileging of inherently limited individual ownership and symbolic buy-outs/transfers. In the last decade, the main activity of the government has been to deal with sectional titles and leasehold arrangements.[26] While this might result in the creation of a small class of new black landowners it will not, and has not, addressed the landlessness and continued impoverishment of most rural dwellers whose welfare would be best served by a collective approach to land acquisition and use (not exactly a new phenomenon in the African context).

Government's tackling of the fundamental issues of land restitution, compensation and redistribution has been extremely weak. Millions of urban and rural poor who were dispossessed remain in urban and rural ghettos, many completely dependent on assistance from the government. There is no indication of dedicated expenditure for the retention and collective use of large tracts of government owned urban land holdings as a means of dealing with urban homelessness and altering the urban productive landscape has been sorely lacking.

Not only is the budgetary allocation for dealing with this urban/rural economic and social disaster minimal (as evidenced by looking at Table 10) but, when combined with the inadequate provision of other basic services, it is clear that millions of South Africans continue to live under an economic and social apartheid.

Table 10: National Department of Land Affairs – Programme Expenditure (1996-2002)[27]

Expenditure (R –Millions)	*1996/97*	*1997/98*	*1998/99*	*1999/2000*	*2000/01*	*2001/02*	*2002/03*
Administration	65.0	76.6	93.0	97.2	103.8	98.1	101.8
Restitution	22.4	43.7	46.9	167.8	149.5	187.9	287.8
Land Reform	106.3	195.7	431.0	301.4	423.8	418.9	380.4
Planning & Info	9.3	15.7	35.0	14.1	56.0	58.9	60.9
Public Works	–	–	–	–	5.1	9.4	12.1
Total	203.0	331.7	605.9	580.5	738.2	773.2	843

Once again, the end result of the budgetary approach to the land issue, has 'delivered' a double blow to the expressed desire of the people for

26 Department of Housing, *Annual Report 1999.*
27 Source: Department of Finance, *National Expenditure Survey 2000.*

meaningful socio-economic freedom. It is simply mind-boggling that the entire fiscal commitment to land restitution since 1994 amounts to less than the cost of one of the fighter aircraft that the government has just purchased. When a government lacks the political will to act in the interests of the very people who suffered most under apartheid and who remain economically and socially oppressed, through concrete fiscal support, but has no problem in committing billions of Rands for weapons procurement then there is something desperately wrong with its democratic principles.

Like many other areas of social expenditure, the present approach to the land issue can only serve to further institutionalise land ownership and living patterns in both rural and urban areas that benefit a small elite at the expense of the poor. Most ironically, it is these elites who then exercise almost complete control over the social and economic lives of that poor majority, the very reason why the people of South Africa struggled so long and hard to replace apartheid.

Water

Of all basic human needs, water is the most primary. Without water, there is no life. This has been legally recognised in South Africa with all water resources, at source, being declared a national asset that cannot be privately 'owned'. Despite this, the reality is that private companies actually do own much of the distribution of water and that water provision has become a commodity which can be bought and sold, depending on access and ability to pay. As has been alluded to, earlier in this study, this global trend has resulted in the absolutely ludicrous situation of people being denied access to water simply because they are poor. Of most countries, South Africa knows all too well the consequences of the denial of basic human rights, which makes the present approach to the provision of water even more difficult to comprehend.

Given this complete abrogation of the right of all citizens to water (since there are millions of South Africans who simply do not have access to, or cannot pay for, clean water), the budget has done little more than provide fiscal confirmation to this state of affairs. If water is, in reality, treated as a commodity whose provision is dependent on one's socio-economic status and/or ownership of land, then there can be no expectation that fiscal tools such a the budget will be used as a means to ensure the opposite. This is exactly what the data confirms – i.e., that the government has not taken its own stated commitment seriously. While the data below (which comes from the Department of Water Affairs & Forestry) shows that over four million people have 'benefited' from some kind of public water project, the scale of delivery pales in comparison to budgetary commitments (over time) that, at best, have a very indirect benefit for the majority of South Africans. In a country that is officially categorised as semi-arid, it is scandalous that the annual budgetary commitment of the Water Affairs Department for the1999/00 fiscal year amounts to one fourtieth of the amount spent in the same year on servicing the apartheid debt.

As a direct result of the combination of privatisation of water provision and lack of sustained infrastructural development, it was only a matter of time before serious human consequences were manifested. The recent outbreak of cholera, resulting directly from the policy of making poor people pay for access to clean water, has forced the government to belatedly acknowledge the need for providing free water to the most needy. However, even this promise, made during the last local government elections by the ruling political party, has already come under suspicion as the government appears wedded to its love affair with privatisation and neo-liberal, cost-recovery mechanisms that will result in further impoverishment and human suffering.

Even the budgetary allocations for the public provision of free water in both rural and urban areas give no indication that verbal commitments have been translated into providing the practical means to do so. Instead, South Africans have witnessed spiralling costs, stemming directly from the government's failure to institute block tariff systems and cross subsidisation schemes that would provide the necessary capital to expand provision to the poor.

The present budgetary approach will bring about a further institutionalisation of racial, gender, class and geographical inequality of access and provision. Indeed, it is important to note that the section of the population that is most negatively affected are rural African women, the vast majority of whom spend most of their productive time collecting water for both consumption and basic household needs. The general economic indicators in respect of household access to water and the data on the infrastructural status of clinics provided earlier only provide confirmation of this. There is simply no other way to ensure universal water rights than for the government to carry out its constitutionally prescribed duty and thus for the budget to reflect this through fiscal commitment.

Table 11: National Department of Water Affairs – Programme Expenditure (1996 – 2002)[28]

Expenditure (R –Millions)	*1996/97*	*1997/98*	*1998/99*	*1999/2000*	*2000/01*	*2001/02*	*2002/03*
Administration	96.1	126.9	108.2	137.9	132.3	125.9	127.1
Water Resource Assessment	41.4	47.0	52.3	67.4	78.0	76.4	77.8
Water Resource Planning	68.7	72.5	79.3	108.4	107.2	110.0	113.6
Water Resource Development	279.7	264.8	224.5	319.3	326.5	329.1	329.8
Regional Implementation	533.2	1 415.8	1 935.7	1 578.6	1 527.9	698.7	813.0
Integrated Management	67.4	38.1	49.3	79.0	89.8	94.1	99.4
Water Services	892.6	537.0	54.0	63.9	75.0	74.3	72.7
Total	1 979.1	2 502.1	2 503.3	2 354.5	2 336.7	1 508.5	1 633.4

Public Works

While the general expenditure data shows that the budgetary allocation to 'general economic services' (under which public works falls) has risen in the last several budget cycles, it does not reveal the scale of what needs to be addressed. Nor does it capture the overall decline in real expenditure over time. Given that the entire purpose of public works programmes is to expand infrastructural developmental and to provide sustainable employment and skills development opportunities that benefit the largest possible number of poor people, it does not take sophisticated analysis to determine that the scale of success in South Africa over the last several years has been minimal. Indeed, when set against the massive job losses that have been witnessed over the last several years (an estimated 500 000+ since 1996), the (proud) announcement by Finance Minister Manuel in the 2000 budget speech that several thousand jobs would be created through public works schemes can only be taken as a sign of the government's ideological commitment to further reducing its role in job creation and infrastructural provision.

[28] Source: Department of Finance, *National Expenditure Survey 2000.*

It is ironic that the impetus for this kind of approach has come from the very same quarters of those who utilised massive amounts of government finances to stimulate the economy through large-scale public works and infrastructural expenditure (i.e., the developed countries in the North). This reveals yet another key failing of the budgetary approach. Namely, that there are few, if any, linkages that are made (within the budget) between developmental necessities and fiscal commitment. Rather, what we witness is a direct linkage between fiscal austerity and developmental hopes, with the former being presented as the prerequisite for the latter. This is not a very sound basis for ensuring that basic social services are delivered, nor of tackling the huge social and economic inequalities that plague South Africa.

The few public works programmes that have been funded by government (e.g., Working for Water, the Community Water and Sanitation Programme and the Consolidated Municipal Infrastructure Programme) reflect the very same lack of linkages mentioned above. Each of them is, to a great extent, pursued within a fairly narrow departmental and developmental framework that cannot really address the need for large-scale infrastructural, developmental and job creating projects. The continuation of this developmental and budgetary 'gap' will ensure that effective public works programmes will remain paper promises.

Local Government Grants

Part of federalist compromises reached during the negotiations of the early 1990s allowed for the establishment of a local tier of government that was then constitutionally enshrined with competencies to deliver many of the basic services so desperately needed by the majority of the population. Given the generalised political and administrative chaos inherited at the local level, combined with the massive lack of both human and fiscal resources to actually carry out designated 'delivery' functions, it made sense that the national government, through the budget, would provide sustained fiscal support to local government. However, this has not been the case.

The real 'equitable share' of national revenue that is supposed to be provided to local government (added to conditional grants), has consistently been slashed over the last several years[29] to the point where local government has been forced to rely almost wholly on local-level revenue to fund the delivery of a range of basic services. In turn, this has created

29 Source: Data obtained from Department of Provincial and Local Government, 1999.

a situation where local governments have had to: i) cut back drastically on service delivery targets, with the poor being the hardest hit; ii) prioritise 'cost recovery' mechanisms as a means to gain revenue, resulting in cut-offs of basic services such as water and electricity in those communities least able to afford payment; and iii) privatise the management and delivery of basic services leading to increased charges and the prioritisation of delivery to communities able to pay. It is, unfortunately, the same story that comes out over and again.

The reality of what has happened countrywide, as a direct result of the budgetary cut back of the 'equitable share' of the national fiscus due to local government, is only now beginning to bare its teeth. Entire communities (particularly in poor rural areas) have been denied their rights to basic services, resulting in outbreaks of preventable diseases (e.g. cholera, dysentery) and other knock-on effects such as environmental damage due to collection of wood for fuel, have negatively affected the quality of life. In urban areas, electricity and water cut-offs have left tens of thousands of poor people without basic amenities and have contributed to serious social and environmental urban decay.

This sorry state of affairs is a direct result, once again, of the ideologically driven nature of the budgetary framework, whereby the national government has increasingly removed itself from the sphere of basic service delivery. The ever-dwindling budgetary allocations to local government, have given practical content to the unstated reality of the gradual, but consistent, removal of responsibility, for basic service delivery, from the shoulders of national government. The budget has thus become an effective (if sometimes indirect) tool, for the rapid privatisation and corporatisation of local level services in direct opposition to the overwhelming democratic mandate given to the government by the people.

Military

The year-on-year budgetary allocations for those government departments and agencies in the field of (mis-named) defence and safety/security, has bucked the overall trend of declining real social expenditure in the budget as a whole. In a country with such deep-seated social and economic inequalities, it says a great deal about the priorities of government when the largest single increase in a budget line-item for the last fiscal year is dedicated to expenditure on military weapons.

South Africa does not face any real (or even imagined) external military threat to justify such expenditure. The military expenditure of South Africa is over three times greater than all of its neighbours combined.[30] The exceptionality of the increases is made all the more difficult to accept given the dogged insistence by the Finance Minister over the last several years, that the country can ill afford deficit spending. The real decline in social expenditure over time has most often been explained away as the result of the need to tighten the 'fiscal belt' so as to ensure a decreasing budget deficit and ensure overall fiscal responsibility. Yet, it would appear as though this dictum does not apply when it comes to expenditure for new military toys (Table 12). There is simply no economic logic, not to mention social justification, for such fiscal hypocrisy.

Table 12: Defence Budgets (1996-2004)[31]

Budget Year	*Amount (R Billion)*
1996/97	10.984
1997/98	11.170
1998/99	10.439
1999/00	10.727
2000/01	13.768
2001/02	15.272
2002/03	16.491
2003/04	17.766

The attempts by the Ministries of Defence, Trade & Industry and Finance to defend the most recent military expenditure ring equally hollow. Nowhere in the world do arms suppliers give away their products, as has been intimated in the case of South Africa, by these government departments. Even the most economically illiterate South African understands that capitalist economics does not operate on the principle of loss-making deals and yet, this is precisely what the government would have citizens believe in the 'special' case of their arms procurement package. The double-speak about foreign investment and 'counter-trade' actually paying

30 Source: *SIPRI Yearbook,* (Oxford, 1999), in: *Coalition Against Military Spending – Background Information* (Sept. 2000).

31 Source: Economists Allied for Arms Reduction, *Revisiting the Defence Review: The transformation of the SANDF in light of the corruption allegations and the armaments acquisition package,* Nov. 2000.

for the weapons is simply nonsense as evidenced by budgetary plans already underway to borrow billions to help finance the deal.

Analyses of previous line-item expenditure patterns in the budget have revealed the consistent lack of political will (as expressed through the budget) to effectively meet government's economic and social rights responsibilities. However, it does not take any advanced analytical or statistical skills to conclude that a political will is not lacking when it comes to meeting the needs of the military establishment. Monies have been found very quickly and the fervour with which government has both pursued and defended the arms procurement package speaks volumes of the government's willingness to use the budget as a vehicle for implementing what are, in reality, political decisions. Indeed, the example provided by the massive arms procurement package recently concluded by the government(now estimated to cost in the region of R60 billion), under extremely controversial circumstances, gives lie to government's rationalisations about fiscal 'restraint' and responsibilities as applied to key areas of social expenditure.

Wages/Salaries

Due to the contractionary fiscal approach adopted in successive budgets, there has been every attempt to reduce public sector wages as a percentage of overall budgetary departmental allocations, backed by arguments that doing so is necessary for the fiscal health of the country. In what really amounts to a statistical sleight of hand, (real) declines in personnel expenditure (i.e. through lower wages/salaries and retrenchments) are then used to propagate the argument that the concomitant rise in expenditure on non-personnel components is confirmation that government is increasing capital and infrastructural expenditure (i.e. delivery). In fact, the issue should not be one of looking at the percentages (in relation to overall budgetary allocation) of personnel expenditure since average public sector wage increases are well below inflation. Rather, there should a wider perspective that looks at the needs of the public sector as a whole – including both personnel and non-personnel components alike. If this is not done, then the figures imply that the majority of personnel are getting too much (something that is clearly not the case), and that therefore the solution is to reduce both the wages and numbers of the workforce, thus resulting in the overall percentage of non-personnel expenditure being proportionately increased.

On a more specific level though, it can be determined that over the past several years, the respective gap between rises in wage/salary levels of public sector employees and politicians has seriously widened. While public sector employees have seen below inflation wage increases for the last three years, top national and provincial politicians have received sizeable increases (on an average year-to-year basis, far above inflation) on top of already bloated salaries. Thus, while a public sector enrolled nurse (whose workload has increased due to the personnel retrenchments) now earns an average of R48 829 per annum, each Cabinet Minister earns an average of R518 000 per annum, over 10 times more. These kinds of wage/salary disparities in the public sector are certainly not consistent with principles of labour equality and even worse, are indicative of a persistent political hypocrisy emanating from the top layers of government in relation to the need for general fiscal austerity and specific budgetary restraint.

Towards a People's Budget

The first step in any struggle for a people's budget must be a radical shift in the character of budgetary participation by the people. In this regard, South Africans would do well to look at the example of participatory budgeting that has been instituted in the city of Porto Alegre (Brazil) by a pro-people local and state government that has shown how real democracy can be made to work, both politically and economically. Here, the budgetary system revolves around local populations in each neighbourhood deciding, in popular assemblies that are open to the entire population, the priorities for the public budget allocated to their locality. In other words, it is the people themselves who determine the content of the budget (e.g., whether funds should be used to build a road, subsidise health care or be investing in skills training). Subsequent assemblies then allow the people to monitor the implementation of the chosen budget priorities, while a council made up of delegates elected by the assemblies, manages the distribution of the budget to the different neighbourhoods. Since the budget assemblies are open and transparent, the system enjoys a high degree of legitimacy and popularity.[32]

Even with the difficulties of implementing such a participatory budget process at the national level, there is nothing to stop the government from making the attempt, of believing in the ability of people to make budgetary decisions that, after all, affect them most directly. Similar systems are in operation all around Cuba, and despite the ideological onslaught from powerful capitalist countries and institutions, the degree of popular democratic participation makes most other (democratic) countries appear

---

[32] Michael Lowy, 'A Red Government in the South of Brazil', in: *Monthly Review,* Vol.52, No.6, Nov. 2000.

to be stuck in the feudal phase of decision making. For most South Africans, the necessary shift to a truly participatory budget process would come almost naturally, given the rich and varied history of participatory democracy in people's organisations and movements. Nonetheless, there will have to be a concerted, mass struggle to turn the idea into a living reality – a struggle not so much against an enemy but for a different vision and practice.

Without such a struggle, there will remain a situation where a few politicians and economic advisors/technocrats decide what is best for the people and then merely inform them via budgetary sharing of information and 'consultation' (as is now the case). This is not real governance and it is certainly not real democracy, both of which depend on the extent to which the democratic mandate given to the government is actually sustained and not merely tested (electorally) ever few years.

In the more immediate term though, there are eminently feasible changes that can be made to the content of the budget that would make a huge difference in the daily lives of the most vulnerable and oppressed sections of South Africa society. Many of these changes have been outlined in the course of this study, whether they apply to radical shifts in the tax regime, cancellation and subsequent use of debt capital or increased social and infrastructural expenditure to deliver basic services and redistribute resources. Such changes are not representative of a fiscal irresponsibility, nor are they representative of unmanageable populist sloganeering. They are, rather, concrete and viable ways of giving democratic content to the base rights and needs of South African society and to a politically fundamental and economically necessary commitment to the poor.

A people's approach to the budget must be built on the understanding that a people-oriented society will be to the long-term benefit of all South Africans, irregardless of colour, location and present social and economic standing. A people's budget must be informed by the very history that has given rise to the divisions, inequalities and injustices that now threaten to tear apart the economic and social fabric of the society. For there to be a real change though, a people's budget must begin to radically shift the terrain on which the present budget now operates. Merely playing with numbers and percentages, or arguing about redirection of surpluses is not going to make much of a difference. A people's budget must be unapologetically used in order to alter the productive side of the equation, which is, after all, the real point to an empowerment of the people. Above all, there must be a political will to act, as difficult as this might be in the midst of hostile and powerful forces, for whom radical change is anathema.

As was pointed out at the beginning of this study, a budget can be an extremely powerful and progressive tool in the hands of a people's government willing to carry out its democratic mandate. Indeed, a budget is one of the few weapons available for change in a constricted and unfriendly international economic environment. South Africa has a rich history of progressive struggle for equality and justice and the government that has been entrusted with ensuring the realisation of those struggles, owes its existence to the poor majority that continues to suffer from gross economic inequality and social injustice. Through a political commitment to utilising the budget as a transformative tool to address such inequality and injustice, the government can turn the present situation around. Instead of listening to the voices and worrying about the deep pockets of international/domestic corporate and finance capital, there must be a belief that radical change is possible and an equally strong conviction that this can be achieved through investing in the people of South Africa, not in endlessly trying to placate those in positions of economic power.

However, as much as the struggle for a people's budget, both in process and content, must inculcate all of the above, there is a serious danger that cannot be ignored. Ranged against the struggle for radical socio-economic change is a concerted attempt on the part of government, and within certain intellectual quarters, to embrace a deracialised capitalism that recognises the need for degrees of change but is wholly removed from the overall interests of the poor. This is a direct result of the continued ideological and strategic 'fall-back' that accepts the notion that the best we can do is to further develop capitalism as a platform for some kind of hoped-for alternative far in the future.

There is an almost complete lack of any debate and/or analysis of real socialisation of the commanding heights of the economy (as a means to gain income and thus increase expenditure), or of socialisation of the land (to produce the same result). Likewise there is a deafening silence when it comes to the consideration and application of actual people's mass participation in any budget process (other than occasional pressure tactics).

Is there not a danger of accepting just another, but less restrictive, set of 'constraints' as a means of getting an 'in' with the powers that be? Convincing the political and economic 'bosses' of the day of the veracity and economic logic of 'our' arguments has not, and will not, fundamentally change anything expect that there might be some redirection of expenditure now and then.

The only real way towards a people's budget is through the people themselves, not through better economic arguments (although the collection and analysis of data etc can be used effectively). In other words, through mass mobilisation that is not measured by the occasional electoral turnout but by the extent to which people themselves are involved in the decisions that affect their everyday lives. The majority of South Africans do not have to be convinced that GEAR has not delivered and that all the economic indicators and patterns presently adopted in the budget are not going to deliver the basic services that are their right.

The technical points and political arguments gained from collection and analysis must be taken down to the people (not simply debated and argued out amongst NGOs, intellectuals and within the public sector). Such grassroots democracy can buttress and help sustain struggles that are already happening but which, in most cases, do not go beyond the point of reaction to immediate problems. It is community leaders, rural women, urban youth and workers on the shop floor that need to be taking up these arguments, but to be doing so within a political framework that sees the need for a fundamental change of direction.

It is going to do very little for the poor majority of South Africans if all they are 'presented' with are the economic arguments laid out about deficit:GDP ratios, taxation tables, costing exercises etc. Limiting potential change to the outcomes of essentially elite arguments is not going to empower ordinary people. What will and does, make sense, is combining economic analysis with political and social mobilisation to force change that is based on the experiences of the poor themselves.

That political 'threshold' has to be crossed in order for meaningful change to take place and for work such as this to have real effect. Concretely, this means an all-out intellectual and practical assault on the absolute ideological and technical bankruptcy of attempts to modify a capitalist framework for the long-term benefit of the majority. There will never be a people's budget unless there is a dynamic and sustained people's democracy that reflects, in content and process, people's own struggles and experiences (both past and present).

ACTIONS TO PROMOTE THE REALIZATION OF THE RIGHT TO ADEQUATE HOUSING[1]

Miloon KOTHARI (India)

Approach/Methodology Proposed by the Special Rapporteur

The Special Rapporteur intends to take a constructive approach that will provide solutions aimed at the realization of the human right to adequate housing. While the violations approach yields critical insights into the many dimensions of housing rights (such as through a study of the causes and consequences of forced evictions), it is the Special Rapporteur's intention to focus primarily on identifying where and in what form innovation and strategic cooperation have led to the realization of the rights. The Special Rapporteur intends to draw from them policy suggestions with demonstrated practicality. At the same time the Special Rapporteur will make a critical analysis of the current global fashion of "best practices" from a housing rights perspective.

He will attempt to investigate key dimensions of the right to housing keeping in mind the indivisibility of all human rights, especially the interface between housing as an economic, social and cultural right and critical civil and political rights such as the right to information and the right to the security of the home, without which the right to adequate housing loses its meaning.

In order to fulfil this ambitious mandate, the Special Rapporteur will seek the cooperation and partnership of a variety of individuals, organizations and State institutions. In addition, he expects to engage in active dialogue with United Nations and other intergovernmental agencies, IFIs, human rights treaty bodies and civil society organizations at all possible levels.

Cooperation with Governments

In the extensive work undertaken in the last decade on the right to housing, numerous insights have emerged on the precise nature of State

1 Report of the Special Rapporteur on adequate housing as a component of the right to an adequate standard of living, Mr. Miloon Kothari, submitted pursuant to Commission resolution 2000/9. Ecosoc. Commission on Human Rights. Fifty-seventh session. Item 10 of the provisional agenda. Distr. General , Chapter III, n.87-107.

responsibilities at the international and national levels. The forthcoming reports of the Special Rapporteur will detail the nature of these obligations, which will focus on, *inter alia*:

a) Engaging in a dialogue towards developing further the "core content" of the right to adequate housing, and the State obligations to "recognize, respect, protect and fulfil" the right;
b) Defining and studying the feasibility of indicators and benchmarks to understand better the meaning of "adequacy" in the context of the right to housing as a component of the right to an adequate standard of living;
c) Applying the Limburg Principles and the Maastricht Guidelines;
d) Exploring prospects for domestic justiciability of the right to adequate housing;
e) Analysing globalization pressures, structural adjustments and debt servicing and their effect on States' ability to implement the right to adequate housing; and
f) Developing further the meaning of "international cooperation" in the context of covenanted human rights obligations relating to the right to housing.

International Cooperation

Of particular importance are the obligations for States emerging out of the international legal provisions of international cooperation. These obligations are especially critical given the current global reality of growing income disparities, the related growing civil society unrest, and academic and media attention which have highlighted the policies and guiding principles of bilateral and multilateral institutions that drive economic globalization. The groups, mentioned above, that question the ideological and procedural basis of economic globalization recognize the importance of the "regulatory" role of the State. The link with State obligations under the international human rights instruments is obvious.

With reference to economic, social and cultural rights, particular attention needs to be given to articles 2.1, 11, 15, 22 and 23 of ICESCR, which build upon the foundation for international cooperation in Articles 55 and 56 of the Charter of the United Nations, and the obligation for States parties to recognize the essential role of international cooperation and to reaffirm their commitment to take joint and separate action.

What flows from this is that States' international policies (or policies they contribute to formulating at multilateral forums and institutions) must respect the full realization of people's economic, social and cultural rights. These insights and provisions obviously have implications for trade, investment, finance, debt and structural adjustment policies.

In the context of the right to adequate housing, it is important to keep in mind the obligations enshrined in article 11.1 of ICESCR urging all States parties to "take appropriate steps to ensure the realization of this right, recognizing to this effect the essential importance of international cooperation based on free consent". CESCR further clarified this obligation in General Comment No. 4 for both States and IFIs who must:

"seek to indicate areas relevant to the right to adequate housing where external financing would have the most effect. Such requests should take full account of the needs and views of the affected people" (para. 19).

The Special Rapporteur would like to stress that in this era of increasing interdependence, when it is clear that States acting alone cannot meet their human rights obligations, that it is important to go beyond the discussions of official development assistance or other forms of financial assistance. The "solidarity" and "fraternity" dimensions of international cooperation need urgent attention. In order to ensure that the obligations flowing from the "international cooperation" provisions of international human rights instruments are met, the Special Rapporteur will examine two areas of work:

(a) The need to review existing and potential international economic and other obligations; and
(b) The need to assist, through "joint and separate action", in the improvement of housing and living conditions.

The Special Rapporteur finds the field of "international cooperation" a valuable area of inquiry and action and an under-utilized aspect of international human rights law and relations. He is encouraged by the attention that this issue is gaining in various human rights forums,[2] and, pursuant to resolution 2000/9, would like to contribute to the development of instruments that would be useful to Governments, relevant United Nations bodies, specialized agencies, international organizations in the field of housing rights, non-governmental organizations and international

[2] See in particular the Record of the Workshops on International Trade, Investment and Finance and Economic, Social and Cultural Rights: *The Role of the Committee on Economic, Social and Cultural Rights,* 6 May and 19 August 2000 (CESCR/WK), available on the OHCHR Web site.

financial institutions to counter the adverse effects of economic globalization. The Special Rapporteur would also like to underscore the human rights aspects of international cooperation in the context of the High-level Event on Financing for Development to be held in 2002.

Cooperation with International and Regional Financial and Economic Institutions

An increased focus on poverty and country-owned processes in the policies of the international financial institutions such as the World Bank and IMF is reflected in new instruments such as the Poverty Reduction and Growth Facility (PRGF) of IMF (which replaced the controversial Enhanced Structural Adjustment Facility (ESAF) in November 1999) and the Poverty Reduction Strategy Paper (PRSP) and Comprehensive Development Framework (CDF) processes of the World Bank. The Special Rapporteur is of the view, however, that given the reluctance of these institutions to jettison the narrow macroeconomic perspective that continues to drive these new initiatives, it is unlikely that these policies will contribute to the realization of economic, social and cultural rights in general and the right to adequate housing in particular. The Special Rapporteur will pay particular attention to the changes in policy conditionality as a result of the transformation of ESAF into PRGF and the national responses, and will also review the current debt-relief mechanisms, particularly the Heavily Indebted Poor Country (HIPC) initiative, and their likely effect on the poverty reduction prospects of HIPCs, especially the right to adequate housing. The Special Rapporteur looks forward to working closely with other mandates established by the Commission and the Sub-Commission.

Cooperation with the United Nations Bodies and Human Rights Mechanisms

1. Developing Linkages with Treaty Bodies and Other Mandates

The Special Rapporteur will make every effort to encourage strengthening linkages between his mandate and the treaty bodies, as well as with other mandates established by the Commission and Sub-Commission, including those on food, water, internally displaced persons, migrants, indigenous people, street children, human rights defenders, women and violence, extreme poverty, and the effects of structural adjustment policies and foreign debt. The Special Rapporteur has, during the relatively short period since his appointment, had opportunities for informal exchanges of views with several other special rapporteurs and independent experts, and is convinced that regular consultations among all mandate holders will enrich the normative content of all rights and enhance the impact of thematic mandates. The Special Rapporteur is also grateful to have been given an opportunity to hold a dialogue with CESCR at its twenty-fourth session on 29 November 2000, and appreciated the useful advice and guidance from the Committee members.

2. Inter-agency Consultation

The Special Rapporteur is expected to play a catalytic role in promoting interagency cooperation among United Nations bodies and other international organizations. Towards this end, an inter-agency consultation meeting was organized by OHCHR in cooperation with UNCHS in Geneva on 28 November 2000, for the initial stocktaking of activities undertaken by various agencies relevant to his mandate. The initial assessment revealed that the various aspects of the right to adequate housing were seriously dealt with by several agencies, including UNHCR and UNICEF, and that others were in the process of re-evaluating the housing dimensions of their mandates, keeping in mind the relevance of the human rights approach.

This meeting was also invaluable to the Special Rapporteur in mapping out possible modalities of interaction with United Nations bodies in carrying out his mandate, and as such he requests OHCHR to organize such an inter-agency consultation on a regular basis.

3. Integrating the Right to Adequate Housing in the Operational Activities of the United Nations

The Special Rapporteur recognizes the important role the United Nations system has, through the effective use of the United Nations Development Assistance Framework (UNDAF) and Common Country Assessment (CCA) processes, in responding to the needs of its member States and in promoting greater realization of all human rights at the field level. In this context, he is aware that OHCHR has been actively promoting rights-based approaches through the CCA/UNDAF. While the current CCA indicator covers housing statistics in terms of sufficient living space, disaggregation of indicators beyond gender and geography, such as discrimination and exclusion with regard to race, religion and ethnicity, are necessary to achieve more meaningful analysis of the enjoyment of the right to adequate housing. Towards this end, the Special Rapporteur looks forward to working with OHCHR, UNCHS and the United Nations Development Group in further refining CCA/UNDAF as a tool to promote, in the context of the right to adequate housing: (a) free, active and meaningful participation; (b) the empowerment of women; (c) accountability by all partners; and (d) non-discrimination and attention to the rights of vulnerable people and communities.

In this context, the Special Rapporteur notes with interest the recent launching of the Global Campaign for Secure Tenure by UNCHS and attaches importance to strengthening cooperation between the two offices and with other partners, including civil society, for operationalizing the campaign for the further realization of the right. The Special Rapporteur will seek to ensure that this campaign evolves conceptually from the current narrow focus to embrace the wider requirements of the right to adequate housing. This reassessment needs to include also a wider participation of civil society organizations that are directly working from a housing rights-based perspective across the world.

The Special Rapporteur welcomed the opportunity to attend a joint meeting on technical cooperation held on 28 November 2000 between OHCHR and UNCHS, at which it was revealed that the vast majority of field activities and projects of both agencies were not conceptualized and made operational from a housing as a human rights perspective. As such, the Special Rapporteur will review the technical cooperation activities of all relevant agencies, particularly OHCHR and UNCHS.

4. Cooperation with Regional Human Rights Bodies and National Human Rights Institutions

The Special Rapporteur intends to forge a working relationship with regional human rights mechanisms and national human rights institutions, with a view to understanding the extent of the work on the right to housing by these bodies and, where necessary, encouraging more work on this right. The need, for example, for national human rights institutions to focus more on economic, social and cultural rights is evident. An attempt will also be made to bring to the attention of these bodies violations of the right to housing that come to the notice of the Special Rapporteur.

Cooperation with Civil Society

The Special Rapporteur acknowledges, and is inspired by, the genius and innovation that characterizes civil society in respect of housing rights and hopes to act as a conduit for this wisdom by bringing the voices of the poor to the ear of the international community, in particular through popular expressions such as poetry, case studies and stories.

Over the past decade, expertise has developed within civil society on a range of areas relevant to the mandate of the Special Rapporteur. These include conceptual work and standard-setting, human rights education and learning materials, strategies for alternative planning from slum settlements, community finance, formation of campaigns, documentation of violations and so forth.

The Special Rapporteur will develop methodologies for collaboration with the various levels of ongoing efforts. Some of these may include:

(a) Development of questionnaires on monitoring the realization of housing rights and assessing violations;
(b) Developing an urgent action response mechanism;
(c) Encouraging increased use of the United Nations system including alternative reporting procedures; and
(d) Encouraging the development of human rights education materials, including training manuals and so forth.

Preliminary Conclusions and Recommendations

Given the information that is already available to the Special Rapporteur, it is clear that housing and living conditions across the world are deteriorating. Therefore, the creation of the Special Rapporteur's mandate is a welcome step that could lead to a better understanding of the structural reasons for this state of affairs and act as a catalyst for institutionalizing housing rights. The Special Rapporteur is of the view that a forthright approach in the mandate that draws upon the considerable wisdom that rests with Governments, the United Nations and other international agencies, civil society and the professional community can result in concrete policy recommendations aimed at alleviating the enormous shortfall in the global realization of the human right to adequate housing.

Accordingly, the Special Rapporteur intends to promote the linkages between the right to adequate housing as a component of the right to an adequate standard of living, and the global review processes of United Nations conferences including the five-year review of the Habitat Agenda (Istanbul +5) in June 2001, the 10-year review of the World Summit for Children in September 2001, the Third United Nations Conference on Least Developed Countries (LDC-III) in May 2001 and the High-level Event on Financing for Development in 2002. This report has already highlighted issues to be raised at these conferences.

The following recommendations, respectfully made to the Commission, will allow the Special Rapporteur to fulfil his mandate effectively:

(a) Given the consistent interest that the United Nations General Assembly has shown on the subject, the Special Rapporteur requests the Commission to make it possible to report annually both to the Commission and to the General Assembly;
(b) The Special Rapporteur places importance on the need to undertake further studies, based on the development of a research agenda, on the effects of globalization processes, including liberalization, deregulation and privatization, with a particular focus on housing. The Commission could request the Special Rapporteur to convene an expert seminar, in collaboration with OHCHR, UNCHS and the United Nations Research Institute for Social Development, to address these issues and initiate a process that will enable the Special Rapporteur to make policy recommendations;
(c) Given that the critical issue of women and housing rights will be a consistent theme during the course of the mandate, the Special Rapporteur requests the Commission also to make it possible for him to report annually to the Commission on the Status of Women;
(d) The Commission may wish to entrust the Special Rapporteur with the tasks of seeking, receiving and responding to information on all aspects of the realization of the right to adequate housing, in particular urgent calls/action in cases of serious violations of the right to adequate housing, including forced evictions or discriminatory policies and measures that impact upon the realization of the right to adequate housing;
(e) Given the wide scope of his mandate and the scale of the housing crisis, including the differential impacts on vulnerable groups, in the world today, the Special Rapporteur requests that he be permitted to submit periodically, in addition to the annual report, thematic reports that highlight different dimensions of the problems and solutions that are called for in order to develop an accurate assessment and a result-oriented thrust to the mandate. These thematic reports could focus on developing the link between the right to adequate housing as a component of the right to an adequate standard of living and issues such as forced evictions and resettlement, international cooperation, indicators and benchmarks.

THE GAP BETWEEN POLICY AND IMPLEMENTATION

Joe Louis WASHINGTON (United States of America)

It is an honor for me to share a few brief thoughts with you this afternoon. I will strive to be as concise as possible because I truly believe the most important sharing happens when we can dialogue with one another about our concrete experiences. Thus, I hope to identify some issues and concerns for our on-going reflection and dialogue.

I take a somewhat broader view when looking at the gap between policy and implementation. I'm sure we are all familiar with the myriad of traditional assumptions concerning the gap between policy and implementation. This usually refers to various events or obstacles that prevent well crafted social policies and human rights norms from being translated into effective mechanisms for the protection of human rights and human dignity. I want to add to the discussion, my concern for an often-neglected earlier gap or disconnect that frequently occurs. This gap entails policies that do not address at the onset – the priority, real and/or felt needs of the most vulnerable segments in society. If these policies do not address the 'real' needs, it becomes difficult, if not impossible, to conceive how implementation can be truly effective. I will return to this point later in my comments.

Four basic assumptions comprise the bulk of my presentation. *First*, human rights *are* universal, inalienable, interdependent and interrelated, but ... Practical priorities must often be identified that meet the immediate human needs of the most vulnerable segments of the population if human rights are to be meaningful in people's daily lives. Miloon Kothari spoke of one aspect of this point when he mentioned human rights serving as a floor for which no one should be allowed to drop below. Venita Govender also emphasized the notion of goals and needs in the context of the South Africa experience.

When I speak of human needs, I am referring to what has been characterized as social goods essential to human subsistence. These include: food, clothing, shelter, health care, identity, and education, just to name a few. Many of you will immediately note the majority of these items are also protected as economic, social and cultural rights. The point I want to raise is the importance of language and the need for those of us committed to support vulnerable populations to demystify human rights language. For me, our challenge is to serve as translators and interpreters in order to identify the real and felt needs of the vulnerable populations and link those to relevant human rights instruments and mechanisms. Thus, whether we use human rights, human needs or other language, the ultimate result must be the protection and empowerment of human dignity.

Let me share a brief example to underscore this last point. I recently visited a Native American or First Nations reservation to assist a friend on several projects. She is a member of the tribe, an attorney and conducts a great deal of human rights advocacy in the international arena. Thinking about my upcoming presentation, I asked her how does she talk to people on the 'res' about the existence and purpose of internationally protected human rights? She replied that she uses words or terms in their local language that reflect the sacred and inherent principles embedded in various human rights instruments. She went on to emphasize the importance of demystifying human rights language in order to make it accessible to the people on the ground and related to their daily reality. Thus, when I inquired how she dealt with bridging the gap or disconnect between lofty human rights principles versus actual implementation on the ground, she offered the following key elements:

- Education and awareness;
- Preparing tribal members for the sustained effort often required before concrete results materialize;
- Adopting and/or bringing forth long standing traditional indigenous principles clearly reflective of human rights norms and standards; and
- Mobilizing local pressure to push for the protection of their human dignity and rights at appropriate levels.

In the broader context, when thinking about how to bridge the gap between policy and implementation, I think it is essential that at a minimum, the following occur:

a) an on-going process of broad-based dialogues and consultations be enacted;
b) with those most effected;
c) resulting in appropriate and effective redress;
d) undertaken at various levels by governmental *and* non-governmental actors.

Second, let me suggest we "go back to the future" in order to clarify why gaps may exist between policy and implementation. I suggest we must initially start with our own individual societies, and ultimately think about other societies we may be most familiar. Ask yourself the following questions:

a) Who are the vulnerable populations and groups?
b) Why are they vulnerable?
c) What forms of legal redress are available at the local, national, regional and international levels for them?
d) Are they effective? Why or why not?
e) Do they attempt to address the most critical needs of the most vulnerable population in question?
f) What non-legal forms of redress are available or possible?
g) Are they effective? Why or why not?

I suggest that on one level, this type of critical analysis is essential if we are to comprehensively redress the gap between policy and implementation in a sustained way by clarifying and prioritizing the most important focal points for action. Further, we may discover that the various instruments and mechanisms were designed to address a different need than those most critical to the vulnerable population.

Third, human rights instruments and mechanisms are *essential* for the protection of individual and peoples human rights and human dignity. I want to underscore the vital importance of so-called 'shadow reports' as a tool for community education, empowerment and mobilization both during the preparation of the reports *and* the shadow reports serving as an essential tool in focusing attention on the gap between policy and implementation. The preparation of shadow reports by civil society organizations in Mexico, Brazil and South Africa are excellent examples of the importance and potential of such efforts.

I also strongly suggest that we are yet to test the full potential of various international and regional human rights mechanisms. We should redouble our efforts in that direction and think of creative applications. Here again, the examples of South Africa and Canada in promoting economic, social and cultural rights through what were ostensibly civil and political rights mechanisms offer important lessons.
As we survey the continuing codification of human rights instruments and mechanisms, let me add a cautionary note that we *never forget or lose sight of the human in human rights.* This means, particularly in the area of economic, social and cultural rights, the critical importance of starting from the perspective of the concrete needs of the vulnerable population in question.

Fourth, while advocating for the full utilization of existing mechanisms, let me simultaneously suggest that they alone may prove insufficient to create the type of world we are here to collectively visualize and co-create. Our desired world respects the human dignity of *all* and ensures at a minimum, the basic needs of the most vulnerable populations are met. The complementarity of legalistic rights-based approaches, along with other appropriate approaches, should be pursued to the extent they contribute to the full enjoyment of the individual and people's human rights and human dignity.

My *fifth* and final assumption is that human rights violations, particularly those characterized as gross and systematic, are often the predictable (knowable) result of struggles between various groups and governmental forces for the satisfaction of basic human needs and human rights. The most effective means to prevent and redress human rights violations, incorporates what has been labeled a 'structural approach', geared towards uncovering and addressing the 'root causes' of conflict and violence (expanded here to include violence which might be characterized as physical, structural or cultural). Thus, any policy put forward must not only address the 'trigger' or surface events, but also the underlying root causes.

In closing, let me summarize my presentation and the challenges that lie ahead for us regarding creating a world that respects all human rights, including economic, social and cultural rights. I want to accomplish this by returning again to the use of alternative language and translation. I will briefly recount for each one of us the worldly wisdom that our ancestors left behind.

From China, the saying goes:

> *"A bar of iron, continually ground, becomes a needle."*

From India, the proverb:

> *"If you remove stone after stone, even a mountain will be leveled."*

The clear implication of both of these is the importance of consistent struggle and effort to achieve our goal. In many regards, the sustained struggle for economic, social and cultural rights in the form of such essential items as food, clothing, health care, education, identity and shelter is of utmost importance. Therefore, we must marshal our collective forces to achieve these and other fundamental human rights. A well-known African proverb succinctly makes this point when it states:

> *"When spider webs unite, they can tie up a lion".*

Our Native American or First Nations brothers and sisters remind us that our task is to not only be concerned about the realization of human dignity and human rights in the world today, but also for the seven generations to come. On this point, Gandhi would urge us to keep in mind that:

"The future depends on what we do in the present".

That future starts now!

My final intervention and *our* ultimate challenge in the struggle for promoting economic, social and cultural rights may be effectively summed up by the following folktale. It's from Trinidad and for today's purposes I have taken the liberty of re-titling the story:

Wisdom of the Human Rights' Activist:

> *Once upon a time there was a poor devout man with an old, blind mother and a bitter, barren wife. His life was miserable, so each morning he rose early and went to the temple to pray for the blessing of God to relieve his family's suffering. After twelve years of prayer, he heard a voice – the voice of God. "What one thing do you desire?" God asked. "I don't know," he said. "I really didn't expect you to ask. Do you mind if I go home and ask my mother and my wife?"*
>
> *After receiving permission, he ran home, and first met his mother.*
>
> *"Son, if you will ask God to restore my eyes so that I may see again, you will never be indebted to me for anything."*
>
> *Then the man went to his wife and told her of God's promise. "Forget your mother; she is old and will soon close her eyes for the last time. Ask for a son who may care for us, and perhaps bring us wealth."*
>
> *The mother was listening, and she came with her cane and began to beat the wife. "No, it must be my eyesight." The wife fought back, pulling her hair, and a terrible fight ensued.*
>
> *The poor man ran from the house to a wise adviser, an old man who had mediated many conflicts, and he told him his dilemma. "My mother wants eyesight, my wife wants a son, and I, I wish for a bit of money so we can eat everyday. What shall I ask? Whose needs come first?"*
>
> *The adviser thought for a moment, then answered: "Ah, my friend, you must not choose for any one of your family alone, but for the good of all. Although you may ask only one thing of God, ask wisely. Tomorrow morning you shall say, 'Oh Lord, I ask nothing for myself; my wife seeks nothing for herself; but my mother is blind, and her desire is, before she dies, to see her grandson eating milk and rice from a golden bowl.'"*

CONCLUSIONS

ECONOMIC, SOCIAL AND CULTURAL RIGHTS: GLOBALIZATION OF THE SEARCH FOR ALTERNATIVES AND INTERNATIONAL POLITICAL IMPACTS

Berma KLEIN GOLDEWIJK (The Netherlands)

Introduction

Economic, social and cultural rights represent a very remarkable category of rights: historically neglected, caught into a long standing dichotomy with civil and political rights, and more recently facing the impacts of the global market economy and liberalization. Time has come, indeed, for a globalisation of the search for alternatives. The World Social Forum has created the opportunity to link the different contributions in this respect, and offers a chance to formulate projects in common towards the emergence of global alternative proposals. Adalid Contreras (Bolivia), in his contribution to this book, has made it very clear already that precisely the commonality of problems and issues under globalisation, has prompted the appearance of players with new identities and fresh demands. Civil society actors are interconnecting now, presenting critical thoughts "in order to bring out the full potential of the emergence of citizenship in national, social and political processes, as well as international fora".

Approaches and Instruments for Implementation

Strategies to implement economic, social and cultural rights cannot be limited to the 'monitoring of violations'-approach, which is often used in the field of civil and political rights. Conventional human rights strategies (such as monitoring and enforcement) continue indeed to be very necessary, but appear to have a limited effectiveness in responding to the need to get access to economic, social and cultural rights. In fact, the *accessibility* of these rights has been brought out here as being the core issue. If the strategies that are described in this book need to be more effective in promoting *access* to human rights, they will have to relate closer to the living traditions as well as to the cultural roots and vulnerabilities of the affected subjects. This implies an everyday human rights culture, and thus a lived awareness of human rights principles. The authors of this book clearly stated that the prevalent approach to poverty and hardship has in most cases been development-oriented and resource-led. Integrating a rights-based approach into development processes means that the existing international law is being used to provide a framework for the realization of human dignity and human development. This *might* indeed offer a whole range of new perspectives for people getting better access to their economic, social and cultural rights.

The authors of this book hold as a high priority the further development of instruments and strategies to strengthen the implementation of economic, social and cultural rights. In terms of *instruments*, much has been brought up here about the impacts of national *Civil Society Reports* on State Compliance with the International Covenant on Economic, Social and Cultural Rights. They contribute to establishing a strong relationship between legal reform and social policy transformation. Some examples have been brought up that clearly demonstrate how economic, social and cultural rights have now been recognized as justiciable in legal systems at the national level. Different networks are also pressing courts with test cases that relate to economic, social, and cultural rights. In different countries, new efforts are underway to realize monitoring through the appointment of National Rapporteurs, a model designed on the mandates of the UN Special Rapporteurs who address specific economic, social and cultural rights. These rights are nowadays actively being taken up in public decision- and policy-making. In brief, civil society is now succeeding to accelerate, in a very short period of time, the current implementation processes of economic, social and cultural rights.

It has also become very clear that the further development of *international* instruments can not only be understood in a legislative, administrative or judicial sense. Effective strategies make use of human rights as a *political instrument* that has all potential to contribute to the transformation of the inadequacy of everyday living conditions. In this regard, the Draft Optional Protocol to the International Covenant on Economic, Social and Cultural Rights can indeed be seen as highly relevant. This Optional Protocol ensures that persons and groups who suffer from violations of economic, social and cultural rights would have access to remedies at an international level.

Subjects, Processes and Strategies

Dignity and human security of the individual person and of collective subjects cannot be realized fully and protected effectively in societies where economic, social and cultural rights are ignored or violated. Regaining the basic notion of human dignity, therefore, is especially critical in current times when *us-them* divides are being revived. The authors of this book have reaffirmed their opinion that human dignity needs to be brought to the centre of the international human rights debate.

We are part of a changing international context, which has indeed set the need for more integrated and effective strategies for the implementation of human rights. The authors of this book have given considerable attention to the impacts of economic globalisation on human rights and the living conditions of a whole diversity of subjects. In the field of trade, international financial institutions and human rights, it has been clearly brought out that the benefits of economic globalisation do not reach the poor. The distribution of wealth is unequal. This is recognized in a recent World Bank Report, where it is said that the distribution of the benefits of communication and technology are extraordinarily unequal, whereas wealth and capabilities have never been greater.[1] Indeed, the human rights implications of trade-related agreements, as well as the assessment of policies and programmes of international financial institutions have become central to the human rights community. The authors have explicitly reaffirmed the primacy of human rights obligations under international law over economic agreements and policies. They recommend to fully integrate human rights in current trade negotiations and agreements, and appeal for the needed reform of the existing institutional setting in which international financial institutions operate, in order to guarantee transparency and accountability of their policies. They have presented clear prospects for international economic policies coming closer to human rights priorities.

Concluding. In spite of all the efforts of the human rights community, there seems to remain a persistent uneasiness with economic, social and cultural rights, which is prevalent in courts, in development organisations, among academics, jurists and politicians. This uneasiness continues, even when economic, social and cultural rights have achieved their explicit protection in national law, as in South Africa's new Bill of Rights. In further developing global alternative proposals, this needs to be taken fully into account. It has to be reminded, in this regard, that the United Nations have reiterated the notion of the indivisibility, interdependence and interrelatedness of all human rights on numerous occasions.[2] Economic, social and

---

1 World Bank, *World Development Report 2000/2001: Attacking Poverty*, p. 3; See also the 1995 *Copenhagen Declaration on Social Development.*

2 See also *Vienna Declaration and Programme of Action,* U.N. Doc. A/CONF. 157/23, 12 July 1993; U.N. Doc. E/CN.4/SUB.2/RES/2001/2; U.N. Doc. E/CN.4/SUB.2/RES/2000/8; U.N. Doc. E/CN.4/SUB.2/RES/1999/29; U.N. Doc. E/CN/RES/2001/31; U.N. Doc. E/CN/RES/

cultural rights have indeed to be understood as an indivisible part of human rights. This must have far reaching consequences for their implementation: the indivisibility of human rights will have to lead to the (inter)national recognition of the justiciability of economic, social and cultural rights. Cândido Grzybowski (Brazil), earlier in this book, brought out clearly the global dimension of such views. Indeed, the World Social Forum offers a basic framework to continue such an open dialogue on "issues affecting us all, as well as the initiatives that we are launching and the practices we are developing, the alternative proposals that we can produce, and the networks that we are striving to build up in order to underpin their feasibility".

2001/30, para 4(a)(d); U.N. Doc. E/CN/RES/2000/9, para 3(a)(d); U.N. Doc. E/CN/RES/1999/59.

ANNEXES

INTERNATIONAL COVENANT ON ECONOMIC, SOCIAL AND CULTURAL RIGHTS

Adopted and opened for signature, ratification and accession by General Assembly resolution 2200A (XXI) of 16 December 1966 *entry into force* 3 January 1976, in accordance with article 27

Preamble

The States Parties to the present Covenant,

Considering that, in accordance with the principles proclaimed in the Charter of the United Nations, recognition of the inherent dignity and of the equal and inalienable rights of all members of the human family is the foundation of freedom, justice and peace in the world,

Recognizing that these rights derive from the inherent dignity of the human person,

Recognizing that, in accordance with the Universal Declaration of Human Rights, the ideal of free human beings enjoying freedom from fear and want can only be achieved if conditions are created whereby everyone may enjoy his economic, social and cultural rights, as well as his civil and political rights,

Considering the obligation of States under the Charter of the United Nations to promote universal respect for, and observance of, human rights and freedoms,

Realizing that the individual, having duties to other individuals and to the community to which he belongs, is under a responsibility to strive for the promotion and observance of the rights recognized in the present Covenant,

Agree upon the following articles:

Part I

Article 1

1. All peoples have the right of self-determination. By virtue of that right they freely determine their political status and freely pursue their economic, social and cultural development.

2. All peoples may, for their own ends, freely dispose of their natural wealth and resources without prejudice to any obligations arising out of international

economic co-operation, based upon the principle of mutual benefit, and international law. In no case may a people be deprived of its own means of subsistence.

3. The States Parties to the present Covenant, including those having responsibility for the administration of Non-Self-Governing and Trust Territories, shall promote the realization of the right of self-determination, and shall respect that right, in conformity with the provisions of the Charter of the United Nations.

Part II

Article 2

1. Each State Party to the present Covenant undertakes to take steps, individually and through international assistance and co-operation, especially economic and technical, to the maximum of its available resources, with a view to achieving progressively the full realization of the rights recognized in the present Covenant by all appropriate means, including particularly the adoption of legislative measures.

2. The States Parties to the present Covenant undertake to guarantee that the rights enunciated in the present Covenant will be exercised without discrimination of any kind as to race, colour, sex, language, religion, political or other opinion, national or social origin, property, birth or other status.

3. Developing countries, with due regard to human rights and their national economy, may determine to what extent they would guarantee the economic rights recognized in the present Covenant to non-nationals.

Article 3

The States Parties to the present Covenant undertake to ensure the equal right of men and women to the enjoyment of all economic, social and cultural rights set forth in the present Covenant.

Article 4

The States Parties to the present Covenant recognize that, in the enjoyment of those rights provided by the State in conformity with the present Covenant, the State may subject such rights only to such limitations as are determined by law only in so far as this may be compatible with the nature of these rights and solely for the purpose of promoting the general welfare in a democratic society.

Article 5

1. Nothing in the present Covenant may be interpreted as implying for any State, group or person any right to engage in any activity or to perform any act aimed at the destruction of any of the rights or freedoms recognized herein, or at their limitation to a greater extent than is provided for in the present Covenant.

2. No restriction upon or derogation from any of the fundamental human rights recognized or existing in any country in virtue of law, conventions, regulations or custom shall be admitted on the pretext that the present Covenant does not recognize such rights or that it recognizes them to a lesser extent.

Part III

Article 6

1. The States Parties to the present Covenant recognize the right to work, which includes the right of everyone to the opportunity to gain his living by work which he freely chooses or accepts, and will take appropriate steps to safeguard this right.

2. The steps to be taken by a State Party to the present Covenant to achieve the full realization of this right shall include technical and vocational guidance and training programmes, policies and techniques to achieve steady economic, social and cultural development and full and productive employment under conditions safeguarding fundamental political and economic freedoms to the individual.

Article 7

The States Parties to the present Covenant recognize the right of everyone to the enjoyment of just and favourable conditions of work which ensure, in particular :

(a) Remuneration which provides all workers, as a minimum, with :
  (i) Fair wages and equal remuneration for work of equal value without distinction of any kind, in particular women being guaranteed conditions of work not inferior to those enjoyed by men, with equal pay for equal work;
  (ii) A decent living for themselves and their families in accordance with the provisions of the present Covenant;
(b) Safe and healthy working conditions;
(c) Equal opportunity for everyone to be promoted in his employment to an appropriate higher level, subject to no considerations other than those of seniority and competence;
(d) Rest, leisure and reasonable limitation of working hours and periodic holidays with pay, as well as remuneration for public holidays.

Article 8

1. The States Parties to the present Covenant undertake to ensure :

   (a) The right of everyone to form trade unions and join the trade union of his choice, subject only to the rules of the organization concerned, for the promotion and protection of his economic and social interests. No restrictions may be placed on the exercise of this right other than those prescribed by law and which are necessary in a democratic society in the interests of national security or public order or for the protection of the rights and freedoms of others;

(b) The right of trade unions to establish national federations or confederations and the right of the latter to form or join international trade-union organizations;

(c) The right of trade unions to function freely subject to no limitations other than those prescribed by law and which are necessary in a democratic society in the interests of national security or public order or for the protection of the rights and freedoms of others;

(d) The right to strike, provided that it is exercised in conformity with the laws of the particular country.

2. This article shall not prevent the imposition of lawful restrictions on the exercise of these rights by members of the armed forces or of the police or of the administration of the State.

3. Nothing in this article shall authorize States Parties to the International Labour Organisation Convention of 1948 concerning Freedom of Association and Protection of the Right to Organize to take legislative measures which would prejudice, or apply the law in such a manner as would prejudice, the guarantees provided for in that Convention.

Article 9

The States Parties to the present Covenant recognize the right of everyone to social security, including social insurance.

Article 10

The States Parties to the present Covenant recognize that :

1. The widest possible protection and assistance should be accorded to the family, which is the natural and fundamental group unit of society, particularly for its establishment and while it is responsible for the care and education of dependent children. Marriage must be entered into with the free consent of the intending spouses.

2. Special protection should be accorded to mothers during a reasonable period before and after childbirth. During such period working mothers should be accorded paid leave or leave with adequate social security benefits.

3. Special measures of protection and assistance should be taken on behalf of all children and young persons without any discrimination for reasons of parentage or other conditions. Children and young persons should be protected from economic and social exploitation. Their employment in work harmful to their morals or health or dangerous to life or likely to hamper their normal development should be punishable by law. States should also set age limits below which the paid employment of child labour should be prohibited and punishable by law.

Article 11

1. The States Parties to the present Covenant recognize the right of everyone to an adequate standard of living for himself and his family, including adequate food, clothing and housing, and to the continuous improvement of living conditions. The States Parties will take appropriate steps to ensure the realization of this right, recognizing to this effect the essential importance of international co-operation based on free consent.

2. The States Parties to the present Covenant, recognizing the fundamental right of everyone to be free from hunger, shall take, individually and through international co-operation, the measures, including specific programmes, which are needed :

   (a) To improve methods of production, conservation and distribution of food by making full use of technical and scientific knowledge, by disseminating knowledge of the principles of nutrition and by developing or reforming agrarian systems in such a way as to achieve the most efficient development and utilization of natural resources;
   (b) Taking into account the problems of both food-importing and food-exporting countries, to ensure an equitable distribution of world food supplies in relation to need.

Article 12

1. The States Parties to the present Covenant recognize the right of everyone to the enjoyment of the highest attainable standard of physical and mental health.

2. The steps to be taken by the States Parties to the present Covenant to achieve the full realization of this right shall include those necessary for :

   (a) The provision for the reduction of the stillbirth-rate and of infant mortality and for the healthy development of the child;
   (b) The improvement of all aspects of environmental and industrial hygiene;
   (c) The prevention, treatment and control of epidemic, endemic, occupational and other diseases;
   (d) The creation of conditions which would assure to all medical service and medical attention in the event of sickness.

Article 13

1. The States Parties to the present Covenant recognize the right of everyone to education. They agree that education shall be directed to the full development of the human personality and the sense of its dignity, and shall strengthen the respect for human rights and fundamental freedoms. They further agree that education shall enable all persons to participate effectively in a free society, promote understanding, tolerance and friendship among all nations and all racial, ethnic or religious groups, and further the activities of the United Nations for the maintenance of peace.

2. The States Parties to the present Covenant recognize that, with a view to achieving the full realization of this right :

   (a) Primary education shall be compulsory and available free to all;
   (b) Secondary education in its different forms, including technical and vocational secondary education, shall be made generally available and accessible to all by every appropriate means, and in particular by the progressive introduction of free education;
   (c) Higher education shall be made equally accessible to all, on the basis of capacity, by every appropriate means, and in particular by the progressive introduction of free education;
   (d) Fundamental education shall be encouraged or intensified as far as possible for those persons who have not received or completed the whole period of their primary education;
   (e) The development of a system of schools at all levels shall be actively pursued, an adequate fellowship system shall be established, and the material conditions of teaching staff shall be continuously improved.

3. The States Parties to the present Covenant undertake to have respect for the liberty of parents and, when applicable, legal guardians to choose for their children schools, other than those established by the public authorities, which conform to such minimum educational standards as may be laid down or approved by the State and to ensure the religious and moral education of their children in conformity with their own convictions.

4. No part of this article shall be construed so as to interfere with the liberty of individuals and bodies to establish and direct educational institutions, subject always to the observance of the principles set forth in paragraph I of this article and to the requirement that the education given in such institutions shall conform to such minimum standards as may be laid down by the State.

Article 14
Each State Party to the present Covenant which, at the time of becoming a Party, has not been able to secure in its metropolitan territory or other territories under its jurisdiction compulsory primary education, free of charge, undertakes, within two years, to work out and adopt a detailed plan of action for the progressive implementation, within a reasonable number of years, to be fixed in the plan, of the principle of compulsory education free of charge for all.

Article 15
1. The States Parties to the present Covenant recognize the right of everyone :

   (a) To take part in cultural life;
   (b) To enjoy the benefits of scientific progress and its applications;

(c) To benefit from the protection of the moral and material interests resulting from any scientific, literary or artistic production of which he is the author.

2. The steps to be taken by the States Parties to the present Covenant to achieve the full realization of this right shall include those necessary for the conservation, the development and the diffusion of science and culture.

3. The States Parties to the present Covenant undertake to respect the freedom indispensable for scientific research and creative activity.

4. The States Parties to the present Covenant recognize the benefits to be derived from the encouragement and development of international contacts and co-operation in the scientific and cultural fields.

Part IV

Article 16

1. The States Parties to the present Covenant undertake to submit in conformity with this part of the Covenant reports on the measures which they have adopted and the progress made in achieving the observance of the rights recognized herein.
2. (a) All reports shall be submitted to the Secretary-General of the United Nations, who shall transmit copies to the Economic and Social Council for consideration in accordance with the provisions of the present Covenant;
   (b) The Secretary-General of the United Nations shall also transmit to the specialized agencies copies of the reports, or any relevant parts therefrom, from States Parties to the present Covenant which are also members of these specialized agencies in so far as these reports, or parts therefrom, relate to any matters which fall within the responsibilities of the said agencies in accordance with their constitutional instruments.

Article 17

1. The States Parties to the present Covenant shall furnish their reports in stages, in accordance with a programme to be established by the Economic and Social Council within one year of the entry into force of the present Covenant after consultation with the States Parties and the specialized agencies concerned.

2. Reports may indicate factors and difficulties affecting the degree of fulfilment of obligations under the present Covenant.

3. Where relevant information has previously been furnished to the United Nations or to any specialized agency by any State Party to the present Covenant, it will not be necessary to reproduce that information, but a precise reference to the information so furnished will suffice.

Article 18
Pursuant to its responsibilities under the Charter of the United Nations in the field of human rights and fundamental freedoms, the Economic and Social Council may make arrangements with the specialized agencies in respect of their reporting to it on the progress made in achieving the observance of the provisions of the present Covenant falling within the scope of their activities. These reports may include particulars of decisions and recommendations on such implementation adopted by their competent organs.

Article 19
The Economic and Social Council may transmit to the Commission on Human Rights for study and general recommendation or, as appropriate, for information the reports concerning human rights submitted by States in accordance with articles 16 and 17, and those concerning human rights submitted by the specialized agencies in accordance with article 18.

Article 20
The States Parties to the present Covenant and the specialized agencies concerned may submit comments to the Economic and Social Council on any general recommendation under article 19 or reference to such general recommendation in any report of the Commission on Human Rights or any documentation referred to therein.

Article 21
The Economic and Social Council may submit from time to time to the General Assembly reports with recommendations of a general nature and a summary of the information received from the States Parties to the present Covenant and the specialized agencies on the measures taken and the progress made in achieving general observance of the rights recognized in the present Covenant.

Article 22
The Economic and Social Council may bring to the attention of other organs of the United Nations, their subsidiary organs and specialized agencies concerned with furnishing technical assistance any matters arising out of the reports referred to in this part of the present Covenant which may assist such bodies in deciding, each within its field of competence, on the advisability of international measures likely to contribute to the effective progressive implementation of the present Covenant.

Article 23
The States Parties to the present Covenant agree that international action for the achievement of the rights recognized in the present Covenant includes such methods as the conclusion of conventions, the adoption of recommendations, the furnishing of technical assistance and the holding of regional meetings and technical meetings for the purpose of consultation and study organized in conjunction with the Governments concerned.

Article 24
Nothing in the present Covenant shall be interpreted as impairing the provisions of the Charter of the United Nations and of the constitutions of the specialized agencies which define the respective responsibilities of the various organs of the United Nations and of the specialized agencies in regard to the matters dealt with in the present Covenant.

Article 25
Nothing in the present Covenant shall be interpreted as impairing the inherent right of all peoples to enjoy and utilize fully and freely their natural wealth and resources.

Part V

Article 26
1. The present Covenant is open for signature by any State Member of the United Nations or member of any of its specialized agencies, by any State Party to the Statute of the International Court of Justice, and by any other State which has been invited by the General Assembly of the United Nations to become a party to the present Covenant.

2. The present Covenant is subject to ratification. Instruments of ratification shall be deposited with the Secretary-General of the United Nations.

3. The present Covenant shall be open to accession by any State referred to in paragraph 1 of this article.

4. Accession shall be effected by the deposit of an instrument of accession with the Secretary-General of the United Nations.

5. The Secretary-General of the United Nations shall inform all States which have signed the present Covenant or acceded to it of the deposit of each instrument of ratification or accession.

Article 27
1. The present Covenant shall enter into force three months after the date of the deposit with the Secretary-General of the United Nations of the thirty-fifth instrument of ratification or instrument of accession.

2. For each State ratifying the present Covenant or acceding to it after the deposit of the thirty-fifth instrument of ratification or instrument of accession, the present Covenant shall enter into force three months after the date of the deposit of its own instrument of ratification or instrument of accession.

Article 28
The provisions of the present Covenant shall extend to all parts of federal States without any limitations or exceptions.

Article 29
1. Any State Party to the present Covenant may propose an amendment and file it with the Secretary-General of the United Nations. The Secretary-General shall thereupon communicate any proposed amendments to the States Parties to the present Covenant with a request that they notify him whether they favour a conference of States Parties for the purpose of considering and voting upon the proposals. In the event that at least one third of the States Parties favours such a conference, the Secretary-General shall convene the conference under the auspices of the United Nations. Any amendment adopted by a majority of the States Parties present and voting at the conference shall be submitted to the General Assembly of the United Nations for approval.

2. Amendments shall come into force when they have been approved by the General Assembly of the United Nations and accepted by a two-thirds majority of the States Parties to the present Covenant in accordance with their respective constitutional processes.

3. When amendments come into force they shall be binding on those States Parties which have accepted them, other States Parties still being bound by the provisions of the present Covenant and any earlier amendment which they have accepted.

Article 30
Irrespective of the notifications made under article 26, paragraph 5, the Secretary-General of the United Nations shall inform all States referred to in paragraph I of the same article of the following particulars:
(a) Signatures, ratifications and accessions under article 26;
(b) The date of the entry into force of the present Covenant under article 27 and the date of the entry into force of any amendments under article 29.

Article 31
1. The present Covenant, of which the Chinese, English, French, Russian and Spanish texts are equally authentic, shall be deposited in the archives of the United Nations.

2. The Secretary-General of the United Nations shall transmit certified copies of the present Covenant to all States referred to in article 26.

THE EARTH CHARTER

March 2000

Preamble

We stand at a critical moment in Earth's history, a time when humanity must choose its future. As the world becomes increasingly interdependent and fragile, the future at once holds great peril and great promise. To move forward we must recognize that in the midst of a magnificent diversity of cultures and life forms we are one human family and one Earth community with a common destiny. We must join together to bring forth a sustainable global society founded on respect for nature, universal human rights, economic justice, and a culture of peace. Towards this end, it is imperative that we, the peoples of Earth, declare our responsibility to one another, to the greater community of life, and to future generations.

Earth, Our Home

Humanity is part of a vast evolving universe. Earth, our home, is alive with a unique community of life. The forces of nature make existence a demanding and uncertain adventure, but Earth has provided the conditions essential to life's evolution. The resilience of the community of life and the well-being of humanity depend upon preserving a healthy biosphere with all its ecological systems, a rich variety of plants and animals, fertile soils, pure waters, and clean air. The global environment with its finite resources is a common concern of all peoples. The protection of Earth's vitality, diversity, and beauty is a sacred trust.

The Global Situation

The dominant patterns of production and consumption are causing environmental devastation, the depletion of resources, and a massive extinction of species. Communities are being undermined. The benefits of development are not shared equitably and the gap between rich and poor is widening. Injustice, poverty, ignorance, and violent conflict are widespread and the cause of great suffering. An unprecedented rise in human population has overburdened ecological and social systems. The foundations of global security are threatened. These trends are perilous – but not inevitable.

The Challenges Ahead

The choice is ours: form a global partnership to care for Earth and one another or risk the destruction of ourselves and the diversity of life. Fundamental changes are needed in our values, institutions, and ways of living. We must realize that when basic needs have been met, human development is primarily about being more, not having more. We have the knowledge and technology to provide for all and to reduce our impacts on the environment. The emergence of a global civil society is creating new opportunities to build a democratic and humane world. Our environmental, economic, political, social, and spiritual challenges are interconnected, and together we can forge inclusive solutions.

Universal Responsibility

To realize these aspirations, we must decide to live with a sense of universal responsibility, identifying ourselves with the whole Earth community as well as our local communities. We are at once citizens of different nations and of one world in which the local and global are linked. Everyone shares responsibility for the present and future well being of the human family and the larger living world. The spirit of human solidarity and kinship with all life is strengthened when we live with reverence for the mystery of being, gratitude for the gift of life, and humility regarding the human place in nature.

We urgently need a shared vision of basic values to provide an ethical foundation for the emerging world community. Therefore, together in hope we affirm the following interdependent principles for a sustainable way of life as a common standard by which the conduct of all individuals, organizations, businesses, governments, and transnational institutions is to be guided and assessed.

Principles

I. Respect and Care for the Community of Life

1. Respect Earth and life in all its diversity.

a. Recognize that all beings are interdependent and every form of life has value regardless of its worth to human beings.
b. Affirm faith in the inherent dignity of all human beings and in the intellectual, artistic, ethical, and spiritual potential of humanity.

2. Care for the community of life with understanding, compassion, and love.

a. Accept that with the right to own, manage, and use natural resources comes the duty to prevent environmental harm and to protect the rights of people.
b. Affirm that with increased freedom, knowledge, and power comes increased responsibility to promote the common good.

3. Build democratic societies that are just, participatory, sustainable, and peaceful.

a. Ensure that communities at all levels guarantee human rights and fundamental freedoms and provide everyone an opportunity to realize his or her full potential.
b. Promote social and economic justice, enabling all to achieve a secure and meaningful livelihood that is ecologically responsible.

4. Secure Earth's bounty and beauty for present and future generations.

a. Recognize that the freedom of action of each generation is qualified by the needs of future generations.
b. Transmit to future generations values, traditions, and institutions that support the long-term flourishing of Earth's human and ecological communities.

In order to fulfill these four broad commitments, it is necessary to:

II. Ecological Integrity

5. Protect and restore the integrity of Earth's ecological systems, with special concern for biological diversity and the natural processes that sustain life.

a. Adopt at all levels sustainable development plans and regulations that make environmental conservation and rehabilitation integral to all development initiatives.
b. Establish and safeguard viable nature and biosphere reserves, including wild lands and marine areas, to protect Earth's life support systems, maintain biodiversity, and preserve our natural heritage.
c. Promote the recovery of endangered species and ecosystems.
d. Control and eradicate non-native or genetically modified organisms harmful to native species and the environment, and prevent introduction of such harmful organisms.
e. Manage the use of renewable resources such as water, soil, forest products, and marine life in ways that do not exceed rates of regeneration and that protect the health of ecosystems.
f. Manage the extraction and use of non-renewable resources such as minerals and fossil fuels in ways that minimize depletion and cause no serious environmental damage.

6. Prevent harm as the best method of environmental protection and, when knowledge is limited, apply a precautionary approach.

a. Take action to avoid the possibility of serious or irreversible environmental harm even when scientific knowledge is incomplete or inconclusive.
b. Place the burden of proof on those who argue that a proposed activity will not cause significant harm, and make the responsible parties liable for environmental harm.
c. Ensure that decision making addresses the cumulative, long-term, indirect, long distance, and global consequences of human activities.
d. Prevent pollution of any part of the environment and allow no build-up of radioactive, toxic, or other hazardous substances.
e. Avoid military activities damaging to the environment.

7. Adopt patterns of production, consumption, and reproduction that safeguard Earth's regenerative capacities, human rights, and community well-being.

a. Reduce, reuse, and recycle the materials used in production and consumption systems, and ensure that residual waste can be assimilated by ecological systems.

b. Act with restraint and efficiency when using energy, and rely increasingly on renewable energy sources such as solar and wind.
c. Promote the development, adoption, and equitable transfer of environmentally sound technologies.
d. Internalize the full environmental and social costs of goods and services in the selling price, and enable consumers to identify products that meet the highest social and environmental standards.
e. Ensure universal access to health care that fosters reproductive health and responsible reproduction.
f. Adopt lifestyles that emphasize the quality of life and material sufficiency in a finite world.

8. Advance the study of ecological sustainability and promote the open exchange and wide application of the knowledge acquired.
a. Support international scientific and technical cooperation on sustainability, with special attention to the needs of developing nations.
b. Recognize and preserve the traditional knowledge and spiritual wisdom in all cultures that contribute to environmental protection and human well-being.
c. Ensure that information of vital importance to human health and environmental protection, including genetic information, remains available in the public domain.

III. Social and Economic Justice

9. Eradicate poverty as an ethical, social, and environmental imperative.
a. Guarantee the right to potable water, clean air, food security, uncontaminated soil, shelter, and safe sanitation, allocating the national and international resources required.
b. Empower every human being with the education and resources to secure a sustainable livelihood, and provide social security and safety nets for those who are unable to support themselves.
c. Recognize the ignored, protect the vulnerable, serve those who suffer, and enable them to develop their capacities and to pursue their aspirations.

10. Ensure that economic activities and institutions at all levels promote human development in an equitable and sustainable manner.
a. Promote the equitable distribution of wealth within nations and among nations.
b. Enhance the intellectual, financial, technical, and social resources of developing nations, and relieve them of onerous international debt.
c. Ensure that all trade supports sustainable resource use, environmental protection, and progressive labor standards.
d. Require multinational corporations and international financial organizations to act transparently in the public good, and hold them accountable for the consequences of their activities.

11. Affirm gender equality and equity as prerequisites to sustainable development and ensure universal access to education, health care, and economic opportunity.

a. Secure the human rights of women and girls and end all violence against them.
b. Promote the active participation of women in all aspects of economic, political, civil, social, and cultural life as full and equal partners, decision-makers, leaders, and beneficiaries.
c. Strengthen families and ensure the safety and loving nurture of all family members.

12. Uphold the right of all, without discrimination, to a natural and social environment supportive of human dignity, bodily health, and spiritual well being, with special attention to the rights of indigenous peoples and minorities.

a. Eliminate discrimination in all its forms, such as that based on race, color, sex, sexual orientation, religion, language, and national, ethnic or social origin.
b. Affirm the right of indigenous peoples to their spirituality, knowledge, lands and resources and to their related practice of sustainable livelihoods.
c. Honor and support the young people of our communities, enabling them to fulfill their essential role in creating sustainable societies.
d. Protect and restore outstanding places of cultural and spiritual significance.

IV. Democracy, Nonviolence, and Peace

13. Strengthen democratic institutions at all levels, and provide transparency and sustainability in governance, inclusive participation in decision-making, and access to justice.

a. Uphold the right of everyone to receive clear and timely information on environmental matters and all development plans and activities which are likely to affect them or in which they have an interest.
b. Support local, regional and global civil society, and promote the meaningful participation of all interested individuals and organizations in decision making.
c. Protect the rights to freedom of opinion, expression, peaceful assembly, association, and dissent.
d. Institute effective and efficient access to administrative and independent judicial procedures, including remedies and redress for environmental harm and the threat of such harm.
e. Eliminate corruption in all public and private institutions.
f. Strengthen local communities, enabling them to care for their environments, and assign environmental responsibilities to the levels of government where they can be carried out most effectively.

14. Integrate into formal education and life-long learning the knowledge, values, and skills needed for a sustainable way of life.

a. Provide all, especially children and youth, with educational opportunities that empower them to contribute actively to sustainable development.
b. Promote the contribution of the arts and humanities as well as the sciences in sustainability education.

c. Enhance the role of the mass media in raising awareness of ecological and social challenges.
d. Recognize the importance of moral and spiritual education for sustainable living.

15. Treat all living beings with respect and consideration.
a. Prevent cruelty to animals kept in human societies and protect them from suffering.
b. Protect wild animals from methods of hunting, trapping, and fishing that cause extreme, prolonged, or avoidable suffering.
c. Avoid or eliminate to the full extent possible the taking or destruction of non-targeted species.

16. Promote a culture of tolerance, nonviolence, and peace.
a. Encourage and support mutual understanding, solidarity, and cooperation among all peoples and within and among nations.
b. Implement comprehensive strategies to prevent violent conflict and use collaborative problem solving to manage and resolve environmental conflicts and other disputes.
c. Demilitarize national security systems to the level of a non-provocative defense posture, and convert military resources to peaceful purposes, including ecological restoration.
d. Eliminate nuclear, biological, and toxic weapons and other weapons of mass destruction.
e. Ensure that the use of orbital and outer space supports environmental protection and peace.
f. Recognize that peace is the wholeness created by right relationships with oneself, other persons, other cultures, other life, Earth, and the larger whole of which all are a part.

The Way Forward

As never before in history, common destiny beckons us to seek a new beginning. Such renewal is the promise of these Earth Charter principles. To fulfill this promise, we must commit ourselves to adopt and promote the values and objectives of the Charter.

This requires a change of mind and heart. It requires a new sense of global interdependence and universal responsibility. We must imaginatively develop and apply the vision of a sustainable way of life locally, nationally, regionally, and globally. Our cultural diversity is a precious heritage and different cultures will find their own distinctive ways to realize the vision.
We must deepen and expand the global dialogue that generated the Earth Charter, for we have much to learn from the ongoing collaborative search for truth and wisdom.

Life often involves tensions between important values. This can mean difficult choices. However, we must find ways to harmonize diversity with unity, the exercise of freedom with the common good, short-term objectives with long-term goals. Every individual, family, organization, and community has a vital role to play. The arts, sciences, religions, educational institutions, media, businesses, nongovernmental organizations, and governments are all called to offer creative leadership. The partnership of government, civil society, and business is essential for effective governance.

In order to build a sustainable global community, the nations of the world must renew their commitment to the United Nations,fulfill their obligations under existing international agreements, and support the implementation of Earth Charter principles with an international legally binding instrument on environment and development.

Let ours be a time remembered for the awakening of a new reverence for life, the firm resolve to achieve sustainability, the quickening of the struggle for justice and peace, and the joyful celebration of life.

WORLD SOCIAL FORUM CHARTER OF PRINCIPLES

The committee of Brazilian organizations that conceived of, and organized, the first World Social Forum, held in Porto Alegre from January 25th to 30th, 2001, after evaluating the results of that Forum and the expectations it raised, consider it necessary and legitimate to draw up a Charter of Principles to guide the continued pursuit of that initiative. While the principles contained in this Charter – to be respected by all those who wish to take part in the process and to organize new editions of the World Social Forum – are a consolidation of the decisions that presided over the holding of the Porto Alegre Forum and ensured its success, they extend the reach of those decisions and define orientations that flow from their logic.

1. The World Social Forum is an open meeting place for reflective thinking, democratic debate of ideas, formulation of proposals, free exchange of experiences and interlinking for effective action, by groups and movements of civil society that are opposed to neoliberalism and to domination of the world by capital and any form of imperialism, and are committed to building a planetary society directed towards fruitful relationships among Mankind and between it and the Earth.

2. The World Social Forum at Porto Alegre was an event localized in time and place. From now on, in the certainty proclaimed at Porto Alegre that "another world is possible", it becomes a permanent process of seeking and building alternatives, which cannot be reduced to the events supporting it.

3. The World Social Forum is a world process. All the meetings that are held as part of this process have an international dimension.

4. The alternatives proposed at the World Social Forum stand in opposition to a process of globalization commanded by the large multinational corporations and by the governments and international institutions at the service of those corporations' interests, with the complicity of national governments. They are designed to ensure that globalization in solidarity will prevail as a new stage in world history. This will respect universal human rights, and those of all citizens – men and women – of all nations and the environment and will rest on democratic international systems and institutions at the service of social justice, equality and the sovereignty of peoples.

5. The World Social Forum brings together and interlinks only organizations and movements of civil society from all the countries in the world, but intends neither to be a body representing world civil society.

6. The meetings of the World Social Forum do not deliberate on behalf of the World Social Forum as a body. No-one, therefore, will be authorized, on behalf of

any of the editions of the Forum, to express positions claiming to be those of all its participants. The participants in the Forum shall not be called on to take decisions as a body, whether by meetings, nor does it intend to constitute the only option for interrelation and action by the organizations and movements that participate in it. The participants in the Forum shall not be called on to take decisions as a body, whether by vote or acclamation, on declarations or proposals for action that would commit all, or the majority, of them and that propose to be taken as establishing positions of the Forum as a body.

7. Nonetheless, organizations or groups of organizations that participate in the Forum's meetings must be assured the right, during such meetings, to deliberate on declarations or actions they may decide on, whether singly or in coordination with other participants. The World Social Forum undertakes to circulate such decisions widely by the means at its disposal, without directing, hierarchizing, censuring or restricting them, but as deliberations of the organizations or groups of organizations that made the decisions.

8. The World Social Forum is a plural, diversified, non-confessional, non-governmental and non-party context that, in a decentralized fashion, interrelates organizations and movements engaged in concrete action at levels from the local to the international to built another world.

9. The World Social Forum will always be a forum open to pluralism and to the diversity of activities and ways of engaging of the organizations and movements that decide to participate in it, as well as the diversity of genders, ethnicities, cultures, generations and physical capacities, providing they abide by this Charter of Principles. Neither party representations nor military organizations shall participate in the Forum. Government leaders and members of legislatures who accept the commitments of this Charter may be invited to participate in a personal capacity.

10. The World Social Forum is opposed to all totalitarian and reductionist views of economy, development and history and to the use of violence as a means of social control by the State. It upholds respect for Human Rights, the practices of real democracy, participatory democracy, peaceful relations, in equality and solidarity, among people, ethnicities, genders and peoples, and condemns all forms of domination and all subjection of one person by another.

11. As a forum for debate, the World Social Forum is a movement of ideas that prompts reflection, and the transparent circulation of the results of that reflection, on the mechanisms and instruments of domination by capital, on means and actions to resist and overcome that domination, and on the alternatives proposed to solve the problems of exclusion and social inequality that the process of capitalist globalization with its racist, sexist and environmentally destructive dimensions is creating internationally and within countries.

12. As a framework for the exchange of experiences, the World Social Forum encourages understanding and mutual recognition among its participant organizations and movements, and places special value on the exchange among them, particularly on all that society is building to centre economic activity and political action on meeting the needs of people and respecting nature, in the present and for future generations.

13. As a context for interrelations, the World Social Forum seeks to strengthen and create new national and international links among organizations and movements of society, that – in both public and private life – will increase the capacity for non-violent social resistance to the process of dehumanization the world is undergoing and to the violence used by the State, and reinforce the humanizing measures being taken by the action of these movements and organizations.

14. The World Social Forum is a process that encourages its participant organizations and movements to situate their actions, from the local level to the national level and seeking active participation in international contexts, as issues of planetary citizenship, and to introduce onto the global agenda the change-inducing practices that they are experimenting in building a new world in solidarity.

Approved and Adopted in São Paulo, on April 9, 2001, by the Organizations that make up the World Social Forum Organizating Committee, Approved with Modifications by the World Social Forum International Council on June 10, 2001.

WORLD SOCIAL FORUM ORGANIZATING COMMITTEE:

ABONG – Brazilian Association of Non-Governmental Organizations
ATTAC – Association for the Taxation of Financial Transactions for the Aid of Citizens
CBJP – Brazilian Justice and Peace Commission, National Council of Bishops (CNBB)
CIVES – Brazilian Business Association for Citizenship
CUT – Central Trade Union Confederation
IBASE – Brazilian Institute for Social and Economic Studies
CJG – Centre for Global Justice
MST – Movement of Landless Rural Workers

ORGANIZATIONS THAT TOOK PART IN THE MEETING OF THE WORLD SOCIAL FORUM ADVISORY COUNCIL IN SÃO PAULO ON JUNE 10, 2001:

International and Regional Networks and Organizations:

- 50 Years Is Enough Network
- ALAI – Agencia Latinoamericana de Información
- ALAMPYME – Associação Latino Americana de Pequenos e Médios Empresários
- Alliance for a Responsible United World

- Aliança Social Continental
- ALOP – Associação Latino Americana de Organismos de Promoção
- AIDC – Alternative Information & Development Centre /Jubilee South Africa
- Articulación Feminista Marco Sur
- APC – Association for Progress in Communications
- ATTAC – Argentina, France, Paraguay, Sweden, Switzerland
- CADTM- Comité pour L´Anullation de la Dette du Tiers Monde
- Caritas International
- CEAAL – Consejo de Educacion de Adultos de America Latina
- CEDAR International – Forum ESCR – Centre for Dignity and Rights
- CIDSE – Coopération Internationale pour le Développement et la Solidarité
- CLACSO – Conselho Latinoamericano de Ciências Sociais
- CONAIE – Equador
- WCL – World Confederation of Labour
- The Other Davos – Switzerland
- Enda – Senegal
- Focus on the Global South
- World Forum of Alternatives / Tricontinental Centre
- Friends of the Earth
- Genoa Social Forum
- Grito dos Excluídos/as Continental
- IPS – Inter Press Service
- IFG – International Forum on Globalization
- International Rivers Network
- Jubilee South / Dialogue 2000
- Network Institute for Global Democratization
- OCLAE – Organización Continental Latinoamericana de Estudiantes
- ORIT – Organización Regional Interamericana de Trabajadores
- People's Summit of the Americas – Quebec
- PIDHDD – Plataforma Interamericana de Derechos Humanos, Democracia y Desarrollo
- Red Mujeres Transformando la Economía
- Rede APM/Libro de Piedras Siglo 21
- Dawn Network
- Latin American and Caribbean Black Women's Network
- REPEM – Red de Educacion Popular entre Mujeres
- Social Watch
- Third World Network
- Via Campesina
- World March of Women

Representatives of the following organizations, which are deciding internally whether to join the Council, took part as observers:

- AFLCIO- American Federation of Labor-Congress of Industrial Organizations
- CES – Confederação Européia de Sindicatos / ETUC – European Trade Union Confederation
- CIOSL – Confederação Internacional de Organizações Sindicais Livres

The following organizations/networks took part as guests:

- CTA – Central de Trabajadores Argentinos
- Federació de Cooperatives de Catalunya / Red Europea de Socieconomía Solidária
- Fons Català de Cooperació al Desenvolupament/Foro Regional Barcelona
- FORO ALCE/Desenvolupament Comunitari

A representative of the following organization took part as an international observer:

- North South XXI Foundation

The following organizations could not attend but supported the formation of the Council:

- Arab NGO Network for Development
- Cedetim – Centre d´Etudes et d´ Initiatives de Solidarité Internationale
- FIAN – Foodfirst Information and Action Network
- FNTG – Funders Network on Trade & Globalization
- IATP – Institute for Agriculture and Trade Policy
- International Gender and Trade Network
- Public Citizen's Global Trade Watch
- Red Mujer y Habitat LAC
- Unimondo/Oneworld Italy

Representatives of the host governments of the WSF2002 in Porto Alegre were present as observers:

- Rio Grande do Sul State Government
- Porto Alegre Municipal Government

Representatives of the following organizations/networks were present as Brazilian national observers:

- Arquitetos Solidários
- Comitê Gaúcho do FSM
- Comitê Rio de Janeiro do FSM
- Fórum Mundial de Educação

ENDORSING NETWORKS

NATIONAL HUMAN RIGHTS MOVEMENT
MNDH, Movimento Nacional de Direitos Humanos
(Brasília, Brazil)

Organized by civil society, Brazil's National Human Rights Movement (MNDH – *Movimento Nacional de Direitos Humanos*) is a nationwide non-profit entity that functions as a democratic, ecumenical, supraparty network. Established in 1982, it today interlinks more than 320 member entities all over Brazil, forming the nation's leading tool for fostering and promoting human rights.

Main objective: ushering in a human rights culture that affirms their universal, indivisible and interdependent nature is the key element required for the exercise of citizenship. Based on the *Struggle for Life against Violence*, its Action Programme is designed to promote human rights to their full universal, indivisible and interdependent scope, grounded on the principles established by the Charter of Olinda (1986).

The activities of Brazil's National Human Rights Movement (MNDH) are divided into separate areas clustering a wide variety of actions:
Capacity-building: training and educational activities to qualify the militants of this Movement and others defending human rights in general.
Studies and Research: permanent monitoring of the status of human rights and their progress, with special attention to certain high-priority areas, in order to produce feedback for the actions of the Movement in general and more particularly shaping its stance and guiding its political propositions.
Political Representation and Lobbying: as a social player, it represents Brazilian society in matters related to human rights, not as its sole spokesperson but rather as a leading mouthpiece for civil society. To do so, it issues denunciations through local and international mechanisms, followed by ongoing oversight and lobbying activities.
Social Mobilization: buttressing and building up its permanent legitimacy as a player speaking out on human rights issues in Brazil, it must deploy the tools needed to mobilize society as a whole – particularly organized civil society – on core issues, monitoring and participating in the activities resulting from the mobilization of civil society.

INTER AMERICAN PLATFORM OF HUMAN RIGHTS, DEMOCRACY AND DEVELOPMENT
PIDHDD, Plataforma Inter-Americana de Derechos Humanos, Democracia y Desarrollo (La Paz, Bolivia)

A plural, convergent and autonomous association of various Latin American and Caribbean's civil society organisations, concerned with human rights and grouped in National Chapters. Supports the processes of society-building, developing strategies of demandability and social monitoring while striving to ensure that the States comply with their obligations and commitments regarding human rights in general and economic, social and cultural rights in particular.

The *general objective* is to contribute to the development of a rights-based and peace-based culture with justice in society; and contribute to a social and political consensus as regards the integrality of human rights, democracy and development, by means of the mobilisation of civil society, producing concepts and actions for demanding human rights, in particular economic, social and cultural rights.

Specific objectives:
- to strengthen a conceptual, methodological and operational proposal on the links between development, democracy and the demandability of ESCR;
- to impact on the programmes of the international forum and on the national public policies in favour of ESCR;
- to promote and to support wide social alliances among human rights organisations, development NGO's and social organisations, in order to develop social demandability actions of ESCR;
- institutional consolidating and positioning of the PIDHDD.

CEDAR INTERNATIONAL FORUM FOR THE IMPLEMENTATION OF ECONOMIC, SOCIAL AND CULTURAL RIGHTS
Centre for Dignity and Rights (The Hague, The Netherlands)

Vision
Cedar International's logo is a spiral curve that connects human dignity and human rights. Whereas dignity is the source of human rights law, the main function of human rights law is to protect dignity. This interaction is realized through processes of the implementation of rights.
Human dignity is central because it
- points to an area of being human where the vulnerable and fragile dimensions of life have the first priority;
- provides a critical standard and basic norm to adjudicate any person, group, organisation, institution or structure that denies fundamental freedoms and human equality, and thus humiliates and dehumanises people;
- offers a decisive indicator for the sustainability of efforts to realise human development and human rights.

Mission
Cedar International was created to encourage concerted interventions towards a more effective implementation of economic, social and cultural rights. As an International Forum, the Cedar network consists of Regional Cedars in Africa, Asia, Latin America and is in process of being extended to Eastern/Central Europe and the Middle East. The facilitating office, Cedar International (The Hague), supports the development of innovative approaches, advocates for new instruments and

contributes to integrated strategies for the implementation of economic, social and cultural rights.

Cedar International is committed to the implementation of ESC rights and has defined as its core tasks:

1. to advance human *rights-based approaches* to poverty and development. Such approaches consist of relating the standards and mechanisms of international human rights law to (inter)national policies and practices. Indeed, economic, social and cultural rights advance the right to common goods to which most poor people have never had access to, such as adequate housing, food and good health conditions;
2. to contribute to the development of *new instruments* for the implementation of economic, social and cultural rights, such as Civil Society Reports and the Draft Optional Protocol. Indeed, there is the need to further develop the institutional protection mechanisms at the same time as the contents of these rights are advanced and interpreted;
3. to develop *multi-actor strategies* that are integrated and effective.

Cedar International is housed at the TMC Asser Institute for Research on International Law, The Hague.

NOTES ON CONTRIBUTORS
in order of appearance

VIRGINIA DANDAN (Philippines),
Artist, Professor of Fine Arts, and presently the Dean of the College of Fine Arts, University of the Philippines, the premier institution of learning in the fine arts in the Philippines, Diliman, Quezon City. She is also the current Chairperson of the United Nations Committee on Economic, Social and Cultural Rights, where she has been a member for the last ten years. Her firm conviction that the most powerful tool for the protection and promotion of human rights is through education has led her to explore innovative learning in human rights education particularly among indigenous and rural communities. She recently established the Asia Pacific Learning Institute for Human Rights.
Education as her springboard for action in her quest for the full enjoyment by all of their human rights. Editor of the Arts Quarterly, published by the President's Committee on Culture and the Arts under the Office of the President, University of the Philippines.

MILOON KOTHARI (India)
Leading activist/scholar on housing and land rights working from New Delhi, India. Currently he is the UN Special Rapporteur on adequate housing as a component of the right to an adequate standard of living. This UN independent mandate involves reporting to the UN Commission on Human Rights on the status throughout the world of these rights and to undertake action, in collaboration with NGO's, Governments and relevant UN and other international bodies to promote housing and land rights. He is also the Convener of the Habitat International Coalition's Housing and Land Rights Committee and the Executive-Director of 'SAMMAN' Centre on Economic, Social and Cultural Rights. In these capacities he is working closely with NGO's and Community groups and campaigns on housing rights and against forced evictions to promote the housing and land rights approach and to apply international human rights law at the local, national and regional levels. www.unhchr.ch/html/menu2/i2ecohou.htm

BERMA KLEIN GOLDEWIJK (The Netherlands)
Programme Director, Cedar International, at TMC Asser Institute for Research on International Law, The Hague. Former positions: core staff of the human rights programme on Development, Law and Social Justice (DL&SJ), Institute of Social Studies (ISS). Associate Professor researching urban poverty and practice-oriented theory, Catholic Theological University, Utrecht. Senior Researcher/Senior Policy Advisor, Cebemo/Cordaid. Senior Researcher (PhD) at the Faculty of Theology and Lecturer in Development Studies at the Third World Centre, Catholic University, Nijmegen. Recent publications: co-author of *Where Needs meet Rights. Implementing Economic, Social and Cultural Rights*, Geneva 1999; *God and the Goods, Global Economy in a Civilizational Perspective*, Geneva 1998.

CÂNDIDO GRZYBOWSKI (Brazil)
Director-General, Brazilian Institute for Social and Economic Analyses (IBASE – *Instituto Brasileiro de Análises Sociais e Econômicas*), Rio de Janeiro, Brazil, which he joined in 1990 as its Policies and Planning Director. One of the main initiators and coordinators World Social Forum. Sociologist and philosopher, with a post-doctoral degree from the Institute of Latin American Studies and the Economics Department, University College, London University; PhD in Economic and Social Development, *Institut d'Étude du Développement Economique et Social, Université de Paris I, Panthéon, Sorbonne*; Degree in Philosophy, *Faculdade de Filosofia, Ciências e Letras*, Ijuí, Rio Grande do Sul State, Brazil.

PAULO CÉSAR CARBONARI (Brazil)
Master of Philosophy, Goiás State Federal University (UFG-GO), Brazil. Lecturer in Ethics, Berthier Superior Institute of Philosophy (IFIBE – *Instituto Superior de Filosofia Berthier*), Passo Fundo, Rio Grande do Sul. National Coordinator for Cooperation and Partnership, National Human Rights Movement (MNDH – *Movimento Nacional de Direitos Humanos*) and Executive Secretary of the Brazilian Platform for Economic, Social and Cultural Human Rights and the Brazilian Chapter of the Inter-American Platform for Human Rights: Democracy and Development (PIDHDD – *Plataforma Interamericana de Derechos Humanos: Democracia y Desarollo*).

JAYME BENVENUTO LIMA JR. (Brazil)
Lawyer with a Master's Degree in Law from the Pernambuco Federal University. Representative of the Legal Affairs Advisory Bureau for Grassroots Organisations (GAJOP) and the National Human Rights Movement at the United Nations. Author of the book entitled *Os Direitos Humanos, Econômicos, Sociais e Culturais*, PIDHDD-SBDHDD, 2001; also published in Spanish, La Paz (Plural Editores) 2001. Coordinated the following books: *Extrajudicial, Summary or Arbitrary Executions – An Approximation of the Situation in Brazil*, MNDH, Recife 2001; and *Direitos Humanos Internacionais – Avanços e Desafios no Início do Século XXI*, GAJOP, Recife 2001. Editora Renovar, Rio de Janeiro, 2001.

VENITIA GOVENDER (South Africa)
Born in Johannesburg, studied Law at the University of Durban / Westville, and was active in student politics. Human rights activist and previous Director of the Human Rights Committee, a long-standing NGO. Currently serving as Director of the Ceasefire Campaign (a demilitarisation organisation) in Johannesburg, involved in efforts aimed at narrowing the ever-increasing gap between policy and implementation.

WIETEKE BEERNINK & HARRY DERKSEN (The Netherlands)
Wieteke is a Social Scientist and former activist in the movement for Education for All in the Netherlands. She was Director of various organisations for adult and vocational education from 1985-1996. Next she went on duty at ICCO, Interchurch

Organisation for Development Cooperation, as head of the Africa-Middle East Department. From 2002 onwards she will be working as an independent consultant. Harry spent the past 12 years with ICCO as desk officer for South Africa and the Middle East. For the past few years he has also been working on the development of the ICCO policy on human rights and more specifically on the implementation of a rights-based approach.

Adalid Contreras Baspineiro (Bolivia)
Sociologist and specialist in communications for development. Regional Technical Secretary, Inter-American Platform for Human Rights, Democracy and Development (PIDHDD – *Plataforma Interamericana de Derechos Humanos, Democracia y Desarrollo*), La Paz. Graduate course lecturer at several Latin American universities on Communication Strategies for Development. UNDP Consultant for the Dialogue 21 Programme. UNESCO Consultant for the Culture of Peace Programme. Expert invited by the Office of the United Nations High Commissioner for Human Rights for designing the strategy for Latin America and the Caribbean. Coordinator Cedar Latin America.

Flávia Piovesan (Brazil)
Lecturer in Constitutional Law and Human Rights, Pontifical Catholic University (PUC), São Paulo. Visiting Fellow, Human Rights Programme, Harvard Law School (1995 and 2000). São Paulo District Attorney. Coordinator, Working Group on Human Rights, São Paulo State Attorney-General's Office. Member of the Commission on Justice and Peace. Publications: *Direitos Humanos e o Direito Constitucional Internacional,* São Paulo 1996/2000); *Temas de Direitos Humanos,* São Paulo, 1998.

Areli Sandoval Terán (Mexico)
Degree in International Relations from the National Autonomous University of Mexico (UNAM). Since September 1998, she has worked as a Project Coordinator for social development and economic, social and cultural rights, and as a Researcher for the Citizen Diplomacy Programme (*Programa Diplomacia Ciudadana*) run by DECA Equipo Pueblo, A.C., an NGO promoting social development, established in 1977. At the moment, she also coordinates the Working Group on Economic, Social and Cultural Rights for the Latin-American Association of Promotion Organisations (ALOP – *Asociación Latinoamericana de Organizaciones de Promoción*) with which the Equipo Pueblo organisation has been affiliated since 1994. Coordination Committee Member, Social Watch International Network.

Marcio Alexandro Gualberto (Brazil)
Copywriter and Technical Expert, Federation of Social Welfare and Education Entities (FASE – *Federação de Órgãos para Assistência Social e Educacional*), Rio de Janeiro, Brazil Coordination Committee Member, Brazilian Chapter of the Inter-American Platform for Human Rights, Democracy and Development (PIDHDD – *Plataforma Interamericana de Derechos Humanos, Democracia e Desenvolvimento*). Editor, *Rede Nova Abolicionista* website.

PEDRO CLÁUDIO CUNCA BOCAYUVA (Brazil)
Director, Work and Income Area, Federation of Social Welfare and Education Entities (FASE – *Federação de Órgãos para Assistência Social e Educacional*), Rio de Janeiro, Brazil. Historian with Master's Degree in International Affairs. Studying for PhD in Urban and Regional Planning and Research through IPPUR-UFRJ. In charge of the Economic, Social and Cultural Rights Project run by FASE. Researcher into Integrated Sustainable Local Development for the *Rede DLIS* network.

AZIZ NAZIB AB'SABER (Brazil)
Brazilian ecologist. Emeritus Professor, Physical Geography, University of São Paulo. Former researcher, Brazilian Centre for Analysis and Urban Planning. Member of the Institute of Advanced Studies (*Instituto de Estudos Avançados*), University of São Paulo (IEA-USP) and Editorial Board Member for the *Revista de Estudos Avançados,* a quadrimestral journal produced by IEA-USP. He chaired the SBPC Brazilian Society for Advanced Sciences and is Honorary President of the SBPC. He has authored over 280 works, including articles and books on geography, ecology, politics and poetry.

PATRICIA MORALES (Argentina/The Netherlands)
Coordinator of academic activities for the Earth Charter, Cedar International and Globus (Institute for Globalisation and Sustainable Development), Tilburg University. Studied Philosophy at the University of Buenos Aires and at the Goethe University in Frankfurt, Germany. PhD dissertation on *Derechos humanos y ética de la responsabilidad solidária.* As assistant for human rights to Professor Ruud Lubbers at Tilburg University (1998-2000), she became involved in the Earth Charter process, participating in its research programme and attending conferences. They also produced the *Glossary on Global Principles for the Earth Charter.* She is editor of *Indigenous Peoples, Human Rights and Global Interdependence* (1994); *Towards Global Human Rights* (1996); *Pueblos Indigenas, Derechos Humanos e Interdependencia Global* (1994/2001).

RICARDO VEGA POSADA (Peru)
Director, Puno Peasants Capacity-Building Centre (CCCP – *Centro de Capacitación Campesina de Puno*); Chair, National Board of Directors, Technical Committee, Melgar Peasants Unit Federation (FUCAM – *Federación Unitaria de Campesinos de Melgar*), Rural Coordinator for Peru.

GERTRUDE ROEBELING (The Netherlands)
Studied Tropical Agriculture and Development Economy. Former positions: Manager of several agricultural projects and cooperatives in Venezuela, Brazil and Portugal. Since 1986 she has been a Project Officer for Southern Africa and Brazil with the ICCO co-financing agency, and continued as Manager for Brazil and Southern Cone (Latin America). She initiated and coordinated the advocacy network of 250 partner organisations in the region linking these with a new European network of seven major European donor organisations. Within this context she coordinated two key themes: Human Rights and Institutional

Development. She actively networks with other Dutch co-financing agencies (Novib, Hivos and Cordaid) and backdonors, such as the Ministry of Development / Cooperation (The Hague) and the European Commission (Brussels). Current position: Senior Policy Advisor, ICCO, in charge of issues related to Globalisation, Democracy and Human Rights.

M.C. RAJ (India)
A leading intellectual and activist, he works with Dalit communities in India and helps bring their cause before the international community, particularly through relating street-level struggles to the appearance of liberation theories for the Dalit people of India. He has authored several books, with his most recent publication *Dalitology*, a milestone work that analyses the issues of globalization and the caste system in India. His former position was the Director of Rural Education for the Development of Society (REDS), Tumkur (Karnataka), India. He is Coordinator Cedar South Asia.

FRANCISCO WHITAKER FERREIRA (Brazil)
Architect by training, political leader by vocation, Francisco Whitaker Ferreira was among the many Brazilians exiled by the military dictatorship during the 1960s and 1970s. He spent fifteen years in France and Chile, becoming a specialist in the planning area and returning to Brazil in 1981. Backed by an impressive track-record of engagement through entities linked to the Roman Catholic Church, from his militant student days with *Juventude Universitária Católica* (today the *Pastoral da Juventude*) through to his participation in projects run by the National Brazilian Bishops Conference (CNBB – *Conferência Nacional dos Bispos do Brasil*), Whitaker is now the Executive Secretary of the Brazilian Commission for Justice and Peace (*Comissão Brasileira de Justiça e Paz*) under the aegis of the CNBB, and a member of the Brazilian Organising Committee for the World Social Forum. He also holds a seat on the Editorial Committee of the *Boletim de Análise de Conjuntura,* which is published by the Brazilian Commission for Justice and Peace.

DALE MCKINLEY (South Africa)
PhD. in Politics and African Studies. Political activist and scholar committed to the struggle for justice and equality in South Africa and the globe. He has held numerous positions in the movement in South Africa throughout the 1990s, and has worked as a lecturer, researcher, freelance journalist and community activist. Author of *The ANC and the Liberation Struggle,* London (Pluto Press) 1997, as well as numerous chapters and articles dealing with people's struggles in South and Southern Africa. He presently resides in Johannesburg.

JOE LOUIS WASHINGTON (USA)
Human rights advocate, social critic, poet and peace builder. He serves in various capacities as an international lecturer and trainer in human rights and the settlement of disputes. He is currently a professor at the Scuola Superiore Sant'Anna where he lectures on the Settlement of Disputes and serves as the

Dispute Settlement and Human Rights Officer, International Training Program for Conflict Management (ITPCM), both located in Pisa, Italy.

JACQUES VAN NIEUWENHOVE (Belgium/The Netherlands)
Emeritus Professor University of Nijmegen (The Netherlands), where he lectured on Processes of Change in the Latin American Society and Churches. Former lecturer on Political Ethics and Theology at the Universities of Louvain (Belgium) and Tilburg (The Netherlands). Worked in Burundi, Africa. Former member of the Board of the Justice & Peace Commission in Belgium and The Netherlands. The editors are most grateful for his valuable support in editing this book.

CAROLYN BRISSETT (UK/South Africa/Brazil)
Interpreter / translator for Global Multilingüe, a specialized international communications enterprise in Rio de Janeiro established by Antonio Machado (PhD) and Sergio Xavier Ferreira (MA).